Epica Book 20
Europe's
Best Advertising

DIRECTOR
Andrew Rawlins

EDITOR
Patrick Taschler

ART DIRECTORS
Frédéric Ansermet
Patrick Taschler

SYNOPSES
Mark Tungate

EDITORIAL ASSISTANT
Francelina Pacarić

COVER IMAGE
Tim Flach
(Getty Images)

PUBLISHER
AVA Publishing S.A.
enquiries@avabooks.ch

DISTRIBUTION
North America
Sterling Publishing Co.
www.sterlingpub.com
All other countries
Thames & Hudson Ltd.
sales@thameshudson.co.uk

PRODUCTION
AVA Book Production Pte Ltd.
production@avabooks.com.sg

Printed in Singapore

Contents

"What is European Advertising? The question is similar to the problem of trying to define European culture. Everyone recognizes its existence, but no one can say what it is. My view is that it is more of a patchwork than a single entity: a sum of all our many different cultures in Europe. Similarly, European Advertising is the sum of its many different parts rather than one single phenomenon."

Ronald Beatson
(Epica Book 1)

"The fact that it is increasingly difficult to find marketing solutions through objective analysis and product differentiation means that there is an increasingly important role for creativity in advertising… Creativity in advertising is added value in itself. It is a gift from the brand to the public. Just as a river breaks its banks to irrigate new areas, creativity is the art of pushing boundaries so that new desires can grow."

Marie-Catherine Dupuy
(Epica Book 9)

"To communicate is akin to governing: foresight is all. Some of us imagine that advertising is only the mirror of the societies it seduces. And some of us are wrong. First and foremost, advertising is the early warning system of changes in society. Its genius is to sense our future. Advertising must play the sociologist before setting to its creative tasks."

Jacques Séguéla
(Epica Book 4)

"In my experience, the best ideas come from a) the product, and b) the human condition. And the correct combination of the two will cross any border… All we have to do is generate ideas. Nothing more, nothing less. Safe in the knowledge that ideas generate sales. And selling is what we do, people. Art is for art's sake."

Trevor Beattie
(Epica Book 10)

"In the final analysis it is much more the heart to which we have to make a direct appeal. Creativity therefore continues to be our prime task, although it now needs to be on a far higher plane then ever before. The emotions have to be stimulated, the fascination aroused, and that calls for other talents than the current mode of storytelling and entertaining."

Jean Etienne Aebi
(Epica Book 6)

"It is odd how advertising can so often end up polluting people's minds instead of enriching them. It should be at the front of any advertiser's objectives to endeavour to build a relationship with the consumer based on trust and inspiration. But this is rare… If we want to have a meaningful dialogue with our fellow inhabitants on planet Earth, then we have to be aware that constant change is an unavoidable part of that."

Joakim Jonason
(Epica Book 11)

"Provided the strategy behind the campaign is sound and the target group is correctly identified, exciting advertising obviously sells better then advertising that is lifeless and poorly dramatised… That advertisement which is able to charm, always wins. Whether it is better to appeal to humour or to other strings on the emotional scale is an issue under constant discussion. Those who master this intuitive art, will always be the best."

Knut Georg Andresen
(Epica Book 7)

"Market research has made all advertising much of a muchness, just as the wind tunnel has made all car shapes similar. In research groups, respondents can only tell you about the past or the present. They know nothing of the future… Creatives around the world are working with research that tells them what the consumer prefers. Since we all have access to the same information, our campaigns end up looking identical."

Luis Bassat
(Epica Book 12)

"Exploring peoples' and countries' unique roots, cultures and insights, in combination with planning, might be fruitful advice to consistently produce more original advertising with distinct personality… Based on survival and the need for success within our emerging free-market world economy, our clients will either grow by being innovative or loose their consumer/customer basis by fooling themselves."

Michael Conrad
(Epica Book 8)

"Does award winning advertising sell?. I would like to turn that discussion around… What about the work that doesn't win awards? Or the work that doesn't even pass the first threshold: the work, whose creators themselves don't even think is good enough to be sent to compete in awards shows. This work, too, was dearly paid for by the client and he very rightfully expected it to be excellent and to bring him results."

Ami Hasan
(Epica Book 14)

"If creativity had only a little influence on the success of advertising, the ADC winners would make a negligible showing in competitions based on effectiveness. However, this is far from the case! In fact, of the campaigns that received Effie (advertising effectiveness) awards from Germany's advertising agencies association in the 1990s, a high percentage were also recognised by the ADC for their creative quality."

Sebastian Turner
(Epica Book 15)

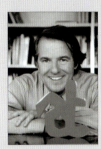

"In a year of downturn like 2002, the greatest risk was to forfeit creativity. Many companies, pushed by the instinct to survive, could have said 'no, thanks' to the most innovative ideas... scared to take risks, lacking courage. Well, in a such difficult year, (our industry) succeeded in demonstrating the value of the creative idea more than ever, its vitality and its irreplaceable importance."

Marco Testa
(Epica Book 16)

"Because although this book will teach you how to do advertising, it will be advertising like the advertising in this book. And as great as it is, the advertising in this book is now the great advertising of the past. The great advertising of the future will be nothing like it. That's why it will be great advertising, of course."

John Pallant
(Epica Book 17)

"After all the theories, buzz words, acronyms, touch points, brilliant media solutions and 'good meetings', all consumers really give a damn about is our ideas. The brilliant creative ones that break through, connect and persuade."

Basil Mina
(Epica Book 18)

"The digital revolution, coupled with the Internet, mobile telephony and interactive television, is rapidly transforming traditional media and the way they're used. People are spending more time at the computer than in front of the TV. Building one-to-one relationships is what it's all about today. All the advertising agencies are aware of this challenge by now... But let's be honest: so far, only a minority of them are making it happen."

Olivier Altmann
(Epica Book 19)

No New Eldorado

When I was invited to write this introduction, I took a look at what my predecessors had written and I said to myself, "How on earth am I going to come up with such brilliant remarks and appear so smart?" And then the moment came when I just had to start writing.

One thing I've noticed is that certain debates become fashionable in the advertising business. Not so long ago the trendy subject was: does creativity sell? Today, in my experience, you hear nothing but talk about new media and integrated campaigns.

There's a lot of waffle spoken about this subject. Of course communication tools are multiplying, but they don't add up to a magic potion or a new Eldorado. Successful advertising can't exist without a big idea. And for a big idea to emerge, two elements need to be united – as all the award winners in this book already know.

The first is the creative team: talented guys and girls given all the means they need to come up with sensational ideas. The second is a structure capable of bringing these ideas to life; in other words, capable of selling them.

If the entire advertising industry concentrated on these two essential factors, if all our energy was spent training creatives and ensuring that their ideas saw the light of day, the world would be full of very rich clients and much-loved brands.

In the end, despite all the fashionable debates, nothing has really changed since Bill Bernbach.

Erik Vervroegen,
Executive Creative Director & Chairman, TBWA\Paris

Epica d'Or (Film)

Epica d'Or (Print)

EPICA D'OR (FILM)   WIEDEN+KENNEDY AMSTERDAM   COCA-COLA "HAPPINESS FACTORY"
EPICA D'OR (PRINT)   SCHOLZ & FRIENDS BERLIN   JOBSINTOWN "WRONG WORKING ENVIRONMENT"

FILM WINNERS

FOOD	TONIC COMMUNICATIONS, DUBAI	NANDO'S RESTAURANT "RAMADAN KAREEM"
CONFECTIONERY & SNACKS	ABBOTT MEAD VICKERS BBDO, LONDON	WRIGLEYS AIRWAVES "ALIEN"
DAIRY PRODUCTS	TRY ADVERTISING AGENCY, OSLO	TINE YOGHURT "TURN AROUND"
ALCOHOLIC DRINKS	ABBOTT MEAD VICKERS BBDO, LONDON	GUINNESS EXTRA COLD "PUB", "FISH" & "MUDSKIPPER"
NON-ALCOHOLIC DRINKS	WIEDEN+KENNEDY AMSTERDAM	COCA-COLA "HAPPINESS FACTORY"
COMMUNICATION SERVICES	GORGEOUS ENTERPRISES, LONDON	VODAFONE "MAYFLY"
TRANSPORT & TOURISM	OGILVY AMSTERDAM	CENTER PARCS EUROPE "EU TOP"
RETAIL SERVICES	KING STOCKHOLM	ICA SUPERMARKETS "PASQUALE" CAMPAIGN
FINANCIAL SERVICES	DUVAL GUILLAUME, BRUSSELS	DEXIA BANK "SUBTITLES"
PUBLIC INTEREST	DUVAL GUILLAUME, BRUSSELS	DOCTORS WITHOUT BORDERS "HUMAN BALL"
AUDIOVISUAL EQUIPMENT & ACCESSORIES	FALLON LONDON	SONY BRAVIA "PAINT"
HOMES, FURNISHINGS & APPLIANCES	LEO BURNETT, MILAN	ARISTON AQUALTIS "UNDERWATER WORLD"
HOUSEHOLD MAINTENANCE	MARKOM LEO BURNETT, ISTANBUL	POLISAN ELEGANS PAINT "BEDROOM"
BEAUTY PRODUCTS	LOWE LONDON	SURE FOR MEN "GO WILD"
TOILETRIES & HEALTH CARE	BOB HELSINKI	PAMOL F PAINKILLER "HEADPLAYER"
CLOTHING & FABRICS	GORGEOUS ENTERPRISES, LONDON	LEVI'S "NEWS STORY"
FOOTWEAR & PERSONAL ACCESSORIES	WIEDEN+KENNEDY AMSTERDAM	NIKE AIR MAX "ENDURE"
	180 AMSTERDAM	ADIDAS INTERNATIONAL "EQUIPO" & "PARTIDO"
AUTOMOBILES	WIEDEN+KENNEDY LONDON	HONDA CIVIC "CHOIR"
AUTOMOTIVE & ACCESSORIES	WIEDEN+KENNEDY LONDON	HONDA CORPORATE IMAGE "IMPOSSIBLE DREAM"
MEDIA	BETC EURO RSCG, PARIS	CANAL+ "MARCH OF THE EMPEROR"
RECREATION & LEISURE	ABBOTT MEAD VICKERS BBDO, LONDON	CAMELOT LOTTERY "BAG OF SMILES"
PROFESSIONAL EQUIPMENT & SERVICES	SCALA JWT, BUCHAREST	SCALA JWT "TAKING IT TO THE STREETS"

PRINT WINNERS

FOOD	DDB LONDON	MARMITE SQUEEZY "LOVE OR HATE" CAMPAIGN
CONFECTIONERY & SNACKS	LEO BURNETT, LISBON	SMINT "SPEAK CLOSER" CAMPAIGN
DAIRY PRODUCTS	ADVICO YOUNG & RUBICAM, ZURICH	SMP-SWISS MILK PRODUCERS "LITTLE OBELIX "
ALCOHOLIC DRINKS	TBWA\PARIS	ABSOLUT VODKA "SEARCH"
NON-ALCOHOLIC DRINKS	DDB&CO, ISTANBUL	CAFE DEL MONDO "SUMATRA" CAMPAIGN
COMMUNICATION SERVICES	FORSMAN & BODENFORS, GOTHENBURG	TELE 2 COMVIQ "MMS" CAMPAIGN
TRANSPORT & TOURISM	DDB PARIS	VOYAGES-SNCF.COM "TOWN NAMES" CAMPAIGN
RETAIL SERVICES	WALKER, ZURICH	FLEUROP-INTERFLORA "MOTHER'S DAY" CAMPAIGN
FINANCIAL SERVICES	DDB AMSTERDAM	ACHMEA INSURANCE "HOME"
PUBLIC INTEREST	WALKER, ZURICH	AMNESTY INT'L "NOT HERE BUT NOW" CAMPAIGN
AUDIOVISUAL EQUIPMENT & ACCESSORIES	SPILBERG, OSLO	HI-FI CLUB "MAKING WAVES"
HOMES, FURNISHINGS & APPLIANCES	SCHOLZ & FRIENDS, HAMBURG	TECHNOPOWER "CLEANING LADIES" CAMPAIGN
HOUSEHOLD MAINTENANCE	TBWA\PARIS	SPONTEX SPONGES "PEA SOUP"
BEAUTY PRODUCTS	JWT PARIS	SUNSILK SHAMPOO "IDENTIKIT" CAMPAIGN
TOILETRIES & HEALTH CARE	SAATCHI & SAATCHI, STOCKHOLM	BIFACID "I LOVE INDIA"
CLOTHING & FABRICS	TONIC COMMUNICATIONS, DUBAI	WONDERBRA "CENSORED"
FOOTWEAR & PERSONAL ACCESSORIES	GREY&TRACE, BARCELONA	PILOT V LIQUID LIGHT "PILOT LIGHT" CAMPAIGN
AUTOMOBILES	TBWA\ISTANBUL	BMW 1 SERIES "REAR WHEEL DRIVE" CAMPAIGN
AUTOMOTIVE & ACCESSORIES	DDB MILAN	AUDI FIRST CHOICE PLUS "HAIR" & "PAPER"
MEDIA	THE BRIDGE, GLASGOW	SCOTTISH DAILY NEWSPAPER SOCIETY CAMPAIGN
RECREATION & LEISURE	BJL, MANCHESTER	THE LOWRY ROCK PHOTO EXHIBITION CAMPAIGN
INDUSTRIAL & AGRICULTURAL	PUBLICIS CONSEIL, PARIS	STIHL CUT-OUT SAWS "CONSTRUCTION" CAMPAIGN
PROFESSIONAL EQUIPMENT & SERVICES	GRABARZ & PARTNER, HAMBURG	STUDIO FUNK "NOISES" CAMPAIGN
PRESCRIPTION PRODUCTS	HUNTSWORTH HEALTH, MARLOW	APTIVUS "THE SMART WAY TO STAY AHEAD" CAMPAIGN

TECHNIQUE WINNERS

DIRECT MARKETING (CONSUMER)	TBWA\GERMANY, BERLIN	PLAYSTATION FORBIDDEN SIREN II "GHOST PHOTOS"
DIRECT MARKETING (B to B)	HTW, LONDON	NATIONAL PHOBICS SOCIETY
MEDIA INNOVATION	SCHOLZ & FRIENDS BERLIN	JOBSINTOWN "WRONG WORKING ENVIRONMENT"
ADVERTISING PHOTOGRAPHY	BBDO STUTTGART	KAMITEI FOUNDATION "MASSAI" CAMPAIGN
ILLUSTRATION & GRAPHICS	WALKER, ZURICH	FLEUROP-INTERFLORA 2005 ANNUAL REPORT
PUBLICATIONS	LIDA, LONDON	TAYLOR LANE "STUDIO PIN-UPS" CALENDAR
PACKAGING DESIGN	DEPOT WPF BRAND & IDENTITY, MOSCOW	ZVEZDA PAINTS

INTERACTIVE WINNERS

WEBSITES (DURABLES)	EURO RSCG 4D, AMSTERDAM	VOLVO CX90 "THE HUNT"
WEBSITES (NON-DURABLES)	FARFAR, STOCKHOLM	SWEDISH ALCOHOL COMMITTEE "HOW TO PARTY"
ONLINE ADS	NORDPOL+ HAMBURG AGENTUR, HAMBURG	RENAULT SAFETY CAMPAIGN "CAR CRASH"
ONLINE FILMS	FRAMFAB DENMARK, COPENHAGEN	NIKE SPORTS APPAREL "THE CHAIN"
INTEGRATED CAMPAIGNS	SPILLMANN/FELSER/LEO BURNETT, ZURICH	MAMMUT SPORTS GROUP "MARY WOODBRIDGE"

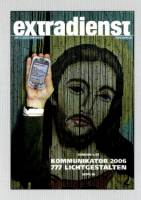

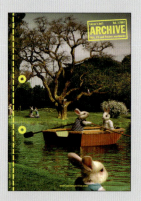

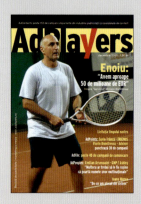

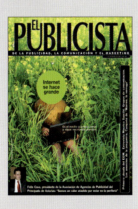

The Jury

The Epica jury is made up of journalists from Europe's leading advertising magazines.

AUSTRIA
Extra Dienst

BELGIUM
Pub

CZECH REPUBLIC
Strategie

DENMARK
Markedsføring

ESTONIA
Best Marketing

FINLAND
Markkinointi & Mainonta

FRANCE
CB News

GERMANY
Lürzer's International Archive
Werben und Verkaufen

GREAT BRITAIN
Creative Review
Marketing Week
The Drum

GREECE
+ Design

HUNGARY
Kreatív

IRELAND
IMJ

ITALY
ADV Express
Pubblicitá Italia
Pubblico

THE NETHERLANDS
Marketing Tribune

NORWAY
Kampanje

POLAND
Media & Marketing Polska

PORTUGAL
Briefing

ROMANIA
AdPlayers

RUSSIA
Advertising Ideas

SLOVAKIA
Stratégie

SERBIA
New Moment

SLOVENIA
MM

SPAIN
El Publicista

SWEDEN
Resumé

SWITZERLAND
Persönlich
Werbe Woche

TURKEY
Marketing Türkiye

Photos: Resumé/Epica

Annual Report

The awards ceremony took place on January 26th, 2007 at the Café Opera in Stockholm. The event was hosted by Resumé, Sweden's leading advertising magazine, and supported by Sveriges Reklamförbund, the Advertising Association of Sweden. More than 400 people attended the event.

Epica celebrated its 20th anniversary in 2006. A total of 703 companies from 45 countries participated in the awards with 5.461 entries, a 10% increase over the previous year.

Wieden+Kennedy Amsterdam won the film Epica d'Or with the Coca-Cola "Happiness Factory" commercial produced by Psyop, New York.

The second Epica d'Or went to Scholz & Friends Berlin for their "Wrong Working Environment" campaign for the online recruitment firm Jobsintown. This marked the first time that an Epica d'Or has been won by a German agency.

Germany was also the most successful country in 2006 with a total of 81 awards, ahead of the UK with 62. Once again, however, the UK took home the most winners finishing on top in 15 categories vs 7 each for Germany and the Netherlands. 2006 was the best year ever for the United Arab Emirates with winners in two categories and for Turkey with three winners. 30 countries won gold, silver or bronze in 2006, four less than the previous year.

With 14 awards, including two winners, TBWA\Paris was the most successful individual agency for the third successive year. Scholz & Friends, Wieden+Kennedy Amsterdam, Abbott Mead Vickers BBDO and Walker, Zurich, each had three winners. DDB was the most successful network, as it was in 2005, with five winners from five countries.

A total of 61 Epica winners were announced in 2006, including the two grand prix. The number of silver and bronze finalists increased 5 % from 379 to 398.

All the winners and finalists are shown in the Epica book, together with a selection of other short-listed entries.

	Entrants	Entries	Winners	Silver	Bronze
Austria	15	73	-	6	4
Belarus	1	1	-	-	-
Belgium	21	205	2	7	6
Bosnia-Herzegovina	1	3	-	-	-
Bulgaria	3	24	-	-	1
Croatia	9	22	-	-	-
Czech Republic	7	25	-	4	1
Denmark	21	72	1	3	5
Egypt	1	1	-	-	1
Estonia	2	6	-	-	-
Finland	22	160	1	3	5
France	44	472	6	28	26
Georgia	1	2	-	-	-
Germany	100	1,111	7	41	33
Greece	17	129	-	-	1
Hungary	10	34	-	2	1
Iceland	5	15	-	-	-
Ireland	7	68	-	-	1
Israel	9	49	-	1	2
Italy	34	262	2	8	6
Kuwait	2	7	-	-	-
Latvia	1	6	-	-	-
Lebanon	3	28	-	1	1
Lithuania	2	4	-	-	-
Luxembourg	1	2	-	-	1
Macedonia	3	7	-	-	1
Netherlands	31	230	7	11	9
Norway	14	79	2	8	8
Poland	13	83	-	2	3
Portugal	11	95	1	1	5
Romania	12	80	1	1	3
Russia	23	77	1	-	1
Saudi Arabia	3	11	-	-	-
Serbia	4	12	-	-	-
Slovakia	7	37	-	-	-
Slovenia	8	24	-	-	-
Spain	27	240	1	5	4
Sweden	85	718	4	24	33
Switzerland	19	337	5	10	14
Tunisia	1	3	-	-	-
Turkey	21	113	3	1	2
Ukraine	11	29	-	1	1
United Arab Emirates	11	103	2	1	3
United Kingdom	59	395	15	22	25
USA	1	7	-	-	-
TOTAL	703	5,461	61	191	207

For more information on the awards and to watch all the film winners and finalists visit www.epica-awards.com

Inside Coke's New World

A look behind the scenes of the Happiness Factory, by Mark Tungate

When Wieden+Kennedy Amsterdam needed a TV spot that would appeal to consumers across the globe, the agency decided to abandon the real world altogether. Instead, it joined forces with a team of animation geniuses to create an alternative universe inside a Coca-Cola vending machine.

"At the time we won the account, Coca-Cola had become like the mountain you live next door to but don't see any more," says Hunter Hindman, creative director on the project along with Rick Condos. "It was so omnipresent that consumers had begun to stop noticing it. Our mission was to bring it back into the foreground."

One of the agency's solutions to this problem was to focus on a key attribute of the brand: its unique glass bottle. "Every time we thought about Coca-Cola, we kept coming back to that iconic bottle and the great taste you get when you drink out of it. So that became the symbol of everything we wanted to do. For Happiness Factory, we imagined the journey of the bottle through the vending machine. In real life, of course, the machines are kind of boring – but we pictured a highly intricate process."

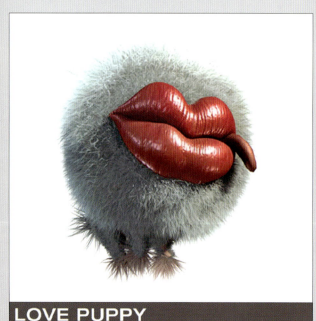

LOVE PUPPY

MORTAR MAN

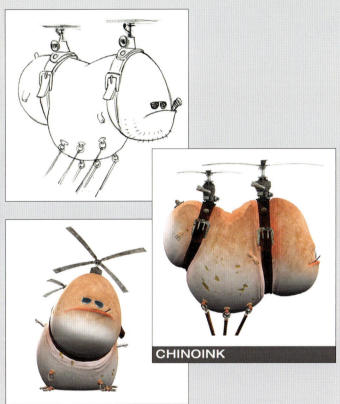

CHINOINK

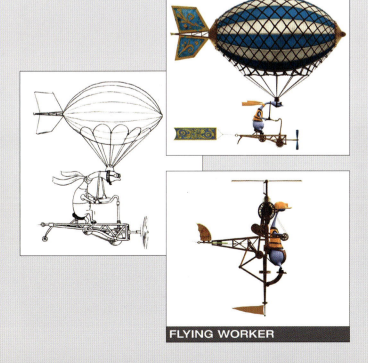

FLYING WORKER

Hindman says the idea "hung around for a long time" before Coke and the agency moved forward with it. "Everyone liked the idea but we weren't really sure how to approach it. Part of the problem was that we didn't know what the new world we wanted to depict would look like. We only knew that we didn't want it to be easy, sugar-coated animation. It had to have a slightly darker side, otherwise contemporary consumers just wouldn't engage with it."

Hindman and Condos remembered Psyop, a New York based computer animation company they had come across in previous jobs at the San Francisco agency Goodby Silverstein, which is known for its technological savvy. When the Wieden+Kennedy team locked themselves into a room to brainstorm the idea with Todd Mueller and Kylie Matulick of Psyop, the pieces began to fall into place.

"One of our reference points was a series of postcards from a particular valley in Australia that has this incredible lush, epic quality. We wanted to merge that fantasy landscape – kind of like the one in Lord of the Rings – with technology. It occurred to us that all of the creatures would have evolved to be perfectly adapted to their allotted tasks. After all, Coke is 120 years old in the real world – who knows how long that is in their time frame?"

Now functioning as a team, Wieden+Kennedy and Psyop began developing ideas for the characters that would populate the vending machine world. Many of the creatures had exaggerated human or animal features mashed up with machine elements. One of the most striking was a cross between a pig and a Chinook helicopter – soon christened a Chinoink – which would carry the bottle with its nipple rings. "You'll notice there's a slightly sado-masochistic element to the spot," laughs Hindman. "We also feed snowmen into a wood chipper. It all fit with our theory that the animation shouldn't be too cute. A factory is hard work and these creatures are totally committed to imbuing the bottle with happiness. It's a labour of love."

More than 15 animators and technicians worked on the spot, which took more than four months to bring to the screen. Wieden+Kennedy call it "an amazing collaborative process".

But the magic didn't end there: audience responses to the film were overwhelmingly positive. Nobody at the agency was entirely prepared for the onslaught of enthusiasm that greeted its release. It was the number one film on the YouTube site for more than two weeks, single-handedly decimating notions that traditional advertising will lose out to Web 2.0.

"It's certainly proof that advertising works if it's entertaining," says Hindman. "And bear in mind that there is hardly a single frame in the spot where either the bottle or the Coke logo are not visible. The spot takes place in a universe where the Coke bottle is the local god."

More than anything, Happiness Factory is proof positive that award-winning advertising is not always about telling a joke. Surreal optimism works too.

Mark Tungate is the author of ADLAND: A Global History of Advertising, published by Kogan Page

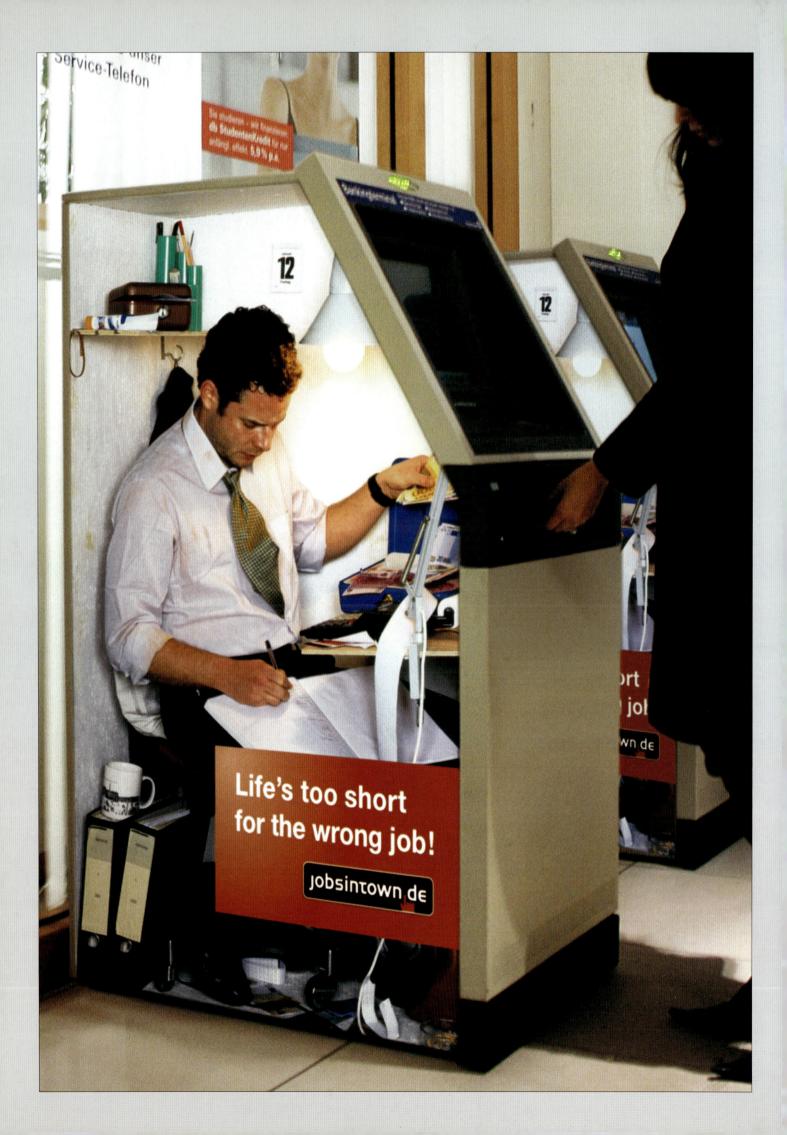

Jobs in Machines

Jan Burney reports on 'wrong working environments'

How do you capture the attention of people engrossed in misery, on their way to a job they detest and unlikely to give a second glance to all the shiny, happy people in adverts that only emphasise the contrast with their own tedious working lives? That was the challenge facing Jan Leube and Matthias Spaetgens, the creative team from Scholz & Friends Berlin, who were handed the brief for a new campaign by Jobsintown, an online recruitment service. The company wanted to become a serious challenger to it's more established rivals - but on a media budget that was considerably smaller.

Leube and Spaetgens convinced their client that only something very special and out of the ordinary would succeed in attracting enough notice and began looking at alternative media as a way round their small budget. Travelling to and from work, and armed with the knowledge that 87% of German employees are dissatisfied with their jobs, they hit on the idea of targeting people when they were most conscious of their discontent - commuting to the work they despised. To grab their attention, they would use these mundane features of our everyday environment - vending machines - and shock people into givng them a second look.

Leube and Spaetgens' series of trompe 'oeil posters plastered to the sides of ATMs, photo booths and vending machines showed people apparently toiling at repetitive tasks - counting and distributing banknotes, developing passport photos, preparing endless cups of coffee - within the tiny, confined space of the cramped booths. Clearly, many of the commuters who thought, "Yeah, that's me," were inspired to act by Jobsintown's message on the posters ("Life's too short for the wrong job"): visits to their website increased by 20% on the previous year.

By choosing booths located in and around metro stations with the highest commuter traffic, the agency maximised the effectiveness of the campaign. Initially, however, they needed all their powers of persuasion to convince these media partners, since the machines had never been used for advertising before.

Ultimately, though, it was the frustrated workers in their claustrophobic booths that not only created an increase in brand awareness for Leube and Spaetgens' client but also persuaded huge numbers of German employees to take action against their own discontent. As a result, the Jobsintown posters might not be the only thing putting a smile on their face as they travel to work: a change of job could be making them feel more like the happy people in the ordinary ads and less like the poor wage slaves who provoked them into contacting Jobsintown.

15

Jan Burney is a writer and lecturer in applied creativity and art history. She has worked as contributing editor to leading advertising industry titles including Lürzer's Archive, Creativity and Graphis, was the editor of Designer magazine, and is the author of books including an acclaimed biography of the Italian designer Ettore Sottsass.

501 **Levi's** PORTATI AD OGNI ESPERIENZA.

Secrets of Sucess

What does it take to be an Epica d'Or winner? Lewis Blackwell reviews the first 20 years

The greatest gift this article could give you is a secret. That secret would be to reveal the magic formula, the 7X equivalent, the knowledge that turns a humble ad into an Epica winner capable of triumphing over the best from Europe and beyond.

That certainly would be a gift worth having. On a regular basis whatever comes out on top at Epica goes on to clean up at many of the awards elsewhere around the world. At the time of writing it's too early to know how the Coke 'Happiness Factory' will perform in the 2007 awards season, but three of the previous four Epica d'Or winners have gone on to top the analysis in the Gunn Report and the last two took Grand Prix at Cannes.

So let's start the revelations on the inner workings of an Epica d'Or.

First, a cracking insight that may seem obvious: good breeding helps. It pays to employ the smart people or work with the smart clients. In other words, if you have an agency like Wieden+Kennedy (four times overall winners) or a pedigree agency-client relationship like 180 Amsterdam and Adidas (twice winners) then this would suggest you have improved your

chances for making good advertising. I could add to that list various other good and famously creative agencies like Mother, Abbott Mead Vickers BBDO, Paradiset DDB in Stockholm, all of whom have also enjoyed the walk to the front for the topmost prize.

But it is worth noting that the Epica d'Or has often helped these established creative stars become established. The reputation has to start somewhere. Even Wieden+Kennedy was only really famous for the Nike work out of the US when they triumphed in the 1994 awards with a product from their relatively recently established Amsterdam office, creators of the spectacular 'The Wall' commercial.

And production pure blood is also aligned with the client and agency breeding. Top tier partners on the execution is always handy and they range from this year's top production team of Psyop, the CGI geniuses behind the winning Coca-Cola spot 'Happiness Factory', to previous big name triumphs for Danny Kleinman, Traktor, Tony Kaye and Paul Weiland.

But I can already hear the rumblings of old ad thinking with the adage: 'Never mind who is behind the ad – it's still nothing if there's not a great idea.' And, of course, that is true. So what are the trends in the most outstanding work? Are there tendencies we can plot so as to help us concoct the likely next Epica d'Or?

Frankly, the diversity of the winning work is a real challenge to analytical skills. It says a lot about the quality of advertising innovation, and perhaps also the openness of Epica juries over the years, that visually and structurally the work could scarcely be more different. Live action one year, animation the next; fine comic writing succeeded by visual extravaganzas…and back again. Nothing easy to plot. But there may be some trends in there somewhere, so let's go in close on a couple of great winners.

Let's turn back the clock and consider the remarkably differing concepts of an idea, and forms of genius, that lay behind the 1990 and 1991 winners.

In 1990 the vote went to the astounding spot 'Egoiste' – a blockbuster, an epic of a commercial, created for Chanel's then new perfume by director and wide-ranging artist Jean-Paul Goude. If you are old enough to remember it, you will, and if not - well, you may still remember it because it so regularly gets re-aired as great content (rather than mere advertising) every time somebody wants to celebrate or criticise the excesses of ad style.

Just to tweak your synapses: it is the spot where you open on a grand hotel (a bit like the Carlton in Cannes, but actually built from scratch as a set on a South American beach, presumably for a fraction of the cost hiring the real hotel…). Then women start flinging open the various bedroom window shutters and shouting 'egoiste'. You pull back and the whole building is full of women opening and shutting the windows in time to this crazy cry. Is it for a man who has seduced them? Or have they run out of the must-have perfume? Whatever, it is astounding, etching the brand name and its desirability onto your memory.

So contrast that with the following year – 1991, a unique moment in Epica history. This was when a print campaign beat all the best commercials of the year to the top honour. This was in fact the only year that this was achieved (as of 2003 separate Epica d'Or have been awarded for film and print ensuring that the best print gets recognised without having to fight the perhaps unfair battle of taking on all the extra seductions of film).

The campaign that managed this remarkable triumph was the 'Fit for whatever' ads for Levi's out of McCann-Erickson, Milan.

Each ad was brutally simple and classic in its construction, dedicated to a photograph that showed the Levi's jeans in unusual, challenging application. In one it was the reins on a horse, in another it appeared as a sumo's mawashi (belt) and in another it swathed a face as a nomad's headdress. The images, by the leading advertising photographer Graham Ford, were quiet masterpieces of ad styling and high production values in which nothing was left to chance, nothing was there that wasn't about impressing us with the idea – that Levi's were fit and fashionable for whatever you threw at them.

Now while the media and the production treatment were remarkably different, there is a very strong connection between the Chanel commercial and the Levi's campaign. Both are excellent celebrations of advertising creatives' ability to lock a complex range of advertising messages together with powerful emotional triggers inside a very clear idea that is bang on brief. They might not look at all the same, but in essence they are the same kind of construction. We are talking about the simple ability to reduce complexity to its simplest, most emotive form.

Both these ads saw their creators find remarkably simple visual ideas. This ability to condense a whole business strategy and complex brief into an image is at the heart of why advertising can work so powerfully on us. It is a masterpiece of reduction akin to the creation of the finest sauce in the Michelin three-star restaurant.

However, you have to wonder if advertising agencies can still focus so much on striving for that purity of an idea. In the age where conventional advertising is less central to some of the media planning, where 'branded content' is spoken about as the buzzphrase ahead of mainstream advertising for increasing numbers of clients, where does the great reductive idea sit? Who needs a single image or a 30-second mind-blowing film when they are trying to fill up websites and even their own TV channels with content?

There are some very real challenges coming through for advertising creativity, of which the highlights will, I trust, be marked out and recorded in the next 20 years of Epica. But we have had some intimations of where things can go, and why great advertising talents are likely to still be central one way or other in shaping brand awareness.

Consider, for example, the delightful Honda 'Grrr' commercial that took the Epica d'Or in 2004. This cute piece of animation ushered in a new way of messaging about a car brand. There was the potential to extend that look and tonality across websites and print, across other content. The same could be said for this year's Coca-Cola spot 'Happiness Factory'.

Mother's 2001 Epica d'Or triumph with the hilarious set of low-cost spots for the cable channel QTV, 'The Danster' campaign, was also as much content as it was straightforward advertising. There was a rich character and attitude in the campaign that could easily have been built out into other areas. Indeed, Mother seem to now be making a point of inventing powerful characters (even wrestling one back from a former client to use elsewhere).

However, we don't have to clutch for connections in recent winners in order to make this point about how you can take outstanding advertising and integrate it with broader brand developments. Right from the beginning the very first Epica d'Or points the way to how great advertising and great branding are often very long-term in their thinking, even if in itself a commercial or print ad is only used relatively briefly.

Back in 1987, when Epica was only a few months old and just setting out on its mission to show no fear or favour in picking the true best of Europe, the jury convened and cogitated in some modest hotel. (We've always done it for the pleasure of discussing great ads rather than any excessive hospitality. Thank you, Andrew, for keeping us all pure.)

After some days, the white smoke arose. The winner was BMP of London with its still astounding commercial for The Guardian newspaper, 'Points of View'. Shot by Paul Weiland and written by the late great John Webster, the film shows how you need to get the whole picture to truly understand things… how different perspectives alter your interpretation of an action. It does this through appearing to show a skinhead first running away from the police, then attacking somebody, when in fact it turns out he is saving a man from a pallet of falling bricks. You have to see it to believe it.

This film looks pretty much as fresh today as then – and, remarkably, could even be used now because that is still a message so universal and relevant that it is on-brand for the newspaper.

My point of view is that the great winners of Epica d'Or stand out as content beyond their specific advertising remit. They are powerful because they connect in intense form and that kind of genius will continue to be invaluable to our culture and commerce. Epica can evolve over another 20 years in rewarding the very best, whatever media our advertising evolves into.

As to the secrets I promised… I think I can perhaps reveal only one overlooked factor behind all the genius of the greatest ads.

EPICA D'OR WINNERS 1987 – 2006

FILM WINNERS

1987	Boase Massimi Pollit, London	The Guardian, "Points of View"
1988	DDB Needham, London	Tate Gallery Liverpool, "Modern Art"
1989	DMB&B, London	Royal Mail, "Letters of Love"
1990	Chanel, Paris (in-house)	Egoiste, "Egoiste"
1992	Lowe Howard-Spink, London	Reebok, "Second Year Running"
1993	Abbott Mead Vickers BBDO, London	Dunlop, "Tested for the Unexpected"
1994	Wieden+Kennedy, Amsterdam	Nike, "The Wall"
1995	Faulds Advertising, Edinburgh	BBC Radio Scotland Campaign
1996	Ogilvy & Mather, London	Guinness, "Bicycle"
1997	Pirella Göttsche Lowe, Milan	Superga, "The Challenge"
1998	Paradiset DDB, Stockholm	Thomson Holidays Campaign
1999	Lowe Howard-Spink, London	The Independent, "Litany"
2000	180 Amsterdam	Adidas, "Adidas Makes You Better"
2001	Mother, London	QTV, "The Danster" Campaign
2002	Euro RSCG MCM, Milan	Peugot 206, "The Sculptor"
2003	Wieden+Kennedy, Amsterdam	Nike, "Musical Chairs"
2004	Wieden+Kennedy, London	Honda, "Grrr"
2005	Abbott Mead Vickers BBDO, London	Guinness, "Noitulove"
2006	Wieden+Kennedy, Amsterdam	Coca-Cola, "Happiness Factory"

PRINT WINNERS

1991	McCann-Erickson, Milan	Levi's, "Fit for Whatever" Campaign
2003	180 Amsterdam	Adidas Rugby, "Self-Portraits" Campaign
2004	BDDP & Fils, Paris	Les Echos, "Understand the World" Campaign
2005	Foote Cone & Belding, Lisbon	Grande Reportagem, "Flags" Campaign
2006	Scholz & Friends, Hamburg	Jobsintown, "Wrong Working Environment"

All kinds of ideas are possible, all kinds of talent, and all kinds of clients and products might be associated with a winner.

But one thing is very clear: there is not a single winner which does not result in effortless display hiding immense amounts of hard graft. So it helps to be a genius, and it helps to work with similar talents… but there won't be a great result without pushing the work to a standard of execution that only a certain amount of pain can deliver.

So our little secret is that perhaps a tendency to sado-masochism in the creative teams is the key factor that binds, very tightly, all the Epica d'Or winners together.

Lewis Blackwell is renowned as a commentator on creativity. His work as SVP group creative director of Getty Images, and formerly Editor-in-chief and publisher of Creative Review, has led him to work with agencies around the world. He is the author of bestselling books, is on the faculty of the School for Creative Leadership at Steinbeis University, Berlin, and looks back fondly on many years spent in a darkened cell as an Epica judge.

Agency	Tonic Communications, Dubai
Creative Directors	Vincent Raffray Khaled Gadallah
Copywriter	Vincent Raffray
Art Director	Peter Walker
Production	Filmworks, Dubai
Directors	Vincent Raffray Peter Walker
Producer	Tim Smythe
Client	Nando's Restaurants, "Ramadan Kareem"

This spot from Dubai depicts a young man sitting on a terrace restaurant overlooking the sea. He holds a succulent leg of Nando's chicken only centimetres away from his open mouth. His gaze is fixed on the middle distance. As the camera's point of view changes, we see that he is watching the setting sun. It's Ramadan, and only when the sun finally goes down can he sink his teeth into the tasty chicken.

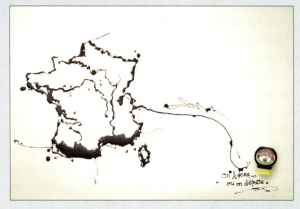

Agency   DDB London
Creative Director Jeremy Craigen
Copywriter   Thierry Albert
Art Director   Damien Bellon
Client   Marmite Squeezy

Agency	Beattie McGuinness Bungay, London
Creative Director	Trevor Beattie
Copywriter	Trevor Beattie
Art Director	Bil Bungay
Production	Partizan, London
Director	Michael Gracey
Producers	Ella Sanderson
	Jane Oak
Client	McCain Oven Chips, "Sunflower Park"

In this homage to Lionel Bart's award-winning musical Oliver, a young man in the kitchen of a large household begins singing about his love of chips: "Chips, glorious chips!" All the kitchen workers join in and – as the boy dances his way through the house – everyone seems to share his passion for the humble French fry. Finally he emerges into the street, where the Hollywood spectacular climaxes in a chorus of "Five per cent faaaat!"

Agency	Saatchi & Saatchi Russia, Moscow
Creative Director	Stuart Robinson
Copywriter	Irina Gorshkova
Art Director	Stuart Robinson
Production	Pandora Films, St. Petersburg
Director	Dmitry Khonin
Producers	Olga Ivanova
	Ekaterina Barmak
Client	Ryabushka Eggs, "Asleep"

A couple of Russian farmers trudge through the snow to a chicken coop. As they unlock the door and step inside, we see that it resembles a boarding school, with rows of comfy-looking beds. In each bed is a chicken, sleeping soundly on a soft pillow. "It's time they were up!" says the man gruffly. "Five more minutes," pleads his wife tenderly, as the coddled chickens snooze on. The best eggs come from the happiest chickens.

Agency	Leo Burnett Paris
Creative Directors	Stephan Ferens
	Jean-François Goize
Copywriter	Céline Lescure
Art Director	Guillaume Quéré
Production	The Gang Films
Director	Joachim Back
Producer	Christophe Demeure
Client	Charal Meat, "Too Late"

In a scenario resembling the film The Shining, a man drives determinedly through a snowy landscape. Why is he haunted by images of his wife? What's the mysterious brown paper bag sitting significantly on the passenger seat? Finally the man is alone in a remote farmhouse, the bag on the table in front of him. His wife's car screeches up outside and she breaks down the door, pleading hysterically: "No John – don't leave us!" It's too late: John has already taken his first bite. Every day, because of Charal beef, vegetarians vanish.

Agency	TBWA\España, Madrid	**Agency**	Ogilvy & Mather, Frankfurt
Creative Directors	Agustin Vaquero Guillermo Gines Angel Iglesias	**Creative Directors**	Simon Oppmann Peter Roemmelt
Copywriter	Vicente Rodriguez	**Copywriter**	Peter Roemmelt
Art Director	Gonzalo Vergara	**Art Director**	Simon Oppmann
Client	Whiskas Cat Food	**Client**	Globus Rutan Cat Food

Agency	DDB Oslo
Copywriter	Torbjørn Kvien Madsen
Art Director	Rune Markhus
Production	Motion Blur
Director	Stefan Treschov
Producers	Espen Horn
	Cyril Boije
Client	Gilde Meat, "Beef"

As a man cycles to the supermarket, every animal and object seems to repeat the same refrain. A bird, a yapping dog, a mobile phone, even the beeping traffic signal, in various tones and pitches they all seem to sound like: "Beef! Beef!" Finally the man arrives at the supermarket. As the cashier scans his packets of meat, even the till seems to sing happily: "Beef! Beef!" Beef this good can give you a one-track mind.

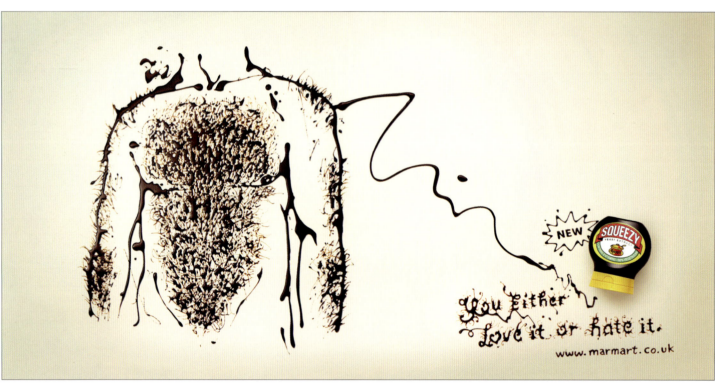

Agency	DDB London
Creative Director	Jeremy Craigen
Copywriter	Thierry Albert
Art Director	Damien Bellon
Client	Marmite Squeezy

Agency	Young & Rubicam, Frankfurt	Agency	TBWA\Paris
Creative Directors	Helmut Schulte	Creative Director	Erik Vervroegen
	Christian Daul	Copywriter	Jean-François Bouchet
Art Director	Bruno Petz	Art Director	Jessica Gérard-Huet
Photographer	Bruno Petz	Photographer	Achim Lippoth
Client	Erasco Soup	Client	Harry's Bread

Agency	Medina Turgul DDB, Istanbul	Agency	.start, Munich
Creative Director	Kurtcebe Turgul	Creative Director	Marco Mehrwald
Copywriter	Gokhan Erol	Copywriter	Bernd Nagenrauft
Art Director	Timsal Unsal	Art Director	Gesine Schmidt
Client	Pastavilla	Photographers	Volker Dautzenberg
			Manfred Kirchmayr
		Client	Burger King

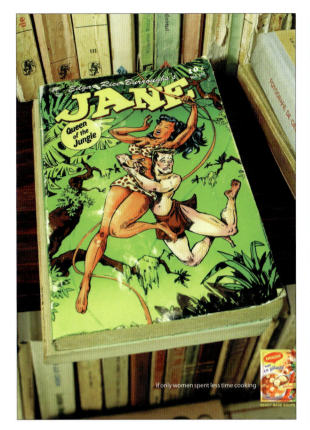

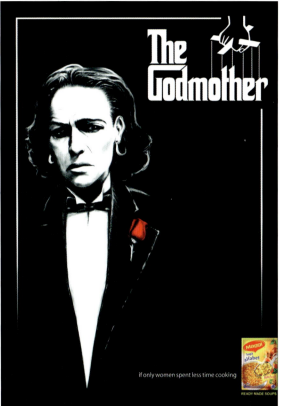

Agency	McCann Erickson Romania, Bucharest
Creative Directors	Adrian Botan
	Alexandru Dumitrescu
Copywriter	Radu Pilat
Art Director	Monica Stanescu
Client	Maggi Soups

Everybody wants to be a dog
Eukanuba

McDonald's in Birkerød re-opens in 2 weeks

McDonald's in Birkerød re-opens in 3 weeks

28 **Food**

Agency	Leo Burnett & Target, Bucharest	**Agency**	DDB Denmark, Copenhagen
Creative Director	Bogdan Naumovici	**Creative Director**	Poul Mikkelsen
Copywriter	Mihai Costache	**Art Directors**	Mikkel Moeller
Art Director	Ghica Popa		Tim Ustrup
Photographer	Tudor Cuciuc	**Client**	McDonald's
Client	Eukanuba Dog Food		

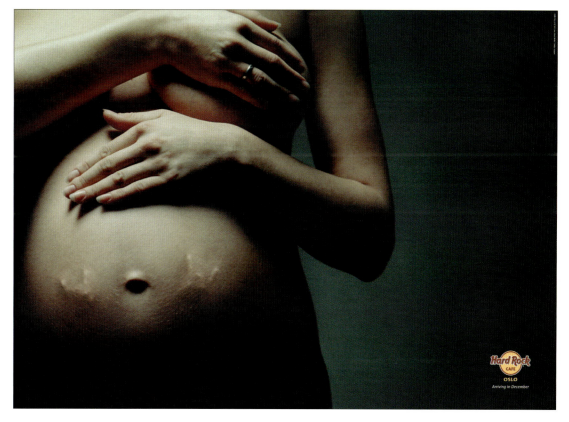

Agency	DDB Amsterdam		**Agency**	DDB Oslo
Creative Directors	Joris Kuijpers		**Copywriter**	Torbjørn Kvien Madsen
	Dylan de Backer		**Art Directors**	Joachim Bjørndahl
Copywriter	Robert den Bremer			Rune Markhus
Art Director	Edward Romunde		**Photographer**	Nick White
Client	McDonald's		**Client**	Hard Rock Café

Agency	Shalmor Avnon Amichay/Y&R, Tel Aviv	**Agency**	TBWA\Paris
Creative Directors	Gideon Amichay	**Creative Director**	Erik Vervroegen
	Yoram Levi	**Copywriters**	Daniel Perez
Copywriter	Yair Sheinberg		Ghislaine de Germon
Art Director	Tal Riven		Stephane Gaubert
Client	Heinz Ketchup	**Art Directors**	Javier Rodriguez
			Isabelle Monot
		Photographer	Cingy Gravelat
		Client	Dentastix

KIKKOMAN. THE FOOD-JAPANIZER.

KIKKOMAN. THE FOOD-JAPANIZER.

Das Gute daran ist das Gute darin

Agency	Cayenne Werbeagentur, Düsseldorf	Agency	Young & Rubicam, Frankfurt
Creative Director	David Moore	Creative Director	Christian Daul
Copywriter	Claudia Korpadi	Copywriter	Christian Daul
Art Director	Regina Wysny	Art Director	Bruno Petz
Photographer	Carlfried Verwaayen	Photographer	Marc Wuchner
Client	Kikkoman	Client	Erasco Spaghetti

32 Food

Agency	Leo Burnett, Brussels
Creative Directors	Jean-Paul Lefebvre
	Michel De Lauw
Art Director	Mathieu Dubray
Illustrator	Michel Denis
Client	Heinz Hot Ketchup

Nejma Sunflower. Cooking and frying oil.

White Tuna Ortiz
Rod-caught
one by one

Agency	Memac Ogilvy Tunisia, Tunis	Agency	Grey & Trace, Barcelona
Creative Director	Nicolas Courant	Creative Directors	Jürgen Krieger
Copywriter	Nicolas Courant		Quim Crespo
Art Director	Gérald Héraud	Art Director	Alex Martín
Photographer	Anis Cherif	Client	Ortiz Tuna
Client	Nejma Oil		

34 Confectionery & Snacks

Agency	Abbott Mead Vickers BBDO, London
Creative Director	Paul Brazier
Copywriter	Stephen Moss
Art Director	Jolyon Finch
Production	Therapy Films
Director	Guy Manwairing
Client	Wrigleys Airwaves, "Alien"

An alien lands in Britain, where he is greeted by officials. "Make yourself at home," says a military man. The alien takes a packet of Airways Active gum from the man's top pocket and begins to chew one. Suddenly able to predict the future, he sees all the crappy aspects of British life that await him: being crammed into the Tube, going to a bingo night, turning into a couch potato, struggling with flat-pack furniture, a barbecue in the rain. After this sudden insight, the alien scurries back into his flying saucer and takes off. Airwaves make everything clear.

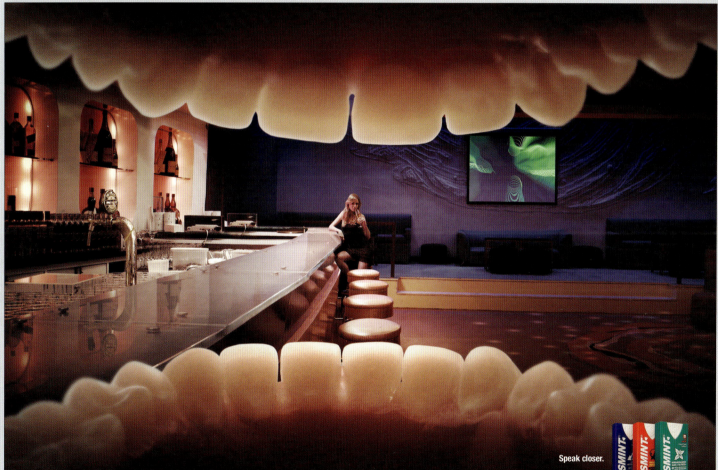

 Confectionery & Snacks **35**

Agency	Leo Burnett, Lisbon
Creative Director	Fernando Bellotti
Copywriter	Marilu Rodrigues
Art Director	Paulo Areas
Photographer	Leo Vilela
Client	Smint Mints

Agency	Leo Burnett, Paris
Creative Directors	Jean-François Goize
	Stephan Ferens
Copywriter	Eric Pierre
Art Director	Damien Boulier
Production	Première Heure
	Uturn
Director	Paf le Chien
Producer	Catherine Guiol
Client	Krisprolls, "Swede",
	"Clog" & "Lulea"

Pity the Swedes! In the first of three spots, we see the impassive expression of a large Swedish man. "Swede in a bad mood", says the caption. Then it switches to "Swede in a good mood". Even when we reach "Swede in love", the man's expression does not change. In the second spot, the clog is presented as the staple item of Swedish footwear. Finally, in the third spot, we see that for most of the winter, the country remains dark. "The most exciting thing about Sweden is the toast", suggest the makers of Swedish breakfast snack Krisprolls.

Agency	Scholz & Friends
	Hamburg
Creative Director	Stefan Setzkorn
Copywriter	Oliver Birkmeier
Art Director	Stefanie Zimmermann
Production	Cobblestone,
	Hamburg
Director	Andreas Hoffmann
Producer	Sabine Schroeder
Client	Chio Chips,
	"The Grandma
	Commercial"

As he ambles along the street distractedly munching his Chio chips, a young man almost bumps into an old lady. He apologises politely and she smiles. Then she tries to grab his packet of crisps. As he struggles to hang on to them, the old woman cries out: "Help!" To onlookers, it seems as if he is trying to rob her! He has no choice but to let go of his crisps. Triumphant, the suddenly sprightly old woman rushes off with his snack.

Agency	DDB Stockholm
Creative Director	Andreas Dahlqvist
Copywriter	Nils-Gustav Thollman
Art Directors	Simon Mogren
	Andreas Dahlqvist
Production	Spader Knekt
Director	Filip Tellander
Producers	Mattias Bengtsson
	Fabian Mannheimer
Client	OLW Potato Crisps,
	"Potato Hunter"

A hushed documentary-style voiceover describes the lives of the amazing free-range potatoes as they enjoy their freedom in the wilderness. When the potato hunters arrive, the lively spuds scatter: but some of them fall victim to the expert potato trappers dispatched by top crisp maker OLW. The scene cuts to a party, where the beautiful people tuck into their OLW crisps, unaware of the savage tale that lies behind their snack.

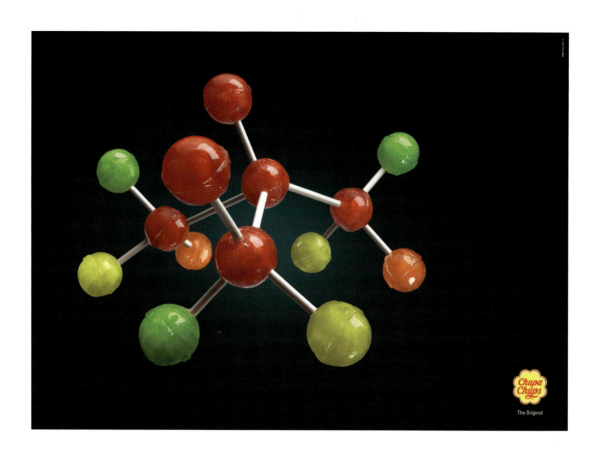

Agency	DDB Spain, Madrid		**Agency**	CLM BBDO, Paris
Creative Directors	Juanra Alfaro		**Creative Directors**	Gilles Fichteberg
	Sergi Zapater			Jean-Francois Sacco
Copywriter	Isahac Oliver		**Copywriter**	Dimitri Guerassimov
Art Director	Xavi Sitjar		**Art Director**	Dimitri Guerassimov
Photographer	Fergus Stothard		**Client**	Freedent White
Client	Chupa Chups			

Agency	Abbott Mead Vickers BBDO, London
Creative Director	Paul Brazier
Copywriter	Mike Nicholson
Art Director	Paul Pateman
Client	Snickers

Agency	JWT Dubai
Creative Directors	John Foster
	Chafic Haddad
Copywriter	Elias Haddad
Art Director	Firas Medrows
Photographer	Daryl Patni
Client	Lion

Agency	Abbott Mead Vickers BBDO, London
Creative Director	Paul Brazier
Copywriter	Jack Stephens
Art Director	Rob Neilsen
Client	Snickers

Long lasting taste **SPORTLIFE**

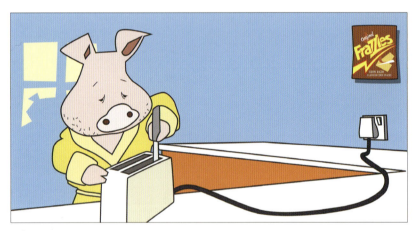

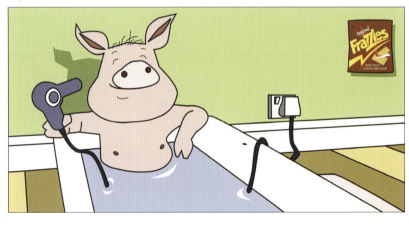

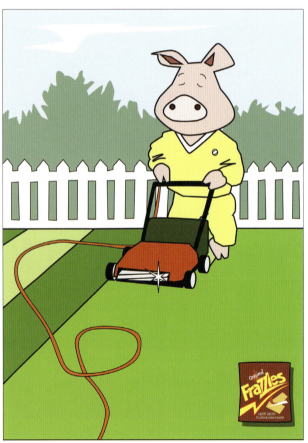

Agency	JWT/PPGH, Amsterdam		**Agency**	Abbott Mead Vickers BBDO, London
Creative Directors	Bart Kooij			
	Nico Akkerman		**Creative Director**	Paul Brazier
Copywriter	Bies Vermeulen		**Copywriter**	Milo Campbell
Art Director	Sebastiaan Kenter		**Art Director**	Sonny Adorjan
Photographer	Nico Garstman		**Client**	Frazzles, Crispy Bacon
Client	Sportlife Chewing Gum			Flavoured Snacks

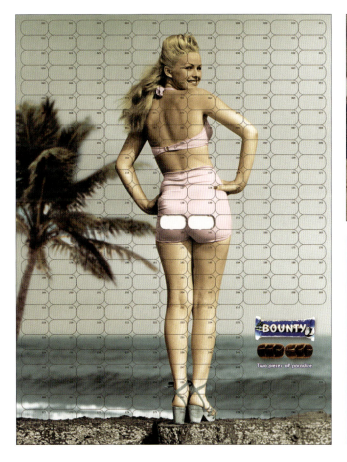

Agency	JWT Italia, Milan
Creative Directors	Pietro Maestri
	Alberto Citterio
Copywriter	Giovanni Salvaggio
Art Director	Stefano Fantini
Photographer	Francesca Garavaglia
Client	Hall's Lozenges

Agency	Tiempo BBDO, Madrid
Executive CD	Andrés Martínez Echeverría
Creative Director	Carlos Alija
Copywriter	Andrés Martínez Echeverría
Art Director	Ricardo Pastor
Client	Bounty

42 **Dairy Products**

Agency	Try Advertising Agency, Oslo
Copywriter	Øystein Halvorsen
Art Director	Einar Fjøsne
Production	Askild Action & Fredrik Fiction
Director	Jesper Andersson
Producers	Fredrik Pryser
	Eivind Moe
	Cecilie Thue
Client	Tine Yoghurt, "Turn Around"

"Turn around," is the first line of Bonnie Tyler's hit song, "Total Eclipse of the Heart", and the soundtrack to this spot. In it, we see various people "turning around" in a panic after forgetting to buy their Tine yoghurt in the supermarket. The scenarios get increasingly extreme: from a woman cycling back up a steep hill to a lady forcing a bus-driver to turn around; and finally the captain of a cruise ship who turns his vessel around after forgetting the delicious yoghurt.

www.swissmilk.ch

Milk. Grow up, stay strong!

Dairy Products 43

Agency	Advico Young & Rubicam, Zurich
Creative Director	Daniel Comte
Copywriter	Christoph Hess
Art Directors	Willem Baumann
	Nicolas Vontobel
Photographer	Julien Vonier
Client	SMP Swiss Milk Producers

Agency	McCann Erickson, Madrid
Creative Director	Luis Diez
Copywriter	Joaquin Barbero
Art Director	Mario Garcia
Photographers	Salva Fresneda
	Bela Alder
Illustrator	Toni Garreta
Client	Magnum Ice Cream

44   Dairy Products

Agency	Gitam BBDO, Ramat-Gan
Creative Directors	Asi Shavit
	Gal Porat
Copywriter	Romem Saranga
Art Director	Gal Porat
Production	Shoshi & Udi, Tel Aviv
Director	Kobi Havia
Producers	Shoshi & Udi
	Maya Meiri
Client	Tnuva Milk, "Magnets"

In this simple but effective spot, a boy takes some milk from the fridge and takes a sip. Suddenly, all the fridge magnets leap off the fridge and stick to his torso. In the pack shot, we learn that the milk is enriched with iron, hence the boy's new 'magnetism'.

Agency	BBDO Oslo
Creative Director	Petter Gulli
Copywriter	Petter Gulli
Art Director	Joachim Haug
Production	Social Club, Stockholm
Director	Henrik Lagerkrantz
Producers	Rickard Edholm
	Rolf Pedersen
Client	Yoplait Yoghurt, "Better in French"

Ah, the joys of French cinema – in which passionate couples are always arguing! This spot takes one such scene and replaces the lyrical French accents with those of working class London. 'You stink of perfume – you bastard!' says the woman, slapping her husband. It turns the whole thing into an episode of the British soap opera East Enders. Some things are better in French, like Yoplait yoghurt for example.

Dairy Products **45**

Agency	ANR.BBDO, Gothenburg	Agency	DDB Paris
Copywriter	Jens Englund	Creative Director	Bertrand Pallatin
Art Director	Andreas Lönn	Copywriter	Frédéric Sounillac
Photographer	Pal Allan	Art Director	Alexandre Veret
Client	Wästgöta Kloster Cheese	Client	Le Petit Camembert

46   **Dairy Products**

Agency	DDB London
Creative Director	Jeremy Craigen
Copywriter	Tim Charlesworth
Art Director	Michael Kaplan
Client	Cravendale Hint Of Milk

The Japanese yoghurt

Agency	Saatchi & Saatchi, Dubai
Creative Director	Ed Jones
Copywriter	Avinash Sampath
Art Director	Andrew Leftley
Photographer	Sunil Raju
Illustrator	Ahmed Kunamed
Client	La Vache Qui Rit

Agency	Volt, Stockholm
Photographer	Pysse Holmberg
Client	Onaka Yoghurt

48 **Alcoholic Drinks**

Agency	Abbott Mead Vickers BBDO, London	
Creative Director	Paul Brazier	
Copywriter	Ian Heartfield	
Art Director	Matt Doman	
Client	Guinness Extra Cold, "Pub", "Fish" & "Mudskipper"	

As in previous years, these three short spots for Guinness Extra Cold take a regular Guinness ad and give it an icy twist. This time, last year's award-winning Noitlulove/Evolution commercial gets the treatment. The original ad showed men devolving into mud-skippers as history rushed backwards. But in that version, there was just one Ice Age. Here there are three: and always at the wrong moment.

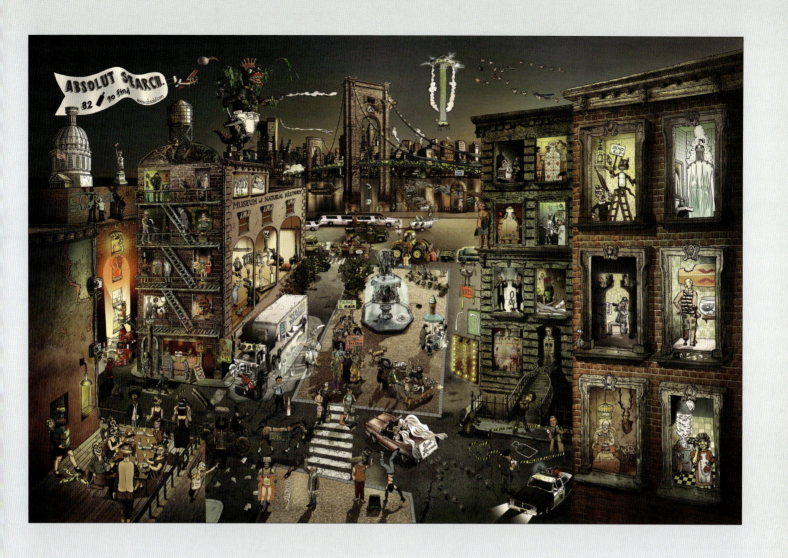

▲ **Alcoholic Drinks** **49**

Agency	TBWA\Paris
Creative Directors	Erik Vervroegen
	Sebastien Vacherot
Copywriter	Marc Platet
Art Director	Nicolas Boyer
Illustrators	Nicolas Boyer
	Alexis Dernov
Client	Absolut Vodka

Agency	180 Amsterdam
Executive CD	Andy Fackrell
Creative Director	Adam Chasnow
Copywriter	Niklas Lilja
Art Director	Antero Jokinen
Production	Knucklehead, London
Director	Rey Carlson
Producers	Tim Katz
	Peter Cline
Client	Amstel, "Filter Life"

Apparently random figures appear on the screen as we learn about the banal things that people are doing right at that moment. 1.037.743.205 are wearing a suit, for example. As the figures count down, the activities become less banal – until we reach the one man who has life all sussed out, relaxing to such a point that a butterfly lands on his big toe. Take life, and then filter out everything you don't like. That's what Amstel does with its pure filtered beer.

50 Alcoholic Drinks

Agency	Irish International, Dublin
Creative Director	Mal Stevenson
Copywriter	Rory Hamilton
Art Director	Jonathon Cullen
Production	Blink
Director	Lynn Fox
Producers	Nick Glendenning
	Noel Byrne
Client	Guinness, "Best Mates"

Two penguins break away from their troupe and trek across the icy wastes. Their mysterious goal is a distant shipwreck. The voiceover explains that when penguins choose their mates – their best mates, naturally – they stick together no matter what. After many trials the penguins arrive at their unlikely destination: which turns out to be a pub. The bar penguin pours a couple of pints of Guinness. But one of the duo realises he doesn't have a wallet. The friendship is about to become strained after all. Guinness drinkers know what matters.

Agency	Leo Burnett, Prague
Copywriter	Richard Kolbe
Art Director	Jiri Langpaul
Production	Dawson Production, Prague
Director	Xavier Mairesse
Producers	Vlastimil Kristl
	Andrea Tomankova
Client	Pilsner Urquell, "Smetana"

The Czech composer Bedrich Smetana is best known for his symphonic poem, My Homeland, written to support the nationalist cause in the 19th century. In this spot, we learn that the composer was inspired by the sunlight shining through a pint of Pilsner Urquell and projecting the drops of moisture on the cold glass onto his page like musical notes. Thus two great Czech treasures are united.

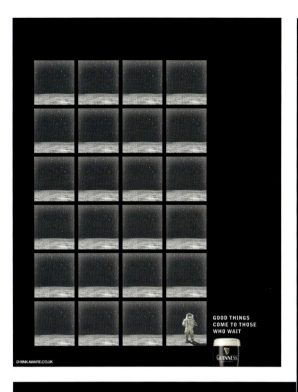

Agency   Abbott Mead Vickers BBDO,
        London
Creative Director Paul Brazier
Copywriter   Andy McAnaney
Art Director   Christian Sewell
Client   Guinness

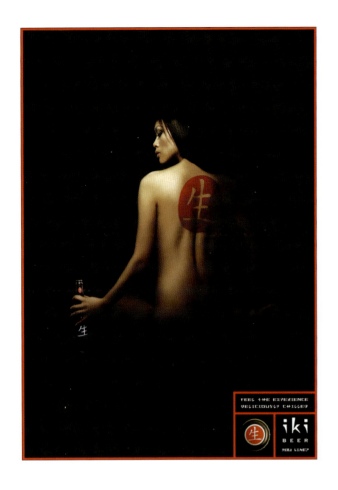

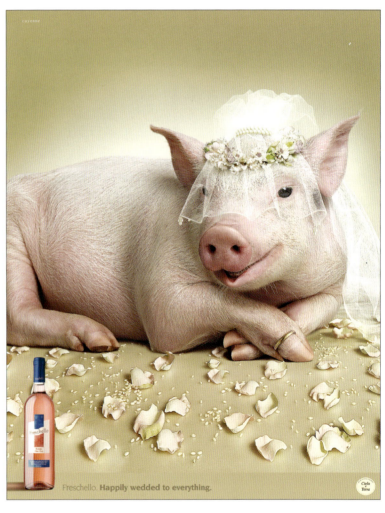

Agency	JWT/PPGH, Amsterdam
Creative Directors	Bart Kooij
	Nico Akkerman
	Christian Visser
Copywriter	Christian Visser
Art Director	Christian Visser
Photographer	Hans Verleur
Client	Iki Beer

Agency	Cayenne Italy, Milan
Creative Director	Giandomenico Puglisi
Copywriter	Sergio Scalet
Art Director	Daniel Fattorini
Client	Freschello Wine

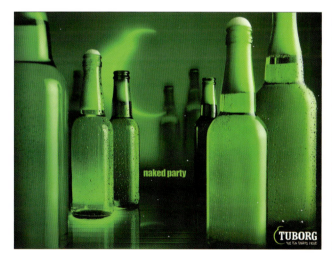

Agency	Irish International, Dublin	Agency	Noble Graphics Creative Studio, Sofia
Creative Director	Mal Stevenson	Photographer	Bliss Worx
Copywriter	Mark Nutley	Client	Tuborg
Art Director	Pat Hamill		
Photographer	Simon Burch		
Client	Guinness		

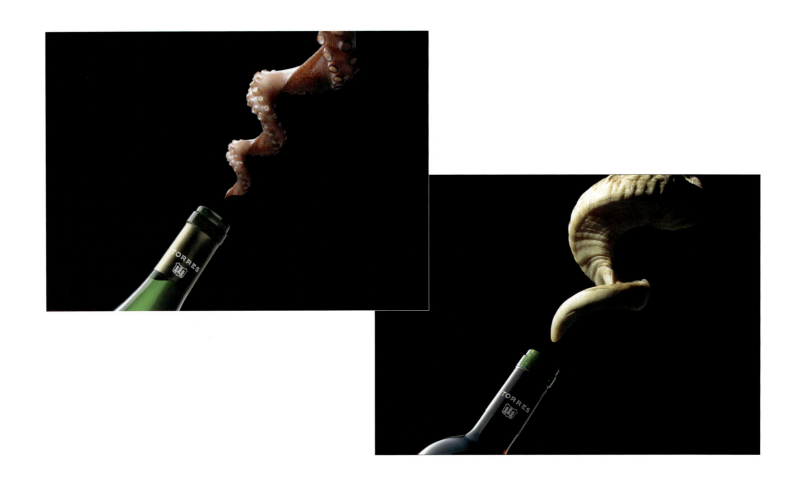

IMMORTALITY BECKONS

Enjoy GUINNESS Sensibly

GUINNESS
HURLING CHAMPIONSHIP

54   **Alcoholic Drinks**

Agency	Grey & Trace, Barcelona	**Agency**	Irish International, Dublin
Creative Directors	Jürgen Krieger	**Creative Director**	Mal Stevenson
	Joan Mas	**Copywriter**	Mark Nutley
	Jose Miguel Tortajada	**Art Director**	Pat Hamill
Copywriter	Jorge Meneclier	**Photographer**	Andy Glass
Art Director	Saül Serradesanferm	**Client**	Guinness
Photographer	Josep Maria Roca		
Client	Torres Wines		

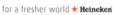
for a fresher world ★ **Heineken**

Agency	Publicis Conseil, Paris	**Agency**	Publicis, Zurich
Creative Director	Olivier Altmann	**Creative Director**	Markus Gut
Art Director	Benoît Blumberger	**Copywriter**	Markus Tränkle
Photographer	Michael Lewis	**Art Director**	Florian Beck
Client	Heineken	**Illustrators**	Flo Wacker
			Björn Burkhard
		Client	Heineken

56 Non-Alcoholic Drinks

Agency	Wieden+Kennedy, Amsterdam
Creative Directors	Rick Condos
	Hunter Hindman
Copywriter	Rick Condos
Art Director	Hunter Hindman
Production	Psyop, New York
Directors	Todd Mueller
	Kylie Matulick
Producers	Boo Wong
	Tom Dunlap
	Darryl Hagans
Music	Human, New York
Client	Coca-Cola, "Happiness Factory"

This joyous spot takes us on a voyage inside a Coke vending machine. It turns out to be a self-contained world, full of fantastical creatures which each have a role in preparing an ice-cold bottle of Coca-Cola for delivery. As the bottle is finally steered into delivery position, the citizens of this amazing universe party like there's no tomorrow. That's why Coke is happiness in a bottle.

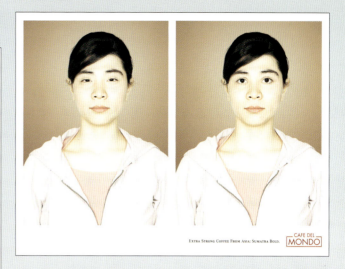

EXTRA STRONG COFFEE FROM ASIA: SUMATRA BOLD.

CAFE DEL MONDO

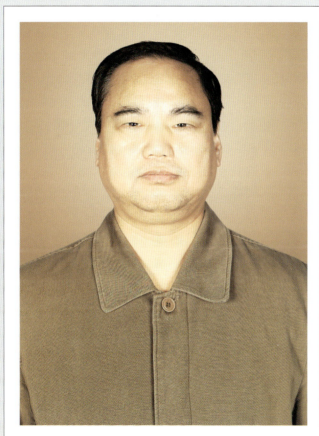

EXTRA STRONG COFFEE FROM ASIA: SUMATRA BOLD.

CAFE DEL MONDO

Non-Alcoholic Drinks **57**

Agency	DDB&Co., Istanbul
Creative Director	Karpat Polat
Copywriter	Karpat Polat
Art Director	Ali Bati
Photographer	Ilkay Muratoglu
Client	Café Del Mondo

Agency	Wieden+Kennedy, Amsterdam
Creative Directors	Rick Condos
	Antony Goldstein
	Hunter Hindman
Copywriters	Rick Condos
	Antony Goldstein
Art Director	Hunter Hindman
Production	MJZ
Director	Dante Ariola
Producers	Debbie Turner
	Natalie Hill
	Chris Weldon
	Tom Dunlap
Music	Eumir Deodato
Client	Coca-Cola, "First Taste"

In an old peoples' home, a man is offered a bottle of Coca-Cola. "I've never had one," he admits, and takes his first sip. With this revelation, he considers all the other things he's never done: told his secret fantasy woman that he loves her, visit a nudist colony, get a tattoo, buy a motorcycle, enjoy a threesome, run with the bulls at a Spanish fiesta…When the scene cuts back to the old people's home, the man's seat is empty. He's gone off to discover the Coke Side of Life.

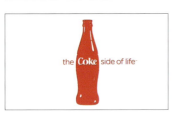

58 Non-Alcoholic Drinks

Agency	Wieden+Kennedy, Amsterdam
Creative Directors	Rick Condos
	Hunter Hindman
	Antony Goldstein
Copywriter	Giles Montgomery
Art Director	Richard Walker
Production	RSA, London
Director	Adam Smith
Producers	Rob Small
	Trudy Waldron
	Sandy Reay
Client	Coca-Cola, "Ringtone"

Sitting on a park bench next to a pretty girl, a young guy suddenly begins mimicking the familiar ring of a cell phone. The girl looks at him strangely. But he carries on with the act, searching through his sports bag for the non-existent phone. He comes up with a bottle of Coke, which he holds to his ear. "Hello?" he says. Then he hands the bottle to the girl: "It's for you." She is clearly charmed by the gesture – as are we.

Agency	Publicis Conseil, Paris
Creative Director	Olivier Altmann
Copywriter	Guilhem Arnal
Art Director	Robin de Lestrade
Production	Première Heure, Paris
Director	Sébastien Chantrel
Producers	Jérôme Rucki
	Patrick Pauwels
	Pierre Marcus
Client	Coca-Cola Light, "The Chase"

A man leaves his can of Coca-Cola Light on the kitchen table, where it is instantly snatched up by his girlfriend. A light-hearted pursuit commences; and as the couple race around their apparently palatial apartment, it's obvious that they too are as light as air, capable of running along walls and ceilings. Finally, the girl accidentally lets go of the can, which floats out through a skylight.

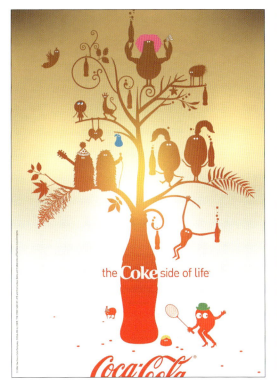

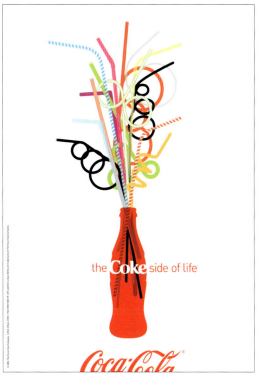

Agency	Wieden+Kennedy, Amsterdam
Creative Directors	Rick Condos
	Hunter Hindman
Copywriter	Rick Condos
Art Director	Hunter Hindman
Illustrators	Genevieve Gauckler
	Hunter Hindman
Client	Coca-Cola

Agency	Airside, London
Creative Directors	Yan Elliot
	Luke Williamson
Client	Coca-Cola

Agency	Wieden+Kennedy, Portland
Creative Directors	Mark Fitzloff
	Hal Curtis
Copywriters	Sheena Brady
	Shannon McGlothin
Art Directors	Sheena Brady
	Shannon McGlothin
Production	Nexus Productions, London
Directors	Alan Smith
	Adam Foulkes
Producers	Julia Parfitt
	Kara McCombe
	Niki Polyocan
Client	Coca-Cola, "Videogame"

Video games like Grand Theft Auto, to which this ad refers, are usually violent. But this is a soft-hearted video game, as we immediately see when the hero pays for his Coke and buys another one for a complete stranger. As the 'game' continues he gives money to a busker, puts out a fire, rescues an old woman from muggers and generally behaves like Mr Nice Guy. Pretty soon, the whole town is rejoicing in a spontaneous outburst of niceness. That's the Coke Side of Life.

60 **Non-Alcoholic Drinks**

Agency	DDB Paris
Creative Directors	Alexandre Hervé
	Sylvain Thirache
Copywriter	Benoît Sahores
Art Director	Cédric Haroutiounian
Production	Les Télécréateurs
Director	Armando Bo
Producers	Erinn Lothe Guillon
	Florence Pottiee Sperry
Client	Lipton Ice Tea Light, "Love Town"

As a conspicuously beautiful jogger runs through town, couples seem to embrace wherever she goes. When she pauses, we see her sip from a can of Lipton Ice Tea Light. Then she runs on, still causing women to jump inexplicably on their loved ones and kiss them passionately. Finally, we realise what's going on: these women don't want their boyfriends to see the jogger, who has a perfect figure thanks to jogging and Lipton Ice Tea – light, of course.

Agency	CLM BBDO, Paris
Creative Director	Anne de Maupeou
Production	Radical Media, London
Director	Tarsem
Producers	Tommy Turtle
	France Monnet
	Jacques Fouché
Client	Pepsi, "Fest"

What should be the Munich Beer Festival turns into a Pepsi fest as various football heroes (Beckham, Ronaldino, Henry) are treated to a display of lederhosen-clad antics on their way to the World Cup in Germany. But the soccer stars still manage to display some fancy footwork and chat up a couple of frauleins, while the oompah band reworks the 1982 pop hit Da Da Da by Trio.

Agency	BBDO Düsseldorf	Agency	Armando Testa, Milan
Creative Directors	Sebastian Hardieck		
	Raphael Milczarek	Creative Directors	German Silva
Copywriter	Felix Lemcke		Ekhi Mendibil
Art Directors	Fabian Kirner		Haitz Mendibil
	Joerg Sachtleben	Copywriters	German Silva
Photographers	Simone Rosenberg		Ekhi Mendibil
	Svenson Linnert		Cristiano Nardo
Client	Pepsi Light	Art Directors	Haitz Mendibil
			Andrea Lantelme
		Photographer	Ellen von Unwerth
		Client	Lavazza Coffee

62   **Non-Alcoholic Drinks**

Agency	Ogilvy & Mather, Paris	**Agency**	TBWA\Paris
Creative Director	Bernard Bureau	**Creative Director**	Erik Vervroegen
Art Director	Thierry Chiumino	**Copywriter**	Jean-François Bouchet
Photographer	Vincent Dixon	**Art Director**	Jessica Gérard-Huet
Client	Perrier	**Photographers**	David Stewart
			Jean-Yves Lemoigne
		Client	Futurlab Energy Drink

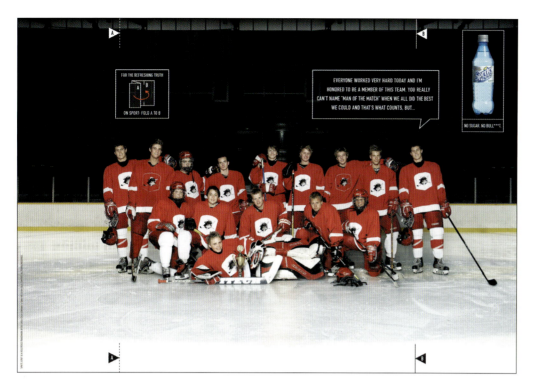

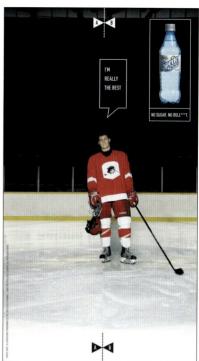

Non-Alcoholic Drinks 63

Agency	Saatchi & Saatchi, Copenhagen
Creative Director	Simon Wooller
Copywriters	Rasmus Petersen
	Lasse Hinke
	Simon Wooller
Art Directors	Rasmus Petersen
	Lasse Hinke
	Simon Wooller
Photographer	Morgan Morell
Client	Sprite Zero

Agency	DDB London
Creative Director	Jeremy Craigen
Copywriter	Ben Tollett
Art Director	Emer Stamp
Client	Copella Apple Juice

Agency	Fortune PromoSeven, Dubai
Creative Directors	Tarek Montasser
	Andre Segone
Copywriters	Pauline Abi Saab
	Herbert
	Ibrahim Mourad
Art Director	Toufic Tawily
Production	Miracle Films, Athens
Director	Charley Stadler
Producers	Annabelle Aronis
	Vito de Haas
	Dina Aly
Client	Nescafé, "Bedridden"

A man gets out of bed but appears to be glued to his mattress – even when he's dressed. This causes many problems, especially when he's getting into his Mini or sharing an elevator. Finally at work, he sips some instant Nescafé. As he visibly wakes up, the mattress slips off of his back and tumbles discreetly out of the window. Outside, we see many other mattresses floating to the ground as Nescafé works its magic.

Agency	McCann Erickson, Paris
Creative Directors	Virginie Caillé-Bastide
	Frédéric Pruvot
Copywriter	Frédéric Pruvot
Art Director	Bernard Exbrayat
Production	Partizan, Paris
Directors	Michel Gondry
Producer	Lionel Courtiaud
Client	Nespresso, "The Boutique"

George Clooney walks into a Nespresso boutique. As he fixes himself a coffee with the handy little Nespresso machine, he hears two beautiful women talking: "Intense, dark, rich…" etcetera. Clooney can't help wondering if they're fantasising about him. Unable to resist, he strolls over and asks them: "You're talking about Nespresso, right?" They confirm. Clooney says, "What else?" and laughs nervously – a little disappointed. Nespresso, like Clooney, is a class act.

Agency	Clemmow Hornby Inge, London
Creative Director	Ewan Paterson
Copywriter	Micky Tudor
Art Director	Micky Tudor
Production	Thomas & Thomas
Director	Jim Gilchrist
Producers	Billy Jones
	Anthony Falco
Client	Tango Clear, "Bravo"

This spot spoofs the now-classic Sony Bravia 'Balls' ad by letting piles of bouncy fruit loose in a hilly street in the north of England. Apart from breaking a window and almost squishing an innocent frog, the rampaging fruit buries a woman in a citrus avalanche. She surfaces from the tangy pile clutching her bottle of Tango, looking amazed. That's what the hit of fruit feels like when you take a sip of Tango: refreshment like no other.

Non-Alcoholic Drinks 65

Agency	Leo Burnett, Lisbon
Creative Director	Fernando Bellotti
Copywriter	Marilu Rodrigues
Art Director	Paulo Areas
Producer	Cristina Almeida
Client	Heredia Coffee

Agency	Ogilvy & Mather, London
Creative Director	Malcolm Poynton
Copywriters	Jon Morgan
	Mike Watson
Art Directors	Mike Watson
	Jon Morgan
Client	Lucozade

66 Communication Services

Agency	BBH, London
Creative Directors	Nick Gill
	Ewan Patterson
Copywriters	Nick Gill
	Ewan Patterson
Art Directors	Nick Gill
	Ewan Patterson
Production	Gorgeous Enterprises, London
Director	Peter Thwaites
DOP	Stuart Graham
Producers	Ben Link
	Davud Karbassioun
Client	Vodafone, "Mayfly"

"The common mayfly has a life expectancy of just one day," says the voiceover, as we see one of the insects hatching out. The narrator tells us that instead of being miserable about this, the fly embraces every single moment of life, filling his day with the things he loves. "He soars, he swoops…" We see the plucky fly teasing bemused animals, indulging in aerial acrobatics, falling in love and joining other mayflies in a colourful mating dance. Humans should be as positive. Vodafone helps us make the most of life.

Communication Services **67**

Agency	Forsman & Bodenfors, Gothenburg
Creative Director	Martin Cedergren
Copywriters	Martin Ringqvist
	Oscar Askelöf
Art Directors	Kim Cramer
	Lars Johansson
Client	Tele2

68   **Communication Services**

Agency	Publicis, Zurich
Creative Director	Ralf Kostgeld
Copywriter	Tom Zürcher
Art Director	Barbara Staub
Client	LTV Yellow Pages

In June 2006, small panel ads were inserted into the editorial content of two well-known nightlife and celebrity magazines. The panels referred to headlines, pictures and captions, giving the existing articles new meanings and "playing" with the media. Similar panels were also placed on the covers of magazines.

Agency	Publicis, Zurich
Creative Directors	Ralf Kostgeld
	Jean Etienne Aebi
Copywriter	Tom Zürcher
Art Director	Ralf Kostgeld
Production	Pumpkin Film, Zurich
Director	Kaspar Wedendahl
Producers	Sonja Brand
	Ines Bossart
Client	LTV Yellow Pages,
	"Elevator" & "Dinner"

These neat black and white spots explain why we might occasionally need the Yellow Pages telephone directory. A man gets into an elevator. Squinting myopically, he pushes a button on a woman's coat. "Optician?" asks the caption. And then, after she's punched him in the jaw, "Dentist?" In the second ad, a man picks his teeth at dinner. Does he need a "dental hygienist"? Incredibly, he reaches over, plucks a hair out of his wife's head, and starts flossing with it. She definitely needs a "dating service".

Agency	Hemisphere Droit, Clichy	Agency	Hasan & Partners, Helsinki
Creative Director	Frank Tapiro	Copywriters	Eka Ruola
Copywriter	Christophe Lafont		Paul Hicks
Art Director	Etienne Batard	Art Director	Nono Alakari
Photographer	Vincent Dixon	Photographer	Magnus Rossander
Client	Virgin Mobile	Client	Wataniya Telecom

Agency	Publicis Conseil, Paris
Creative Director	Olivier Altmann
Copywriter	Guilhem Arnal
Art Director	Robin De Lestrade
Production	Nose, Paris
Director	Sven Super
Producer	Muriel Allegrini
Client	SFR Telecommunications, "Iggy Pop"

Rock star Iggy Pop is asleep in a palatial hotel room when he gets a call. He answers it, leaps out of bed, and starts singing down the phone, rocking out in his usual fashion. Cut to a beach, where we see a man listening to Iggy on his cell phone. As the man's pal appears with some ice creams, he cuts Iggy off. Looking none too pleased, Iggy grunts and goes back to bed. The new music download service from SFR means that you have all the stars at your fingertips.

Agency	Garbergs Reklambyrå, Stockholm
Copywriter	Johan van der Schoot
Art Director	Petter Ödeen
Production	Forsberg & Co
Director	Patrik Forsberg
Producers	Caroline Forsberg
	Jessica Thorelius
Client	Glocalnet, "Blues"

In what appears to be an ancient black and white clip, a blues singer is singing of his woes, as usual. "My woman left me...down this lonesome road," he moans. "Well I feel lower than the deep blue sea...But not as low as Glocalnet, which offers broadband at 249 kroner a month. And I thought I was low! But man, that's low." Glocalnet offers lower prices for broadband.

Agency	Forsman & Bodenfors, Gothenburg
Copywriters	Oscar Askelöf
	Martin Ringqvist
Art Director	Kim Cramer
Production	Acne Film
Directors	Tomas Skoging
	Sebastian Hedin
Producers	Alexandra Flink
	Magnus Kennhed
	Åsa Jansson
Client	Tele2, "Office"

A postman is dragging a giant of a man into an office. It's our old friend Big Bill, still causing trouble wherever he goes. We see that the office is plagued by Big Bills. Meanwhile, another office receives a delivery of a chatty, amiable and easily portable Small Bill. That's because they use Tele2, the phone company that brings you small bills.

Agency	Storåkers McCann, Stockholm
Copywriters	Christian Sundgren
Art Directors	Sofia Ekelund
Client	Telia

If you don't have good mobile coverage in Sweden, your phone calls get cut off in mid-sentence – even in the city. That's why Telia promoted its superior coverage in the Stockholm subway. This lengthy printed monologue led the reader to the payoff: uninterrupted talk with the best coverage in Sweden. The monologues were tailored to suit their environments: an upmarket area had monologues from posh people, for example. You didn't need to read the monologue to get the idea, but the well-written pieces rewarded patience.

Agency	Storåkers McCann, Stockholm
Copywriter	Martin Marklund
Art Director	Enis Püpülek
Production	Esteban
Directors	Alex Brügge
	Markus Ernerot
Producer	Olof Barr
Client	TeliaSonera, "Ski Lift"

On a ski lift, a girl is encouraging her lovelorn friend to call the boy they met last night. "He's got…like, really blue eyes that go on forever," she says, sounding keener than her moody pal. She forces her friend to check her phone in case the love object has called. "Let me see!" In a slight scuffle, the phone falls into the snow below. Where, of course, it begins to ring. Luckily, you can win a new phone at Telia.

72   **Communication Services**

Agency	DDB Oslo
Production	Einar Film, Oslo
Director	Morten Tyldum
Producers	Guri Neby
	Cyril Boije
Client	Telenor, "Sickday"

A young man is browsing in the CD section of a department store. His cell phone rings. When he sees the caller ID, an expression of horror appears on his face. The phone continues to ring as he charges through the store, plunging down escalators and sprinting along aisles. Finally, he arrives at the bedding department, strips off his shirt, and plunges into a bed. He answers his phone. His boss's face appears. "I heard you rang in sick today. When can I expect you back?" Lying in bed, the skiving employee looks convincingly ill. Telenor's phones have gone video.

Agency	Grey London
Creative Director	David Alberts
Copywriters	Lee Brook
	Nick Rowland
Art Directors	Lee Brook
	Nick Rowland
Production	Moxie Pictures, Boston
Director	Errol Morris
Producers	Dawn Laren
	Stephanie Wellesley
	James Guy
Client	AOL, "Good" & "Bad"

Two films narrated by British actor John Hurt take different sides of an argument. Some think the internet is a bad thing: undermining privacy; open to abuse; a market for fake goods, propaganda and dark fantasies. Orwell was right: we are being watched. On the other hand, some think the internet is a good thing: the most powerful educational tool the world has ever known and a forum for free speech. Orwell was wrong: thanks to the internet, it's not the state that has the power, it's us. What do you think?

Agency	Publicis Conseil, Paris
Creative Director	Olivier Altmann
Copywriter	Patrice Lucet
Art Director	Charles Guillemant
Photographer	Jean-Yves Lemoigne
Client	Sagem Mobile Phones

Agency	Lang Gysi Knoll, Bern
Creative Directors	Jean-Marc Demeulemeester
	Daniela Jakab
Copywriter	Lukas Schmid
Art Director	Simone Joerg
Production	Solid & Hauer Films,
	Zurich
Director	Rainer Binz
Producer	Rudi Haller
Client	Swiss Courier, "Hair"

A balding man with a comb-over hairstyle is standing at a bus stop. He seems about to speak to the woman by his side. "Swiss-Kurier picks up your post," says the narrator, as a vehicle whizzes past so fast that the slipstream makes the man's scant hair stand on end. "And then delivers it…" The vehicle flashes in the opposite direction, blowing the man's hair back into place. "Quickly – very quickly indeed," the narrator concludes. The man smiles at the woman, who smiles back.

74 **Communication Services**

Agency	The Fish Can Sing,
	London
Creative Director	Andy Whitlock
Production	Nexus Productions,
	London
Directors	Alan Smith
	Adam Foulkes
Producers	Luke Youngman
	Mo Neef
	David Passey
	Amy Hitchenor
Client	Motorola,
	"Grand Classics"

An animated rabbit character is the link between classic scenes from the history of cinema, as he strolls from the very first flipbook images, through to Charlie Chaplin, Metropolis, Citizen Kane, Hollywood musicals, Hitchcock's Vertigo, The Great Escape, The Graduate, James Bond…right up to Gladiator. The last scene resembles Lost in Translation, as the rabbit sits in a hotel room watching movies on his mobile phone. Movie classics: now on your mobile.

Agency	Lowe London
Creative Director	Ed Morris
Copywriter	Olly Green
Art Director	Greg Milbourne
Production	Gorgeous Enterprises
Director	Chris Palmer
Producers	Rupert Smyth
	Sue Lee Stern
Client	Nokia N93,
	"Film Set"

Actor Gary Oldman explains that thanks to the new Nokia N93 phone's inbuilt video camera, the world becomes your movie set. He takes us on a tour of New York, explaining that all you need to make a movie is – among other things – a spectacular location, dramatic lighting, mystery, drama, conflict and some witty dialogue ("How do I get to Carnegie Hall?" "You gotta practice, lady."). Oh, and of course a leading man.

Agency	Saatchi & Saatchi, Stockholm		**Agency**	Fallon London
Creative Director	Adam Kerj		**Creative Director**	Micah Walker
Copywriter	Adam Kerj		**Copywriter**	Ali Alvarez
Art Directors	Nima Stillerud		**Art Director**	Ali Alvarez
	Gustav Egerstedt		**Illustrator**	Explosm
Photographer	Mejor S Samrai		**Client**	Orange Telecommunications
Client	Motorola Razr Phone			

76 Transport & Tourism

Agency	Ogilvy Amsterdam	Many people have known for years that
Creative Directors	Darre van Dijk	Center Parcs is a world unto itself, but
	Piebe Piebenga	in this spot it finally gains accession to
Copywriters	Edsard Schutte	the EU. As part of the celebrations, a
	Lionell Schuring	delegation of European premiers visits
Art Directors	Jan-Willem Smits	Center Parcs – we recognise Blair, Merkel
	Theo Korf	and Chirac, among others. Blair annoys
Production	Lovo Films, Brussels	everyone when his cell phone goes off
Director	Frank Devos	during a nature trek ("Hello? Cherie?"), but
Producers	Bert Brulez	he makes up for it in his closing speech.
	Brenda Bentz van den Berg	Center Parcs is, he says, "truly a state of
Client	Center Parcs Europe,	happiness".
	"EU Top"	

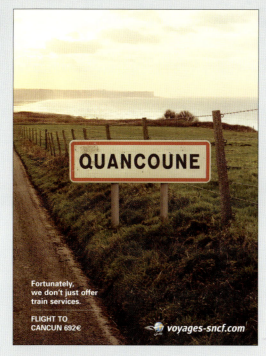

Fortunately,
we don't just offer
train services.

FLIGHT TO
CANCUN 692€

voyages-sncf.com

Fortunately,
we don't just offer
train services.

FLIGHT TO
SHANGHAI 674€

voyages-sncf.com

Fortunately,
we don't just offer
train services.

FLIGHT TO
LOS ANGELES 528€

voyages-sncf.com

Fortunately,
we don't just offer
train services.

FLIGHT TO
NEW YORK 397€

voyages-sncf.com

Transport & Tourism   **77**

Agency	DDB Paris
Creative Directors	Alexandre Hervé
	Sylvain Thirache
Copywriter	Jérôme Langlade
Art Director	Sébastien Pierre
Photographer	Olivier Amsellem
Client	Voyages-sncf.com

78 Transport & Tourism

Agency	Duval Guillaume Brussels
Creative Directors	Peter Ampe Katrien Bottez
Copywriter	Virginie Lepère
Art Director	Frédéric Van Hoof
Photographer	Vincent Fournier
Client	TGV Trains

Agency	BETC Euro RSCG, Paris
Creative Director	Rémi Babinet
Copywriter	Rémi Noel
Art Director	Eric Holden
Production	Première Heure
Director	Hou Hsiao Hsein
Producer	Fabrice Brovelli
Client	Air France, "The Jetty" & "The Pool"

These two spots highlight the soothing ambience of a flight with Air France. In the first, a woman enjoys perfect calm on a jetty overlooking a tranquil lake. When night falls she lies down – and we see that seat 8A on an Air France flight would be just as relaxing.

In the second, a man and woman lounge beside an infinity pool. When the angle of the horizon changes they return to their poolside chairs that are labelled with numbers as if they are actually sitting on an Air France plane.

Agency   BETC Euro RSCG, Paris
Creative Director Rémi Babinet
Copywriter   Rémi Noel
Art Director   Eric Holden
Photographer   Jonathan de Villiers
Client   Air France

GENEVE • MARSEILLE : 2 EXTRA TRAINS EARLY MORNING AND LATE EVENING   *TGV*

Agency	TBWA\Paris
Creative Director	Erik Vervroegen
Copywriter	Clemence Cousteau
Art Director	Javier Rodriguez
Client	SNCF French National Railways

80   Transport & Tourism

Agency	Gitam BBDO, Ramat-Gan
Creative Directors	Asi Shavit
	Gal Porat
	Romem Saranga
Copywriter	Alon Hadad
Art Director	Liat Doanis
Production	Shoshi & Udi, Tel Aviv
Director	Regev Kontas
Producers	Shoshi & Udi
	Liat Moshe
Client	Israir, "Baby"

"An Israir flight to Barcelona", says the caption, above a scene of disgruntled passengers casting irritating glances at a woman nursing a bawling baby. Then we cut to what we are informed is "the competitor's flight to Barcelona": different plane, different passengers, and another woman with her screaming child. "On every flight there is a crying baby," points out the caption. "Why pay more?" With Israir, a flight to Barcelona is only $399.

Agency	Spillmann/Felser/Leo Burnett, Zurich
Creative Director	Martin Spillmann
Copywriters	Martin Spillmann
	Peter Brönnimann
Art Director	Martin Spillmann
Production	Wirz & Fraefel
Director	Ernst Wirz
Producers	Stefan Fraefel
	Sebahat Derdiyok
Client	Swiss Tourism, "Soccer World Cup Alternative"

In the run-up to the World Cup, we see a series of hunky young guys engaging in various activities: farming, conducting trams, logging, even milking a cow. "Dear girls," says the narrator, "why not escape during this summer's World Cup to a country where the men spend less time on football, and more time on you." That's Switzerland.

Non-smoking trains. From 11 December 2005.

Agency	Jung von Matt, Zurich	Agency	Statskog Inhouse, Namsos
Creative Director	Alexander Jaggy	Creative Director	Marek Tachezy
Copywriter	Michael Kathe	Copywriter	Marek Tachezy
Art Director	Lukas Frei	Art Director	Marek Tachezy
Photographer	Mats Cordt	Client	Statskog National Park
Client	SBB Swiss Railways		

Agency	Rapp Collins Zebra, Madrid
Creative Directors	Gustavo Montoro
	Jose Sánchez-Colomer
Copywriter	Carolina Cardona
Art Director	Jaime Sánchez
Client	Maison de la France

Spanish art-lovers can now buy tickets to French museums over the Internet, bringing the two countries that much closer. To illustrate this each ad combines two classic works of art, one Spanish and one French, into a single painting.

LANGLEY
TRAVEL
The skier's travel agency.
Now in Japan.

Agency	Devarrieuxvillaret, Paris	Agency	Goss, Gothenburg
Creative Director	Nicolas Verdeau	Copywriters	Michael Schultz
Art Director	Nicolas Verdeau		Ulrika Good
Photographer	Philip Sinden	Art Directors	Gunnar Skarland
Client	Transilien Suburban railways		Emil Jonsson
			Jan Eneroth
			Mattias Frendberg
			Mimmi Andersson
		Photographer	Lennart Sjöberg
		Illustrators	Fredrik Persson
			Perssons Pixlar
		Client	Langley Travel

Grown ups free of charge when traveling with children.

This summer Stena Line becomes The Children's Boat. Two children incl. one 4-berth cabin. NOK 280. Adults free. Order at www.stenaline.no

Stena Line
Making good time

→ IN THE METRO, HOMO MODERNUS PUTS A MUZZLE ON HIS PET.

RATP

www.objectif-respect.org

→ HOMO MODERNUS DOES NOT PARK IN THE BUS LANE.

RATP

www.objectif-respect.org

Agency	DDB Oslo
Copywriter	Torbjørn Kvien Madsen
Art Director	Rune Markhus
Photographer	Billy Bonkers
Client	Stena Line Cruises

Agency	Human to Human, Paris
Creative Director	Rémi Guilbert
Copywriter	Rémi Guilbert
Art Director	Axel Roy
Photographer	Marc Gouby
Client	RATP Urban Transport System

The toast: 180 seconds at 185°F, not brown nHot enough, not dry, the perfect crunch. Just thick enough to hold the spreading, just warm enough to melt the butter. All in all, one of the thousand things that make you wonder how fantastic a hotel is.

www.nh-hotels.com/customerservice

The sea bream: wild, the freshest. no fish farm. Wet eyes, iridescent skin. Firm but, not hard. deserving animal (he does not know though) for a star table (we don't have less in our restaurants). Over hot. Ready for table twelve: your table. nH

www.nh-hotels.com/restaurants

The Chaise Longue by Le Corbusier: colt leather (no trace smell on the clothes). Made in nHamburg. Ideal for your back. Perfect to be working on your portable or drinking a Bloody Mary: five ounces of tomato, two of vodka, sea salt powder, pepper and three drops of Tabasco. The best advice before flying and leaving our hotel (to visit another of our hotels in any continent).

www.nh-hotels.com/international

The lotion: not too oily, balsamic. With fennel seeds powdered below a hundredth of an inch. No perfume added, only the scent of juniper. Warmed in the hands of the masseur placed gently on your shoulder. Still some stress in the muscles, but less and less, until you are back nH in harmony over a long weekend, of just any weekend.

www.nh-hotels.com/weekend

Transport & Tourism **85**

Agency	Zapping, Madrid
Creative Directors	Uschi Henkes
	Manolo Moreno
	Urs Frick
Copywriters	Manolo Moreno
	Mercedes Lucena
Art Director	Victor Gómez
Client	NH Hotels

Agency	King, Stockholm	
Creative Director	Frank Hollingworth	
Production	Social Club, Stockholm	
Director	Magnus Rösman	
Producer	Magnus Theorin	
Client	ICA Supermarkets, "Pasquale" Campaign	

The long-running ICA supermarket saga is as much loved as many a soap opera, and these are the latest episodes. Staff member Sebastian wonders aloud how the prices of the weekly specials are able to float above the products. Thus we're introduced to Pasquale, the acrobatic French 'price artist' who dangles from the supermarket ceiling, suspending the prices on invisible threads. His family has been in the trade for years, explains the roguish Pasquale. Move a product as far and fast as you like – Pasquale's dexterity ensures that the price always hovers in exactly the right spot.

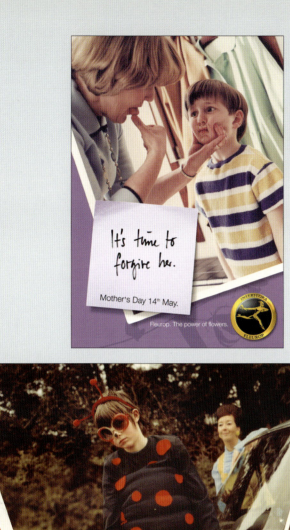

Agency	Walker, Zurich
Creative Director	Pius Walker
Copywriter	Roger Beckett
Art Director	Mieke Haase
Photographer	Uwe Düttmann
Client	Fleurop-Interflora

This feels totally right.

Is it really neccessary to dress up again?

Uncle Ben's

Agency King, Stockholm
Creative Director Frank Hollingworth
Production Social Club, Stockholm
Director Magnus Rösman
Producer Magnus Theorin
Client ICA Supermarkets, "Close Shave"

More scenes from the lives of the oddball staff of an ICA supermarket. In the first, store manager Stig convinces a colleague to shave his head so they can all dress as Buddhists for a Thai food promotion. But then he changes his mind – a little too late.

GRILLMANNEN
EN REKLAMFILMSTRIOLOGI PÅ TV NU

The Barbecue Man? What's that about?

Stig Butikschef

Not being yourself and playing a role is a little scary.

And you get more girls too. I didn't get so many girls earlier...

I have to leave now. I have fresh food on the loading dock.

Nakna Kocken idag 13.0

I chose these delicious hamburgers, that are ready to be cooked, from ICA's own assortment.

"HET MAT" MED NAKNA KOCKEN
www.hetmat.n

I got this downtown, and I thought it might be fun.

Agency King, Stockholm
Creative Director Frank Hollingworth
Production Social Club, Stockholm
Director Magnus Rösman
Producer Magnus Theorin
Client ICA Supermarkets, "Behind the Scenes" & "Naked Chef"

Another spot resembles the "Making Of" segment of a DVD, which takes us behind the scenes of a fictional film called Barbecue Man, set in the store.

Finally, the store hires The Naked Chef for a cooking demonstration. Unfortunately, he turns out not to be Jamie Oliver, of the Naked Chef TV series, but a stripper.

Agency	DDB London
Creative Directors	Adam Tucker
	Justin Tindall
Copywriter	Adam Tucker
Art Director	Justin Tindall
Client	Harvey Nichols

Agency	Heimat, Berlin
Creative Directors	Guido Heffels
	Jürgen Vossen
Copywriters	Till Eckel
	Guido Heffels
Art Directors	Tim Schneider
	Ralf Schmerberg
Production	Triggerhappy Productions, Berlin
Director	Ralf Schmerberg
Producers	Stephan Vens
	Kerstin Breuer
Client	Hornbach Home Improvement Stores, "D.I.Y."

These days, the film suggests, there are timesaving devices for everything: making coffee, polishing shoes, cleaning teeth, exercising, even walking the dog. When was the last time you said "I did it myself?" On the screen, we see a man restoring an old chest of drawers and imagine his sense of achievement when he's finished the job. Maybe we need to visit Hornbach – the home of DIY.

90   **Retail Services**

Agency	Walker, Zurich
Creative Director	Pius Walker
Copywriter	Roger Beckett
Production	Cobblestone, Hamburg
	Social Club, Stockholm
Director	Axel Laubscher
Producers	Pieter Lony
	Markus Ahlm
Client	Fleurop-Interflora, "Kiss" & "Party"

Ah, the trials of teenage years. In the first of these related spots (an appropriate word), a teenage boy is about to kiss his girlfriend for the first time when his mother bursts into his bedroom with a snack. The boy's look of reproach is unmistakeable.

In the second ad, a middle-aged mother dances at her teenage daughter's party, oblivious to the dismay she is causing. Kids – all that was long ago: it's time to forgive her. Remember Interflora on Mother's Day.

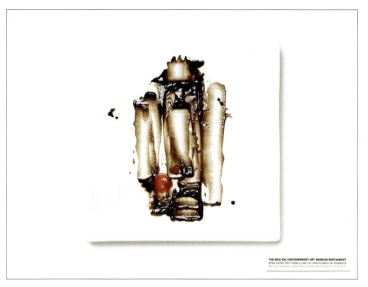

Retail Services 91

Agency	CLM BBDO, Paris
Creative Director	Anne de Maupeou
Copywriter	Dimitri Guerassimov
Art Director	Dimitri Guerassimov
Photographer	Jerome Bryon
Client	MAC/VAL Restaurant

Food just loves to be cooked by Frank Loncin.

Agency	10 Advertising, Antwerp
Copywriters	Heidi Van Damme
	Sebastien Van Reet
Art Directors	Heidi Van Damme
	Sebastien Van Reet
Photographer	Koen Demuynck
Client	Loncin Restaurant

Ehm... mam, I can't sell you this.

It says fakta right here.

We really wish you would stay a little longer

– Now what's it saying?
– It says you bought a garden grill.

fakta
It only takes 5 minutes

Agency	Uncle Grey, Aarhus
Creative Director	Per Pedersen
Copywriters	Thomas Falkenberg
	Anders Tranæs
Art Directors	Rasmus Gottliebsen
	Lone Rasmussen
Production	Lassie Film,
	Copenhagen
Director	Jan Gleie
Producers	Stig Weiss
	Jan Pedersen
Client	Fakta,
	"Private Labels in Fakta"

Fakta will go to any lengths to get its customers to stay a little longer. In this spot, a cashier tries to convince a customer that because a carton of juice has the word 'Fakta' on it, the product belongs to the store – so he can't sell it. The customer protests, so the young man points out: "It says Fakta on my shirt, and I'm not for sale, am I?" At least the debate has kept her there a little longer. Fakta: it only takes five minutes.

Agency	Uncle Grey, Aarhus
Creative Director	Per Pedersen
Copywriter	Thomas Falkenberg
Art Director	Rasmus Gottliebsen
Production	Lassie Film
	Copenhagen
Director	Jan Gleie
Producers	Stig Weiss
	Jan Pedersen
Client	Fakta, "New Scanner"
	& "Robot Arm"

In the first of two spots, the cashier at a Fakta store tests a new head-mounted barcode scanner. Of course it keeps going wrong, insisting that the customer has bought a colour television, and then a garden grill. The errors waste a lot of everyone's time. In another ad, a hapless employee tests a wayward new robot arm which appears to be the exact opposite of time-saving. Shopping at Fakta only takes five minutes, but the store would love it if you stayed a bit longer.

Agency	Lowe Brindfors, Stockholm	Stockholmers can tell what section of
Creative Director	Håkan Engler	the city a person lives in by the way they
Copywriter	Olle Langseth	dress. This insight was the basis of the NK
Art Directors	Magnus Löwenhielm	department store campaign that used 350
	Lina Elfstrand	different posters, each one promoting the
Client	Nordiska Kompaniet	style of clothing appropriate to the district
	Department Store	where the poster appeared.

REALLY GOOD PROJECTORS.

Agency	Dinamo Reklamebyrå, Oslo
Copywriter	Lars Joachim Grimstad
Art Director	Egil Pay
Production	Fantefilm
Director	Mats Stenberg
Producers	Gry Sæthre
	Anita Engen Hjelset
	Tom Ovind
Client	Deal.no, "The Dog"

A man and his dog are watching a golf match on a giant wall screen. When a tree appears on the screen, the dog perks up. It jumps from the sofa, trots over to the screen and pisses on the "tree". The man looks astonished. That's what happens when you buy a really good video projector from deal.no.

It's in you. Let it out!

HORNBACH
Home Improvement Superstores

BM
BYGGMAKKER
Tools heaven

Agency	Heimat, Berlin
Creative Directors	Guido Heffels
	Juergen Vossen
Copywriter	Till Eckel
Art Director	Tim Schneider
Production	Markenfilm, Berlin
Director	Jan Wentz
Producers	Lutz Müller
	Kerstin Breuer
Client	Hornbach Home Improvement Stores, "Window"

Neighbours run for cover when the wall of a suburban house shakes as if being struck by massive blows. A bulge appears, and it seems clear that the wall is about to explode. What terrible creature lurks behind it? Finally, bricks go flying and a ragged hole appears in the wall. A man emerges, clutching a mallet. Looking pleased with his handiwork, he picks up the window frame that is waiting on the doorstep and disappears back into his house to finish the job. Hornbach helps you achieve the impossible.

Agency	DDB Oslo
Copywriters	Camilla Bjørnhaug
	Eirik Hovland
Art Director	Preben Moan
Production	Komet Film
Director	Jens Lien
Producers	Jørgen Mjelva
	Jessica Paine
Client	Byggmakker Tools, "Chain Saw"

A man is looking for a saw in a DIY store. Catching sight of himself in a mirror, he realises he doesn't look very impressive wielding the flimsy implement. He returns with a bigger one. No...still not quite right. It's worse than a woman choosing a handbag! Finally he returns with a chainsaw. Yes, now he looks properly macho – even dangerous. Chainsaws are cool! Bygmakker: it's tools heaven

Agency	Forsman & Bodenfors, Gothenburg
Creative Director	Mathias Appelblad
Copywriters	Rebecka Osvald
	Jörgen Gjaerum
Art Directors	Andreas Malm
	Pål Jespersen
	Pål Eneroth
Photographer	Peter Gherke
Client	Stadium Sports Stores

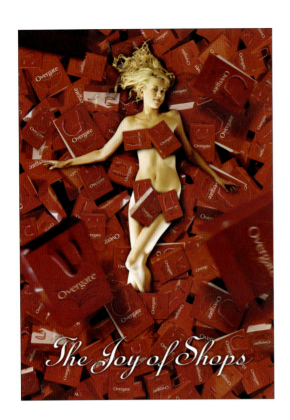

Agency	Family Advertising, Edinburgh
Creative Directors	Kevin Bird
	David Isaac
Copywriter	David Isaac
Art Director	Kevin Bird
Photographer	Mark Seager
Client	Overgate Shopping Centre

Agency	Ogilvy Advertising, Stockholm
Creative Director	Björn Ståhl
Copywriter	Mikael Ström
Art Director	Attila Kiraly
Photographers	Natalie Fobes
	Jeremy Woodhouse
Client	Östermalm Food Market

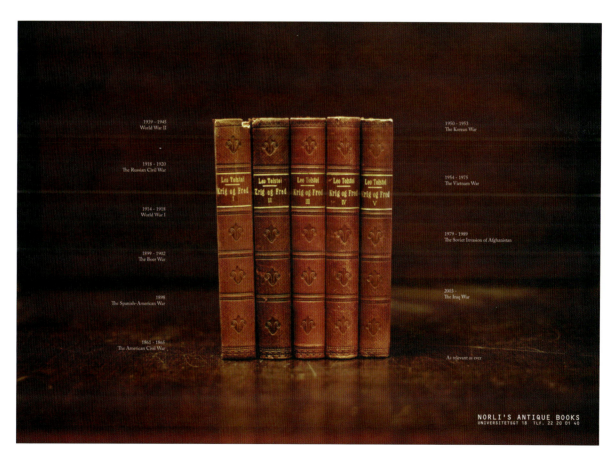

Agency	Åkestam Holst, Stockholm	Agency	SMFB, Oslo
Copywriter	Lotta Lundgren	Creative Directors	Erik Heisholt
Art Director	Jesper Holst		Stig Bjølbakk
Photographer	Oskar Falk	Copywriters	Erik Heisholt
Client	Sturegallerian Shopping Centre		Stig Bjølbakk
		Art Directors	Hans Martin Rønneseth
			Erik Heisholt
		Photographer	Massimo Leardini
		Client	Norli's Antique Books

HARVEY NICHOLS SALE
STARTS 27 DECEMBER

Agency	DDB London	Agency	Heimat, Berlin
Creative Directors	Adam Tucker	**Creative Directors**	Guido Heffels
	Justin Tindall		Juergen Vossen
Copywriters	Grant Parker	**Copywriter**	Gabriel Diakoswky
	Joanna Wenley	**Art Directors**	Mike Brand
Art Directors	Joanna Wenley		Matthias Walter
	Grant Parker	**Photographer**	Matthias Walter
Client	Harvey Nichols	**Illustrator**	Michael Mackens
		Client	Hornbach Colour Mixing Service

Agency	JWT Hamburg	Agency	Ogilvy & Mather, London
Creative Director	Torsten Rieken		
Art Director	Patricia Wetzel	Executive CD	Malcolm Poynton
Photographer	Reinhard Hunger	Creative Partner	Neil Dawson
Client	Perle, Handiwork Agency for Crafts-Women	Copywriters	Nick Simons Jules Chalkley
		Art Directors	Jules Chalkley Nick Simons
		Photographer	Finlay McKay
		Client	Harrods

- Can you pass me the salt?

- Not too much.
You know what the doctor has said.

- The doctor, the doctor...
What does he know?...

- Why don't we go to the seaside this weekend?
What does the weather forecast say?

- It's going to rain cats and dogs
and very cold.

- That reminds me of the winter of '94.
6 inches of snow! Do you remember?

- Definitely! We stayed inside. You were
wearing that low-cut red dress.
And underneath that, a tight black corset that
drove me crazy. I couldn't wait to take off that
dress. You untied your hair sensually,
slowly dropping your dress on the floor...
We were still in shape in those days...
The neighbours complained about the noise.
Yeah, I was 10 years younger and
20 pounds lighter too...
Actually, that black corset - do you still have it?
You wouldn't mind trying it on, would you?
Just to do me a favour... Or the red one.

- Finish your soup, before it gets cold.

A REAL RELATIONSHIP GROWS OVER TIME.

DEXIA
Bank

Agency	Duval Guillaume, Brussels
Creative Directors	Katrien Bottez
	Peter Ampe
Copywriter	Benoit Menetret
Art Director	Jean-Marc Wachsmann
Production	Milly Films
Director	David Luther
Producers	Alain Schwartz
	Marc Van Buggenhout
Client	Dexia Bank, "Subtitles"

An elderly couple lunch together. They have clearly been married for years and know each other so well that verbal communication is no longer necessary; their every gesture speaks volumes. They have an affectionate, bantering relationship. In just a few glances they cover health issues, the weather and even a bit of romantic nostalgia. Great relationships get better over time – just like relationships with a good bank.

Agency	DDB Amsterdam
Creative Director	Martin Cornelissen
Copywriter	Marcel de Jonge
Art Director	Martin Cornelissen
Photographer	Jaap Vliegenthart
Client	Achmea Insurance

This six-page advertisement is inserted right at the beginning of the magazine. The first page asks the reader to fold it out and leave it lying open while turning the following pages. When each page is turned a new disaster unfolds. It ends reassuringly with the tagline: The things you'd rather not think about, we think about. Achmea cares.

Agency	Demner, Merlicek & Bergmann, Vienna
Creative Director	Rosa Haider
Copywriter	Viktoria Farda
Art Director	Germaine Cap de Ville
Production	Close Up, Vienna
Director	Bart Timmer
Producers	Dieter Lembcke
	Maresi McNab
Client	Vienna Insurance Group, "Chocolate Fingers"

A little girl is tucking into an illicit bar of chocolate when her mother calls. Concealing her sticky hands, the girl emerges into the hall, where her mother asks her for help zipping up a splendid white evening dress. The woman turns her back and the girl starts to zip up the dress – pausing for a second to wipe her chocolate-covered fingers on it. The woman dashes out to her party, oblivious of the chocolate marks on her dress. Do you trust your children to look after you in your old age? Better start saving for your pension.

Agency	Lowe Brindfors, Stockholm
Creative Director	Håkan Engler
Copywriter	Martin Bartholf
Art Director	Rickard Villard
Production	Social Club
Director	Jesper Ericstam
Producers	Johan Lindström
	Markus Ahlm
	Sofia Bellini
Client	SEB Bank, "Heroes"

In a series of clips, we see lots of hard-working people from all walks of life – whether surgeons, security guards, taxi drivers or office workers – tapping their feet or singing along with the refrain "Hard work" as they go about the tough business of earning a living. You work hard for your money. So does the SEB Bank.

Agency	Jung von Matt, Hamburg
Creative Directors	Doerte Spengler-Ahrens
	Jan Rexhausen
Copywriters	Maximilano Lueders
	Dylan Berg
Art Directors	Oystein Vic
	Rune Degett
Production	Jo!Schmid, Berlin
Director	Martin Schmid
Producers	André Bause
	Matthias van de Sand
Client	Sparkasse Bank, "Hardselling" & "Chinese"

A young man doesn't seem to be having much luck with his choice of banks. At the first, his enquiries are met with robotic replies concerning special offers, low interest rates and so on. It becomes apparent that the financial advisor is a robot: especially when he blows a fuse and his arm falls off. At the second bank, our hero is confronted with an advisor who speaks to him only in Chinese. Next time he should try Sparkasse bank, which employs real human beings – who speak a language you can understand.

Agency	SWE Advertising, Stockholm
Creative Director	Björn Schumacher
Copywriters	Daniel Vaccino
	Johan Skogh
Art Director	Ann-Marie Wessman
Production	Fladen Film, Stockholm
Director	Måns Herngren
Producers	Johan van der Lancken
	Patrik Ryborn
	Bitte Söderlind
Client	Föreningssparbanken, "Bosse Valentino"

A young man named Bosse Valentino tells the story of his highly eventful life. Born in Italy with a Swedish dad, his red hair made him an outsider – until he moved to Gothenburg, where his dad ran away with the owner of the local pizza parlour. Bosse married and had three kids before his wife ran off with a Swedish football star who played for AC Milan. Trying to win her back at a match, his intentions were misinterpreted by rival supporters who beat him up. Fortunately, in the hospital he met his childhood crush, Giovanna, and fell in love again. Life takes odd twists – best to be financially prepared.

Agency	BBDO Düsseldorf
Creative Director	Carsten Bolk
Copywriter	Andreas Walter
Production	Die Brueder, Berlin
Director	Britta Krause
Producer	Alexander Rosocha
Client	Postbank, "Funny Money"

A man is in the locker room at the gym when a mobile phone goes off. He takes the call. "I just saw this beautiful leather coat at the mall," says a woman's voice. Tying his tie, the man tells her to buy it. She mentions that she has also seen a new Mercedes. Putting on his jacket, he tells her to order it. Now she wants to buy a villa for 1.5 million. "Offer them 1.4," he suggests. The woman hangs up. The man turns to the other guys: "Does anyone know whose phone this is?" Always be prepared for unexpected expenses.

Agency	Lowe, Zurich
Creative Director	Keith Loell
Copywriter	Keith Loell
Art Director	Keith Loell
Production	Th1ng, London
Director	Sylvain Chomet
Producers	Dominic Buttimore
	Sedonie Adams-Grant
	Suzana Kovacevic
Client	Winterthur, "A Town Called Today"

The inhabitants of a town called "Today" are haunted by the shadow of "Tomorrow". This nebulous figure spoils their dinners and casts a pall over their nights. But an elderly woman reassures them that if they plan for tomorrow, they will learn to welcome it – even look forward to its appearance. From then on, the people of today live in happy coexistence with tomorrow. It's all a metaphor for life insurance, of course.

ZURICH

Because change happenz

● ● ● What happens if your car isn't where you left it?

We understand your car's true value.

Because change happenz

ZURICH

● ● ● What happens if you can't retire on your art investments?

We offer options.
At Zurich, we understand people
have different views on what makes
a good investment. Some are better
than others. So we offer a range
of sensible, long-term investment products designed for the realities of an
unstable financial climate. Because we
see people as different, our customers
can choose what suits their taste.
www.zurich.com

Because change happenz

ZURICH

104   **Financial Services**

Agency	Publicis, Zurich		Agency	Publicis, Zurich
Creative Directors	Sacha Moser		Creative Directors	Sacha Moser
	Tim Hoppin			Tim Hoppin
Copywriter	Roland Wetzel		Copywriters	Tim Hoppin
Art Director	Sacha Moser			Roland Wetzel
Production	Stink, London		Art Directors	Sacha Moser
Directors	Oskar Homedal			Lucas Vetsch
	Henry Moore Selder			Martina Wetzel
Producers	Robert Hermann		Photographer	Chris Frazer Smith
	Mungo McLagan		Client	Zurich Insurance
	Daniela Berther			
Client	Zurich Insurance,			
	"Change Anthem - Europe"			

What happens if your invention suddenly
goes global – like the fictional pogo-stick leg
attachments in this film? The spot conjures
up all sorts of alternative futures, including
a world in which cars drive themselves and
stores change configuration every four hours
– from retailer to restaurant, at the flick of a
switch. "Because Change Happenz" nobody
can predict the future, Zurich insurance
understands this.

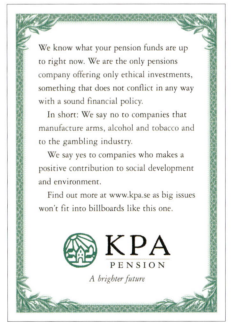

We know what your pension funds are up to right now. We are the only pensions company offering only ethical investments, something that does not conflict in any way with a sound financial policy.

In short: We say no to companies that manufacture arms, alcohol and tobacco and to the gambling industry.

We say yes to companies who makes a positive contribution to social development and environment.

Find out more at www.kpa.se as big issues won't fit into billboards like this one.

KPA
PENSION
A brighter future

Financial Services   **105**

Agency	Abby Norm, Stockholm
Creative Directors	Emil Frid
	Hakan Nyberg
Copywriter	Hakan Nyberg
Art Director	Emil Frid
Photographer	Andreas Kock
Illustrator	Joel Hjertén
Client	KPA Pensions

Agency	DDB Amsterdam
Copywriters	Marcel de Jonge
	Sikko Gerkema
	Nico Akkerman
Art Directors	Martin Cornelissen
	Bart Kooij
Production	Lenzing Brand Films, Amsterdam
Director	Olaf van Gerwen
Producers	Heleen Dankbaar
	Paul Brand
	Yolande van der Meulen
	Chantal Gulpers
Client	Achmea Insurance, "Health"

"Every year," says the narrator, "a million and a half people are injured playing sports. Other people, of course: not you." The spot goes on to depict a series of unlikely accidents that always happen to the other guy, while the hero – who unwittingly causes the mishaps – forever escapes unharmed. "It's important to think carefully about who you choose for your health insurance. For the other people, of course: not for you!"

106   Financial Services

Agency	DDB Amsterdam
Copywriter	Niels Westra
Art Director	Jakko Achterberg
Production	Bonkers, Amsterdam
Director	Matthijs van Heiningen jr.
Producers	Paul Harting
	Vanessa Janssen
Client	Centraal Beheer Insurance, "Witness"

A mobster testifies against the Capo and takes advantage of a witness protection programme, changing his identity and moving to the sleepy town of Omerta Falls. He's just settled in to his new home when the doorbell rings. A huge welcome committee is outside his door, while the mayor tells him that he has become the 100,000th resident of the town, a fact that is being broadcast live on national television at that very moment. His cover blown, the man looks terrified. Need insurance? Just call Centraal Beheer.

Agency	Wirz BBDO, Zurich
Creative Director	Matthias Freuler
Copywriter	Thomas Kurzmeyer
Art Director	Andrea Reinhart
Production	Wirz & Fraefel Productions
Director	Ernst Wirz
Producers	Stefan Fraefel
	Kerstin Reulen
Client	Schweizerische Mobiliar Insurance, "Photographer"

"Dear Sir or Madam," writes a photographer, as we see him setting up a shot of a huge collection of china. "I was photographing the beautiful china collection my aunt wanted to sell." Noticing that one of his studio lights is unplugged, he picks his way gingerly through the maze of objects. "There were 400 pieces." He plugs the light in, but the fuse blows, plunging the room into darkness. Then we hear a CRASH! "Later, there were even more." Yup, insurance comes in handy.

Agency	Saffirio Tortelli Vigoriti, Turin	Circus owners tell an interviewer how a mysterious benefactor has counselled them through various crises: when the clown got depressed, when the "flying woman" got stuck up a tree, when they all caught "sleeping sickness" from a tsetse fly, when one of the midgets grew too tall, and when the fire-eater set the tent ablaze. Who is the man who provided such comfort in hard times? It's the insurance man, of course, from Reale Mutua.
Creative Director	Aurelio Tortelli	
Copywriter	Michela Grasso	
Art Director	Daniele Ricci	
Production	The Family, Milan	
Director	Carl Erik Rinsch	
Producers	Stefano Guaglia	
	Anna Sica	
Client	Reale Mutua Insurance, "Circus"	

Agency	JWT Frankfurt	In this series of ads, which vaguely resembles the hit TV series 24, we enter the tense life of David, who is addicted to online trading. Because money never sleeps, he could conceivably spend his whole life doing deals and making cash – although this does seem to jar with his complex love life and his real job. Nevertheless, as we see David's account balance go up, we can't help wanting to join in.
Creative Director	Mike Ries	
Copywriters	Jan Koehler	
Art Director	Khai Doan	
Production	Jo!Schmid Filmproduktion, Berlin	
Director	Martin Schmid	
Producers	Michael Schmid	
	Marie Louise Seidl	
Client	CMC Markets Online Brokers, "Money Never Sleeps"	

Agency	Springer & Jacoby, Vienna	Life for the new generation is not the same as it was for their grandparents. At four years old, they're already online. At 16, they're writing love letters on their mobiles. At 24, they're cool bosses. At 30, they're relaxed dads. At 40, they're only just emerging from puberty. At 59, they're being envied for their love lives. And at 71, they go on holiday – in space. All these people are alive right now. And they need a new kind of insurance.
Creative Director	Paul Holcmann	
Copywriters	Hans Juckel	
	Jakob Wuerzel	
Art Director	Katharina Haines	
Production	Close Up, Vienna	
Director	Martin Werner	
Producers	Max Wilhelm	
	Melanie Soukup	
Client	Uniqa Insurance, "New Generation"	

Financial Services

Agency	Uncle Grey, Oslo	Agency	McCann Erickson / McEmotion,
Creative Director	Frank Nystuen		Frankfurt
Copywriter	Frank Nystuen	**Creative Directors**	Stefan Herrmann
Art Director	Linn Sandnes		Joerg Hoffmann
Illustrator	Baard Andresen	**Copywriter**	Joerg Hoffmann
Client	American Express Card	**Art Directors**	Stefan Herrmann
			Gerd Stahl
		Photographer	Christoph Herdt
		Client	Domcura Household Insurance

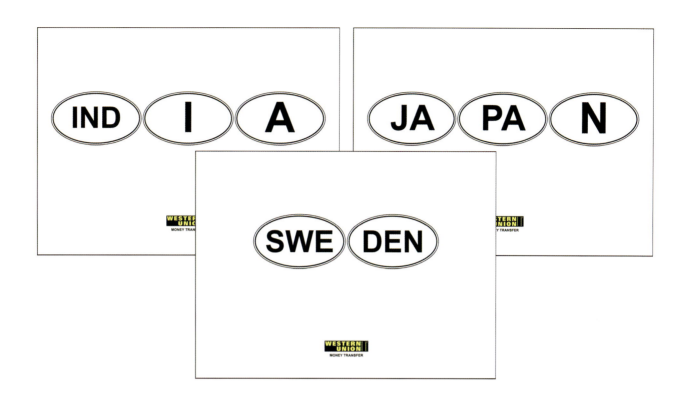

Even small tools can create huge economical damage.   **Hesse & Partner**
                                                             Industry Insurance Brokers

Agency	Leo Burnett & Target, Bucharest	Agency	Ruf Lanz, Zurich
Creative Director	Bogdan Naumovici	**Creative Directors**	Markus Ruf
			Danielle Lanz
Copywriters	Mihai Costache	**Copywriters**	Markus Ruf
	Laura Leonte		Thomas Schöb
Art Director	Ghica Popa	**Art Director**	Katja Puccio
Client	Western Union	**Client**	Hesse & Partner

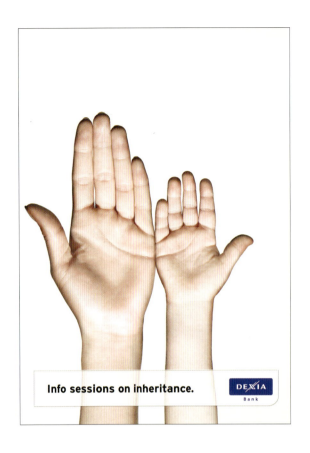

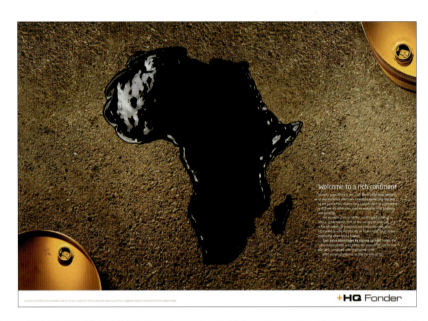

Agency	Duval Guillaume Brussels	Agency	RBK Communication, Stockholm
Creative Directors	Peter Ampe		
	Katrien Bottez	Creative Director	Fredrik Dahlberg
Copywriter	Virginie Lepère	Copywriter	Fredrik Dahlberg
Art Director	Frédéric Van Hoof	Art Director	Erik Larsson
Photographer	Christophe Gilbert	Photographer	Erik Hagman
Client	Dexia Bank	Client	HQ Investment Funds

Agency	Publicis, Zurich	A UBS internal campaign aimed
Creative Director	Markus Gut	at bank employees to address the
Copywriter	Tom Gundy	problem of money laundering.
Art Director	Denis Schwarz	
Photographer	Mathias Zuppiger	
Illustrators	Isabelle Hauser	
	Corinne Bresch	
Client	UBS Bank	

Agency	Duval Guillaume Brussels	In this animated spot, a man is walking down
Creative Directors	Peter Ampe	a dusty street in Africa when he trips and falls.
	Katrien Bottez	As he rolls he knocks over other people, who
	Xavier Bouillon	get tangled up with him in a 'snowball effect'.
Copywriter	Tiny Nys	The rolling ball of humanity grows larger and
Art Director	Alexander Cha'ban	larger, sucking in everybody in its path. It cuts
Production	Caviar	a swathe through the countryside and heads
Director	Andreas Hasle	for the city. Finally it catches up with a woman
Producers	Ingrid & Kato Maes	innocently singing to her baby. Don't let AIDS
	Roxane Lemaire	gain more ground. Support Médecins Sans
	Marc Van Buggenhout	Frontières (Doctors Without Borders).
Client	Médecins Sans Frontières,	
	"Human Ball"	

 Public Interest **113**

Agency	Walker, Zurich
Creative Director	Pius Walker
Art Directors	Marianne Friedli
	Florian Fröhlich
	Carolina Gurtner
Photographer	Federico Naef
Client	Amnesty International

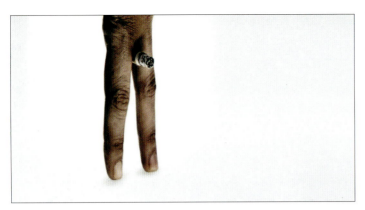

Agency	Abbott Mead Vickers
	BBDO, London
Creative Directors	Paul Belford
	Nigel Roberts
Copywriter	Adam Rimmer
Art Director	Pete Davies
Client	COI - NHS,
	"Fingerlegs - SFX"

Filmed against a stark white background, a pair of fingers holding a smoking cigarette forms the shape of a pair of legs. Party noises and conversation are heard in the background. The narrator explains that thousands of men become impotent because of smoking. "Every cigarette that you smoke causes fatty deposits that restrict the flow of blood to your penis," he says. As if on cue, a long length of ash drops from the cigarette.

114 **Public Interest**

Agency	Ruf Lanz, Zurich
Creative Directors	Markus Ruf
	Danielle Lanz
Copywriter	Markus Ruf
Art Director	Danielle Lanz
Production	Condor Films
Director	Serge Höltschi
Producers	Sina Schlatter
	Martin A. Fueter
Client	Muehlehalde
	Home for the Blind,
	"Stevie Wonder"
	& "Andrea Bocelli"

These two spots show elderly blind people singing hit songs: I Just Called to Say I Love You, by Stevie Wonder, and Con Te Partiro by Andrea Bocelli. Both of these stars were also blind – but not everyone with the affliction can make millions singing. Why not make a donation to Zurich's Home for the Blind?

Agency	Spillmann/Felser/
	Leo Burnett, Zurich
Creative Director	Martin Spillmann
Copywriter	Stefan Ehrler
Art Directors	Martin Spillmann
	Mathias Babst
Production	Will van der Vlugt
	Productions, Amsterdam
Director	Ronald Koetzier
Producers	Marco van Prooijen
	Marlies van Heese
	Sebahat Derdiyok
Client	Helvetas, "Water"

In an African village, we see people going about their daily lives as if they have access to water – but in reality all the utensils they are using are empty. A child's bath, a cup, drinking glasses, a watering can, a tap...they are dry and useless. The water that should be accessible to everyone is not available to these people. Helvetas is fighting so that no-one has to live without water.

Agency	Etcetera, Amsterdam
Copywriter	Stan van Zon
Art Director	Gido van der Vlies
Production	Bij Brand, Amsterdam
Director	Olaf van Gerwen
Producers	Paul Brand
	Patrick Nelemans
Client	NFSG Disability
	Sports Foundation, "Metro"

A girl in a wheelchair confronts the stairwell leading down to ground level from a metro stop. Seemingly resigned, she starts to wheel her chair down the concrete steps. Suddenly, about halfway down, she leaps out of the chair and performs a series of amazing aerial stunts, using the architecture as a frame as she races the tumbling wheelchair down the steps. She soars into the air, landing in the chair just as it arrives at the bottom. The girl is an amputee, but not all disabled people are helpless. This ad was brought to you by the Disabled Sports Foundation.

Agency	Duval Guillaume
	Brussels
Creative Directors	Katrien Bottez
	Peter Ampe
Copywriter	Benoit Menetret
Art Director	Jean-Marc Wachsmann
Production	Lovo Films
Director	François Mercier
Producers	Bert Brulez
	Marc Van Buggenhout
	Dieter Lebbe
Client	ANGCP Organ
	Donations, "Sign Up"

A man is about to sign a document. He notices that his fountain pen has run out of ink. He rummages in his toolbox and finds another fountain pen, but its nib is bent and twisted. That pen is history. He unscrews it: still plenty of ink in the cartridge, though. He picks up the first pen, unscrews it, removes the empty cartridge, and replaces it with the full cartridge from the "dead pen". He signs the document. We then see it's an organ donor form.

Agency	Publicis, Amstelveen
Creative Directors	Joep de Kort
	Massimo van der Plas
Copywriter	Maarten Remmers
Art Director	Wouter Voges
Production	Eyeworks, Amsterdam
Producer	Nathalie Moser
Client	Dutch Ministry of
	Internal Affairs, "Vote!"

This ad uses genuine clips from reality TV shows like Pop Idol and Big Brother. Of course the format depends on votes from the viewers: they decide who wins and who loses, who stays and who goes. In each clip we see a presenter saying, "You have voted in your millions!" or words to that effect. The screen goes black, and some words appear: "So you like to vote?" In that case, you should vote on March 7, the date of the local government elections. The decision is yours.

Agency	Leagas Delaney, Hamburg
Creative Director	Heiko Schmidt
Copywriter	Fabian Klingbeil
Art Directors	Fabian Klingbeil
	Gitta Osthoff
Production	BM8
Producer	Niels Klamroth
Client	International Panda Rescue, "Whales"

We see some cute seals frolicking in the surf. Suddenly the killer whales move in, attacking with brutal savagery and dragging off the young. They even flip the seals through the air with their tails, toying with their prey like cats with helpless mice. The caption says: "Still want to save whales?" Pause. "Save pandas instead."

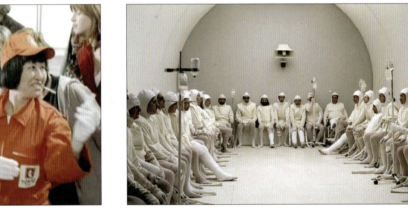

Agency	DraftFCB Paris
Creative Director	Thomas Stern
Copywriter	Dominique Marchand
Art Director	Jean-Michel Alirol
Production	Mr.Hyde
Director	Stephan Prehn
Client	INPES, "Toxic Corp"

Welcome to Toxic Corp, where naïve youngsters are enlisted to become "replacement smokers". As the latest recruits tour the cheerful yet sinister factory, the chirpy narrator explains why the company needs them to become "addicted to nicotine and absorb formaldehyde, arsenic and acetone". The youngsters on the tour seem oblivious to the fact they're almost tripping over the corpses of the smokers they'll be replacing. As tobacco kills one in two smokers, the industry needs as many suckers as it can get.

Agency	Thamesdown CZ, Prague
Creative Director	Viktor Lelek
Copywriter	Ivan Peterka
Art Director	Jan Pohl
Production	Simply Sirena
Director	Kryštof Michal
Producer	Pavel Miler
Client	Greenpeace, "Sperms"

White-clad men sit in a white tube. They look bored, fatigued and unhealthy. Nodding off, one of them drops his crutch. When a red light flashes, they struggle to their feet in unison and we see that they are all sick, elderly or crippled. A door opens at the end of the tube and they straggle out. Most of them fall over before they make it. We've got the idea by now, but the caption confirms it: "Chemicals cause damage to your sperm." For more information, contact Greenpeace.

Agency	Armando Testa, Milan
Creative Directors	German Silva
	Ekhi Mendibil
	Haitz Mendibil
Copywriter	Alessandro Mian
Art Director	Ricard Valero
Graphic Designer	Ricard Valero
Client	Canguro Onlus

Agency	AHA Puttner Red Cell, Vienna
Creative Director	Reinhard Gnettner
Copywriter	Reinhard Gnettner
Art Director	Ivo Kobald
Production	Close Up, Vienna
	SIA, Sofia
Director	Georgi Dimitrov
Producer	Dieter Lembcke
Client	Hilfsgemeinschaft Community for the Blind, "Blind Pilots"

Passengers look dismayed when the pilot and co-pilot board the aircraft. Both men are blind. The passengers have no choice but to stay seated as the plane begins to roll. As it picks up speed, we see that the runway ends in a cliff. The plane gets closer. Just as it is about to go over the edge, the passengers scream. The pilot pulls back on the joystick and the plane soars into the air. "You know Bob," says the pilot to his colleague, "one day they'll scream too late, and we'll all be killed." He laughs. Hilfsgemeinschaft community for the blind sees the world differently.

118 **Public Interest**

Agency	Saatchi & Saatchi Beirut
Creative Directors	Samer Younes
	Dan Khoueiry
Copywriter	Nizar El Hindi
Art Director	Dan Koueiry
Production	City Films, Beirut
Director	Marc Hadife
Producers	Joyce Hadife
	Eli Zreik
Client	Lebanese Ministry of Social Affairs, "Animals"

We see touching scenes of animals nursing their young. From a koala to a lioness, the animals display nothing but tenderness. Then we see a little girl holding a teddy bear. Her face is a mass of bruises. Some kids wish their parents were animals.

Agency	Leo Burnett, Lisbon
Creative Director	Fernando Bellotti
Copywriters	Fernando Bellotti
	Ricardo Corsaro
Art Directors	Fernando Bellotti
	Paulo Areas
Production	Republika Films
Director	Carlos Manga Junior
Producers	Regina Costa
	Cristina Almeida
Client	IAC-Institute for Support of Abused Children, "Alzheimer's"

Visibly gathering her strength as she enters an old peoples' home, a woman visits her mother, who has Alzheimer's. "An aunt came to visit me," says the elderly lady, who is lost in her thoughts. "I asked her to hide me under the bed." Her daughter looks confused: "Under the bed?" "Yes," says the old lady. "My father should be here soon." An abused child never forgets.

DON'T LEAVE HIM ALONE WITH CHERNOBYL

20 years after the disaster, Chernobyl's landscape reminds one of a barren planet. Even more damage was done to local residents, their bodies and minds alike. Red Cross provides them with both medical and psychological assistance. Recently, radiation linked illnesses have increased. Please support us. Keep up your interest in Chernobyl.

DON'T LEAVE HIM ALONE WITH CHERNOBYL

20 years after the disaster, Chernobyl's landscape reminds one of a barren planet. Even more damage was done to local residents, their bodies and minds alike. Red Cross provides them with both medical and psychological assistance. Recently, radiation linked illnesses have increased. Please support us. Keep up your interest in Chernobyl.

DON'T LEAVE HER ALONE WITH CHERNOBYL

20 years after the disaster, Chernobyl's landscape reminds one of a barren planet. Even more damage was done to local residents, their bodies and minds alike. Red Cross provides them with both medical and psychological assistance. Recently, radiation linked illnesses have increased. Please support us. Keep up your interest in Chernobyl.

Public Interest   **119**

Agency	Leo Burnett Ukraine, Kiev
Creative Director	Jaroslaw Wiewiorski
Copywriters	Tatiana Fedorenko
	Jarek Wiewiorski
Art Director	Pavel Klubnikin
Client	Red Cross/Red Crescent

Agency	MSTF Partners, Lisbon
Creative Directors	Susana Sequeira
	Lourenço Thomáz
Copywriter	João Ribeiro
Art Directors	Vasco Thomáz
	Tomás Lemos
Production	Garage Films, Lisbon
Director	João Nuno Pinto
Producers	Miguel Varela
	Martim Lemos
Client	Portuguese Cardiology Foundation, "Big Belly People"

A nature documentary maker is reporting on a breed called "the big belly people". This breed of human is "spreading everywhere" he says, as we see them lolling around like walruses. Sedentary by nature, the big bellies eat whatever they like and rarely exercise. But their condition puts them at risk from heart disease and diabetes, so they may one day become extinct.

Agency	Saatchi & Saatchi, Stockholm
Creative Director	Adam Kerj
Copywriter	Magnus Jakobsson
Art Directors	Mårten Hedbom
	Gustav Egerstedt
Production	Mister Krister
Director	Jens Sjögren
Producer	Cornelia Opitz
Client	Swedish Armed Forces, "Swedish Au-Pair Girl"

People who want to hire au pair girls make home videos outlining their needs. In the first, an American woman wants help "doing her nails" and looking after her spoiled brat of a son. There will be strictly no music after 5pm, when the family gathers around the piano.

In the second video, a Japanese father expresses himself mainly by shouting – and that's just to indicate pleasure. Expressions of displeasure involve a samurai sword. Of course, girls, you could always join the army, which is now recruiting.

Agency	Nitro, London
Creative Director	Bruce Crouch
Copywriters	Olly Farrington
	Neil Richardson
Art Directors	Neil Richardson
	Olly Farrington
Typographer	Andy Bird
Client	Greater London Authority

Agency	Forsman & Bodenfors,
	Gothenburg
Creative Director	Martin Cedergren
Copywriters	Jacob Nelson
	Anna Qvennerstedt
Art Director	Silla Öberg
Designer	Lotta Dolling
Client	Swedish Ministry of
	Health and Social Affairs

Girlpower is a government campaign to promote sex equality. Letters were sent to various editors asking them to explain specific examples of sexual stereotyping that appeared in their publications. The letters, and responses, were then published on poster sites and on the Girlpower website.

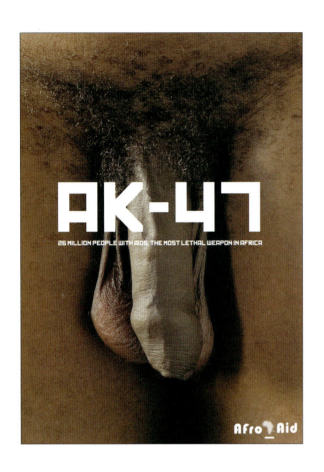

Public Interest

Agency	The Farm, Madrid		**Agency**	Contrapunto, Madrid
Creative Directors	Jose Maria Pujol		**Creative Directors**	Antonio Montero
	Paloma Acedo			Jaime Chávarri
				Iván De Dios
Copywriter	Rosario Garcia		**Copywriter**	Jaime Chávarri
Art Director	Javier Gonzalez		**Art Director**	Iván De Dios
Client	Afro Aid		**Illustrator**	Camilo Puyal
			Client	WWF

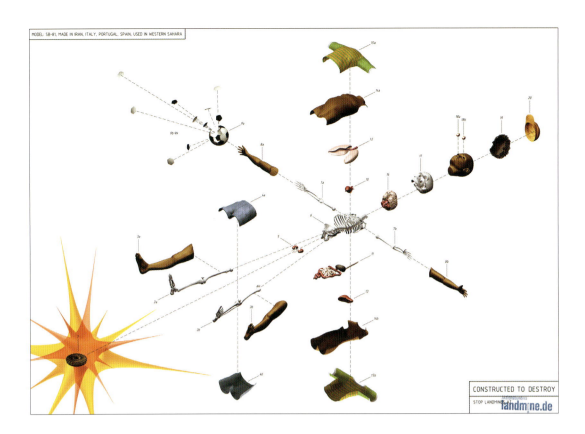

Agency	Scholz & Friends Berlin	**Agency**	Publicis Comunicación España, Madrid
Creative Directors	Matthias Schmidt	**Creative Director**	Nicolás Hollander
	Constantin Kaloff	**Copywriter**	Natalia Vaquero
	Julia Schmidt	**Art Director**	Vanesa Sanz
Copywriter	Birgit van den Valentyn	**Photographer**	Joan Garrigosa
Art Director	Tim Stuebane	**Client**	Survival International
Illustrator	Carolina Cwiklinska		
Client	Actiongroup Landmine.de		

Agency	McCann Erickson, Prague		**Agency**	Euro RSCG Spain, Madrid
Creative Director	Lars Killi		**Creative Directors**	Jose Maria Batalla
Copywriter	Jaromir Fischer			Ana Navarro
Art Director	Alla Havlickova			Maico Garcia
Photographer	Goran Tacevski		**Copywriter**	Ana Navarro
Client	Anabell Foundation		**Art Director**	Maico Garcia
			Photographer	Pep Avila
			Client	Fundación Altarriba

Agency	Ogilvy & Mather, Frankfurt
Creative Directors	Simon Oppmann
	Peter Roemmelt
Copywriter	Peter Roemmelt
Art Director	Simon Oppmann
Photographer	Hana Kostreba
Client	German Foundation for
	Monument Protection

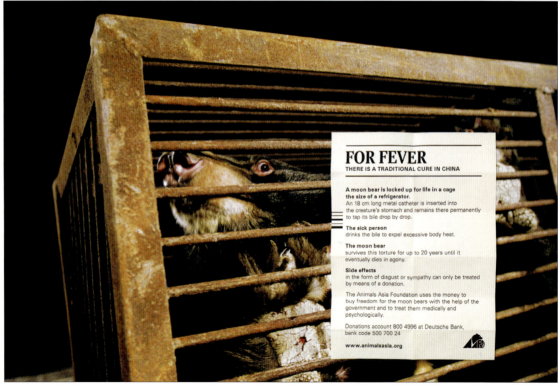

Agency	Duval Guillaume Brussels
Creative Directors	Peter Ampe
	Katrien Bottez
Copywriter	Peter Ampe
Art Director	Katrien Bottez
Photographer	Jimmy Kets
Client	Minority Forum

Agency	Kempertrautmann,
	Hamburg
Creative Directors	Mathias Lamken
	Niels Alzen
Copywriter	Niels Alzen
Art Director	Tim Belser
Photographers	Ursula Meissner
	Alexandra Oetker
Client	Animals Asia Foundation

Agency	Ogilvy & Mather, Frankfurt
Creative Directors	Helmut Himmler
	Lars Huvart
Copywriter	Ales Polcar
Art Director	Till Schaffarczyk
Illustrator	Till Schaffarczyk
Client	OroVerde
	Rainforest Foundation

Agency	BETC Euro RSCG, Paris
Creative Director	Rémi Babinet
Copywriter	Rémi Noel
Art Director	Eric Holden
Production	White
Director	Taryn Simon
Producer	Virginie Chalard
Client	ECPAT, "10 Years"

The camera pushes into a seedy brothel in some unspecified tropical country. The ages of the prostitutes we encounter on our visit flash up on the screen: 13 years, 16 years, 14 years...The camera moves up the stairs and into a bedroom. We see a young girl in bed, and find ourselves in the middle of a police raid. A cop puts his hand over the camera lens. Cut to a police mug-shot, above the line: 10 years. Sex with a minor means prison, no matter which country you're in.

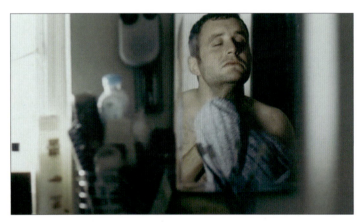

Agency	M&C Saatchi, London
Copywriter	Curtis Brittles
Art Director	Will Bate
Production	Gorgeous Enterprises, London
Director	Vince Squibb
DOP	Simon Chaudior
Producers	Spencer Dodd
	Kate Havers
Client	Transport For London, "The Day You Went To Work"

We see a man getting ready for work, his actions followed by the narrator. "The alarm that always wakes you; the sock you can never find; the tie they make you wear; the girlfriend you kiss goodbye…" We then see the man on his motorbike. "The road you've lived on for years; the mums on the school run…" Suddenly the man swerves to avoid a car door. "The lamppost you slam into; the legs you'll never use again…The day you went to work." Most accidents happen on a familiar journey – never let your attention slip.

Agency	Lyle Bailie International, Belfast
Creative Directors	David Lyle
	Julie Anne Bailie
Copy/Art Directors	David Lyle
	Julie Anne Bailie
Production	Rawi Macartney Cole, London
Director	Syd Macartney
Producers	Ruck Strauss
	Sonia Laughlin
Client	National Safety Council, "Just One"

In a bar, a young man buys a drink for an attractive girl. He is about to sip his own pint when she looks at him disapprovingly. He begins to reflect on the horrendous decisions he may force others to make if he has a car accident on the way home. Who to cut out of the wreckage first? Whether to stop first aid? How to find a school for a disabled child? Whether to pay for plastic surgery? Suddenly disgusted, the man shoves the pint aside. The girl smiles at him. Never have even one drink if you plan to drive.

Agency	Saatchi & Saatchi, Brussels	Agency	Saatchi & Saatchi, Dubai
Creative Director	Philip Vandenberghe	Creative Director	Ed Jones
Copywriter	Patrick De Win	Copywriter	Avinash Sampath
Art Director	Paul Van Biesen	Art Director	Andrew Leftley
Photographer	Koen Demuynck	Photographer	David Bramley
Client	All Dog Training	Illustrator	Ahmed Kunamed
		Client	Re-Lebanon.org

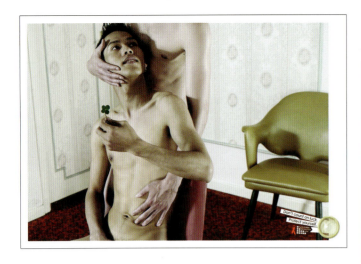

130 **Public Interest**

Agency	Euro RSCG Brussels
Creative Directors	Jean-Luc Soille
	Daniel Van Vlasselaer
Copywriter	Stéphane Daniel
Art Director	Hugo Battistel
Photographer	Frank Uyttenhove
Client	Plateforme Prévention SIDA

Well done. You are now one of the few who are not afraid to get close to an HIV positive person.

AN INITIATIVE LED BY THE FRENCH MINISTER FOR HEALTH AND THE NATIONAL HEALTH EDUCATION INSTITUTE TO INTEGRATE PEOPLE WHO ARE HIV POSITIVE.

Agency	BETC Euro RSCG, Paris	Well done. You are now one of
Creative Director	Stéphane Xiberras	the few who are not afraid to get
Copywriter	Sylvie Charhon	close to a HIV positive person. (This
Art Director	Gérald Schmite	poster was used exclusively on bus
Photographer	Ben Hasset	shelters and other sites that could
Client	INPES-AIDS Prevention	be approached by pedestrians.)

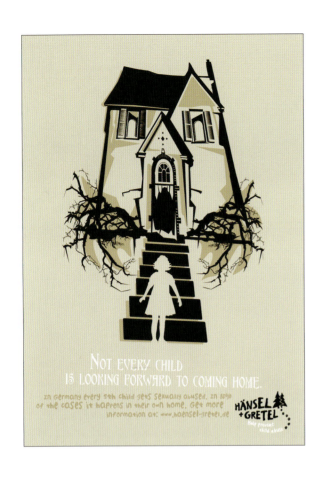

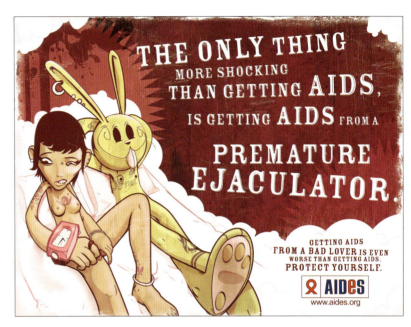

Agency	Scholz & Friends Hamburg	Agency	TBWA\Paris
Creative Directors	Marcus Korell	Creative Director	Erik Vervroegen
	André Klein	Copywriter	Jean-François Bouchet
Art Director	Carolin Rathgeber	Art Directors	Jessica Gérard-Huet
Illustration	Insect, London		Eve Roussou
Graphic Design	Mareike Ledeboer	Illustrator	Aisk One
Client	Hänsel & Gretel Foundation	Client	AIDES
			AIDS Awareness Association

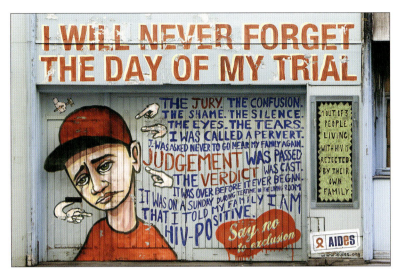

Agency	TBWA\Paris
Creative Director	Erik Vervroegen
Copywriter	Véronique Sels
Art Director	Ingrid Varetz
Client	AIDES
	AIDS Awareness Association

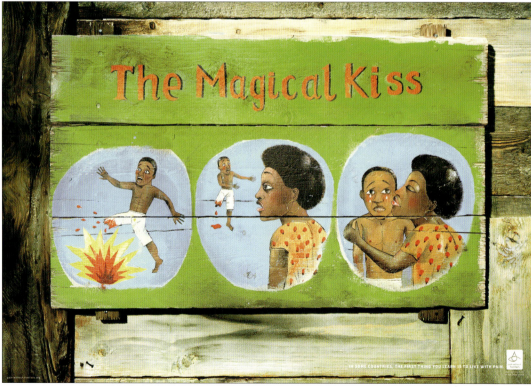

Agency	TBWA\Merlin, Bucharest	Agency	BDDP & Fils, Paris
Creative Director	Cristian Munteanu	Creative Directors	Manoëlle Van Der Vaeren
Copywriter	Radu Olteanu		Laurent Bodson
Art Director	Catalin Scripca	Copywriters	Mathieu Degryse
Photographer	Carioca		Yves-Éric Deboey
Client	Red Cross	Art Directors	Yves-Éric Deboey
			Mathieu Degryse
		Photographer	Yann le Pape
		Illustrator	Olaf Hajek
		Client	Pain Without Frontiers

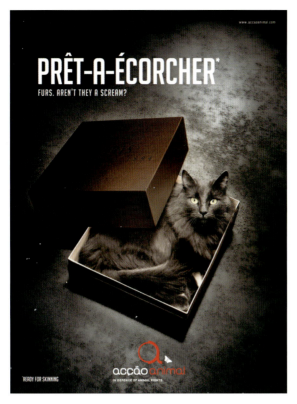

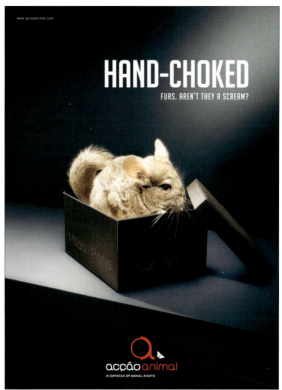

Agency	BBDO Portugal, Lisbon	Agency	Leo Burnett, Brussels
Creative Director	Pedro Bidarra	Creative Directors	Jean-Paul Lefebvre
Copywriter	Nuno Leal		Michel De Lauw
Art Directors	André Moreira	Copywriter	Wim Corremans
	Ivo Purvis	Art Director	Alex Gabriels
Photographer	Pedro Claudio	Photographer	Frieke Janssens
Client	Acção Animal	Client	Bite Back

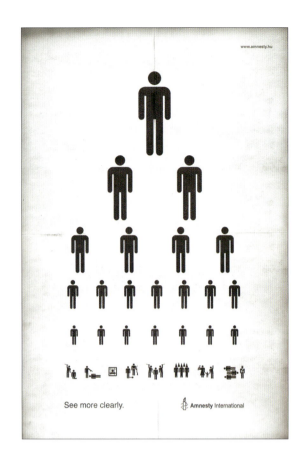

Agency	DDB Budapest	Agency	JWT, Dubai	These double page magazine ads
Creative Director	Milos Ilic	Creative Directors	John Foster	were used exclusively in centrefolds
Copywriters	Lukasz Brzozowski		Chafic Haddad	where the staples were visible
	Rodrigo Fernandes	Copywriter	Jeremy Filgate	
	Chris Hill	Art Director	Subha Naidu	
Art Directors	Lukasz Brzozowski	Photographer	Suresh Subramanian	
	Rodrigo Fernandes	Illustrator	Jomy Varghese	
Client	Amnesty International	Client	Amnesty International	

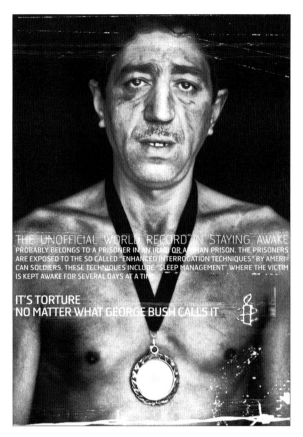

THE UNOFFICIAL WORLD RECORD IN STAYING AWAKE
PROBABLY BELONGS TO A PRISONER IN AN IRAQI OR AFGHAN PRISON. THE PRISONERS
ARE EXPOSED TO THE SO CALLED "ENHANCED INTERROGATION TECHNIQUES" BY AMERI-
CAN SOLDIERS. THESE TECHNIQUES INCLUDE "SLEEP MANAGEMENT" WHERE THE VICTIM
IS KEPT AWAKE FOR SEVERAL DAYS AT A TIME.

IT'S TORTURE
NO MATTER WHAT GEORGE BUSH CALLS IT

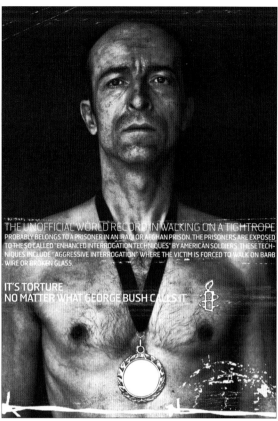

THE UNOFFICIAL WORLD RECORD IN WALKING ON A TIGHTROPE
PROBABLY BELONGS TO A PRISONER IN AN IRAQI OR AFGHAN PRISON. THE PRISONERS ARE EXPOSED
TO THE SO CALLED "ENHANCED INTERROGATION TECHNIQUES" BY AMERICAN SOLDIERS. THESE TECH-
NIQUES INCLUDE "AGGRESSIVE INTERROGATION" WHERE THE VICTIM IS FORCED TO WALK ON BARB
WIRE OR BROKEN GLASS.

IT'S TORTURE
NO MATTER WHAT GEORGE BUSH CALLS IT

A SIGNATURE IS MORE POWERFUL THAN YOU THINK. WWW.AMNESTY.ORG

Agency	BBDO Denmark, Copenhagen
Copywriter	Jesper Hansen
Art Directors	Olga Bastian
	Jesper Isholm
Photographers	Martin Soeby
Client	Amnesty International

Agency	TBWA\Paris
Creative Director	Erik Vervroegen
Copywriters	Ghislaine De Germon
	Clémence Cousteau
Art Directors	Marianne Fonferrier
	Julien Boissinot
	Bérengère Hours
	Nicolas Hurez
Photographer	Marc Gouby
Client	Amnesty International

Here in my country you can't walk like an animal,

Agency	McCann Erickson Portugal, Lisbon
Creative Directors	Diogo Anahory
	José Carlos Bomtempo
Copywriter	Fábio Seidl
Art Director	Diogo Mello
Client	Amnesty International, "Accident"

Walking down the street, a man bumps into a young black guy. The man lets rip with a torrent of racial abuse, much to the dismay of everyone around him. "…and take the Brazilians, the Chinamen and all that crap…" he adds, but hardly has time to finish his sentence when he is run down by a car. He wakes up in hospital, where he is tended by a black doctor. How far does your prejudice go? Respect immigrants.

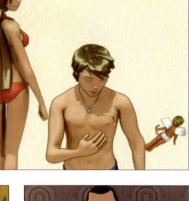

Agency	Leo Burnett Warsaw
Creative Director	Martin Winther
Copywriters	Michael Lars White
	Maciej Porebski
Art Directors	Marcin Serafin
	Jakub Zielecki
Production	Dynamo, Warsaw
Directors	Maciej Majchrzak
	Marcin Serafin
Producer	Janusz Wlodarski
Client	Wolontariat, "Carpet"

The whole neighbourhood vibrates as a big muscular guy beats a carpet, raising clouds of dust. He's already gotten through several carpet beaters and from the size of his biceps, we can assume the carpet has had a damn good seeing to. Finally certain every mote of dust has been beaten out, the man rolls up the carpet and slings it over his shoulder. Then we see that he was doing it as favour for another man, who is wheelchair bound. Helping makes you stronger.

Agency	TBWA\Paris
Creative Director	Erik Vervroegen
Copywriter	Veronique Sels
Art Director	Eve Roussou
Production	Wanda
Director	Wilfried Brimo
Client	AIDES, "Sugar Baby Love"

This animated spot follows a young gay man who seems singularly unlucky in love. His encounters grow ever more bizarre until he is finally beaten up in an alley. Fortunately – as occasionally happens in these kinds of stories – he falls in love with his doctor at the hospital. Even more fortunately, throughout all his love affairs he has always worn a condom. Protect yourself – and live long enough to find the right one.

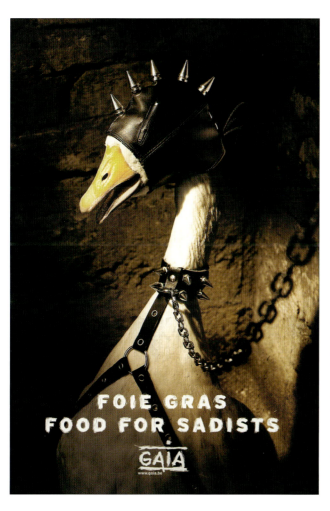

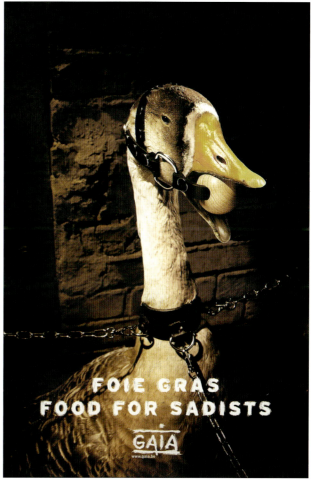

Agency	Design Group, Poole	Agency	Duval Guillaume Brussels
Creative Director	Tony Hill	Creative Directors	Peter Ampe
Copywriters	Liam Forrest		Katrien Bottez
	Tony Hill	Copywriter	Tom Berth
Art Directors	Peter Lee	Art Director	Geert De Rocker
	Simon Tame	Photographer	Kris Van Beek
Photographer	Spiro Politis	Client	Gaia
Client	British Heart Foundation		

Does smoking make you hard?

Not if it means you can't get it up.

Every cigarette you smoke causes fatty deposits that restrict the flow of blood to your penis. Less blood means less of an erection, and if you keep on smoking, things will only get worse.

Text HARD to 84118 for a free information pack. Texts will be charged at your standard rate. Call 0800 169 0 169 www.stayinghard.info

NHS

If you have any concerns about impotence please contact your GP

www.freemylungs.be   Passive smoking kills   free my lungs

www.freemylungs.be   Passive smoking kills   free my lungs

140   Public Interest

Agency	Abbott Mead Vickers BBDO, London		Agency	Duval Guillaume Brussels
Creative Directors	Paul Belford		Creative Directors	Peter Ampe
	Nigel Roberts			Katrien Bottez
Copywriter	Adam Rimmer		Copywriter	Tanguy Gallis
Art Director	Pete Davies		Art Director	Nicolas France
Client	COI-NHS, Anti-Smoking		Photographer	Grégor Collienne
			Client	Free My Lungs

Congestion tax in
Stockholm.

To reduce congestion,
increase accessibility and
improve environment.

Agency	Contrapunto, Madrid	Agency	Blomquist Annonsbyrå, Stockholm
Creative Directors	Antonio Montero	Copywriter	Janne Akerblom
	Jaime Chávarri	Art Director	Fredrik Gustafson
	Iván De Dios	Photographer	Peter Phillips
Copywriters	Jaime Chávarri	Client	Stockholm Congestion Tax
	Lis Torrón		
Art Director	Iván De Dios		
Client	WWF		

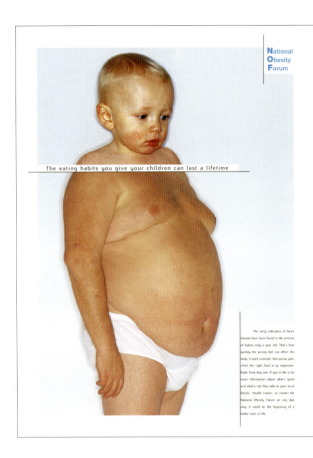

The eating habits you give your children can last a lifetime

The early indicators of heart disease have been found in the arteries of babies only a year old. That's how quickly the wrong diet can affect the body. A stark reminder that giving your child the right food is so important. Right from day one. If you'd like a bit more information about what's good and what's not then talk to your local Doctor, Health Visitor, or contact the National Obesity Forum on 0115 846 2109. It could be the beginning of a better start in life.

THINK ABOUT WHAT IT CONSUMES BEFORE BUYING.
CHECK WWW.ENERGYVORES.BE

THINK ABOUT WHAT IT CONSUMES BEFORE BUYING.
CHECK WWW.ENERGYVORES.BE

142   **Public Interest**

Agency	The Union, Edinburgh
Creative Director	Andrew Lindsay
Copywriter	Michael Hart
Art Director	Don Smith
Photographer	Euan Myles
Client	National Obesity Forum

Agency	Leo Burnett Brussels
Creative Directors	Jean-Paul Lefebvre
	Michel De Lauw
Copywriter	Wim Corremans
Art Director	Alex Gabriels
Photographer	Frieke Janssens
Client	Belgian Government
	Public Services

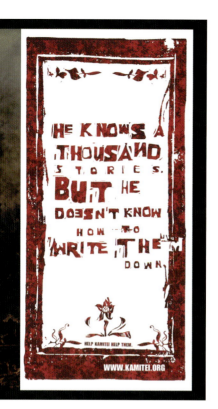

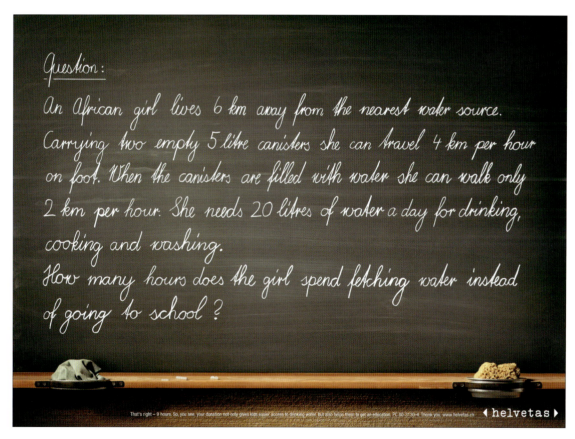

Agency	BBDO Stuttgart	**Agency**	Spillmann/Felser/Leo Burnett, Zurich
Creative Directors	Armin Jochum	**Creative Director**	Martin Spillmann
	Andreas Rell	**Copywriter**	Stefan Ehrler
Copywriters	Andreas Rell	**Art Director**	Patrik Rohner
	Achim Szymanski	**Photographer**	Jonathan Heyer
	Ono Mothwurf	**Client**	Helvetas
Art Director	Armin Jochum		
Photographer	Aernout Overbeeke		
Illustrators	Marcus Widmann		
	Julia Stackmann		
Client	Kamitei Foundation		

Public Interest

Agency	Ogilvy & Mather Istanbul	**Agency**	Lowe, Zurich
Creative Director	Tibet Sanliman	**Creative Directors**	Valentina Herrmann
Copywriter	Ergin Binyildiz		Beat Egger
Art Director	Can Pehlivanli	**Copywriters**	Beat Egger
Photographer	Nejat Talas		Keith Loell
Client	WWF	**Art Directors**	Valentina Herrmann
			Fernando Perez
		Photographers	J. Sutton-Hibbert
			Roger Grace
		Client	Greenpeace

Agency	Leagas Delaney Italia, Milan	Agency	Serviceplan, Munich
Creative Directors	Stefano Campora	Creative Director	Ekki Frenkler
	Stefano Rosselli	Copywriters	Carlos Obers
Copywriter	Michelangelo Cianciosi		Christine Deinhart
Art Director	Eustachio Ruggieri	Art Director	Sybille Stempel
Photographer	Fulvio Bonavia	Photographer	Camillo Büchelmeier
Client	Saab Road Safety	Client	Child Health Foundation

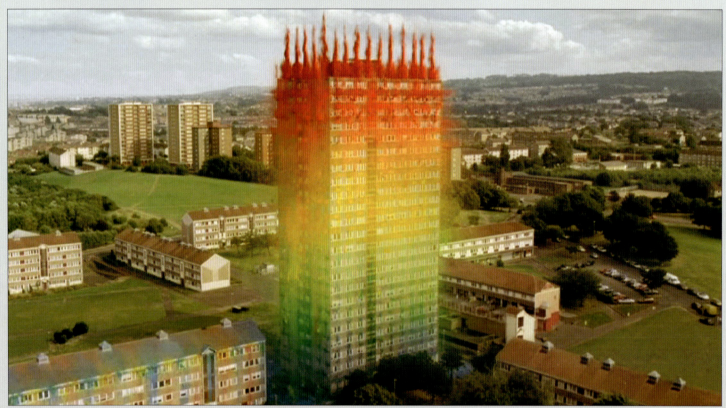

Colour

like no other

146 **Audiovisual Equipment & Accessories**

Agency	Fallon London	In this sequel to the hit "Balls" spot for
Executive CDs	Richard Flintham	Sony Bravia televisions, a drab council
	Andy McLeod	estate gets drenched in colour thanks to
Creative Director	Juan Cabral	explosions of paint. Colours are blasted out
Art Directors	Juan Cabral	of cannons and bombshells of colour burst
	Richard Flintham	in the air. The brilliantly choreographed
Production	Academy Films	paint-fest is punctuated by the surreal
Director	Jonathan Glazer	image of a clown who runs briefly across
Producers	Simon Cooper	the foreground. When the last paintball has
	Nicky Barnes	exploded and the scene has fallen silent,
Client	Sony Bravia, "Paint"	multicoloured rain falls gently from the sky.
		The Sony Bravia: colour, like no other.

 Hi-Fi club

Audiovisual Equipment & Accessories   **147**

Agency   Spilberg, Oslo
Creative Director   Frode Karlberg
Copywriter   Frode Karlberg
Art Director   Jørgen Marthinsen
Client   Hi-Fi Club

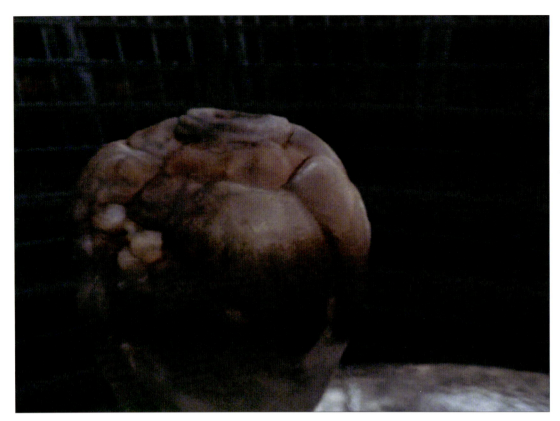

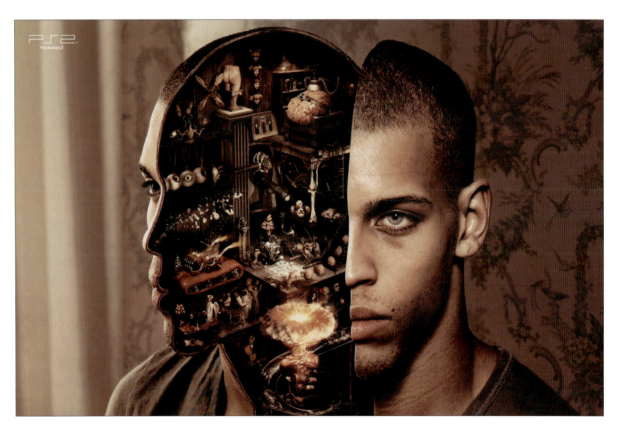

　Audiovisual Equipment & Accessories

Agency	TBWA\Paris	This highly surreal ad takes us inside the
Creative Director	Erik Vervroegen	body of a man playing the PlayStation
Copy/Art Directors	Sebastien Vacherot	2 videogame. His heart is squeezed by
	Jessica Gérard-Huet	a giant fist and his head explodes with
	Loïc Cardon	unlikely Bosch-style images: a robot
Production	Def 2 Shoot	dog using his tongue as a treadmill,
Director	Thomas Marqué	disembodied bottoms being slapped and
Client	Sony PlayStation2,	nipples tweaked, the heads of clowns
	"Head"	being fired from cannons, and his own
		brain being electrocuted. No wonder he
		looks a bit stunned.

Agency	TBWA\Paris
Creative Director	Erik Vervroegen
Copy/Art Directors	Sebastien Vacherot
	Jessica Gérard-Huet
	Ingrid Varetz
	Loïc Cardon
	Gregory Barry
Photographer	Yann Robert
Client	Sony PlayStation2

Agency	TBWA\Paris	Art Directors	Bjoern Ruehmann
Creative Director	Erik Vervroegen		Joakim Reveman
Copywriters	Xander Smith		Marianne Fonferrier
	Ghislaine De Germon		Cedric Moutaud
	Daniel Perez		Eve Roussou
	Matthew Branning		Emmanuel Courteau
		Photographers	Hans Starck
			Dimitri Daniloff
			Marc Da Cunha Lopes
		Client	Sony PlayStation2

Agency	Tonic Communications, Dubai
Creative Directors	Vincent Raffray
	Khaled Gadallah
Copywriter	Vincent Raffray
Art Director	Peter Walker
Production	Velocity South Africa
Director	Adrian De Sa Garces
Producers	Melina McDonald
	Arnaud Verchere
Client	Sony Wega Televisions, "Kick"

Unlikely though it may seem, these two guys can do football tricks with an old portable TV set. After bouncing the thing around for a while and generally showing off their skills, one of them whams the old telly against a wall, where it shatters to bits. Make room for the new Wega portable TV, from Sony.

150   **Audiovisual Equipment & Accessories**

Agency	McCann Erickson, San Francisco
Creative Directors	John Boiler
	Glenn Cole
	Scott Duchon
	Geoff Edwards
Copywriter	Scott Duchon
Art Director	Goeff Edwards
Production	Gorgeous Enterprises, London
Director	Frank Budgen
Producer	Alicia Bernard
Client	Xbox, "Jump Rope"

In an example of urban virtuosity, a bunch of people show off their incredible skills with a skipping rope. Nearly every passer-by seems endowed with grace and skill as they hop, leap, dance and even cycle through the swiftly arcing rope. Great experiences are accessible to everyone. Xbox 360 – jump in.

Agency	McCann Erickson, San Francisco
Creative Directors	John Boiler
	Glenn Cole
	Scott Duchon
	Geoff Edwards
Copywriter	Mat Bunnell
Art Director	Nate Able
Production	Gorgeous Enterprises
Director	Frank Budgen
Producers	Alicia Bernard
	David Verhoef
Client	Xbox, "Water Balloons"

A solitary water balloon bursts on a grim housing estate. Then another is hurled – and then a couple more. The battle escalates and suddenly we're in the midst of a full-scale water fight. Young kids, teenagers and adults alike hurl water balloons at one another. They can't seem to decide whether to scream, laugh, run, hide or come back with more ammo. It all looks great fun, everyone gets soaked and life becomes a bit more exciting for a while. Xbox 360 – jump in.

Something wrong with your favourites? CHANGE YOUR STEREO! **Hi-Fi** klubben

Something wrong with your favourites? CHANGE YOUR STEREO! **Hi-Fi** klubben

PSP WHITE IS COMING

yourPSP.com

Agency	Uncle Grey, Aarhus	**Agency**	Tequila\, Amstelveen
Creative Director	Per Pedersen	**Creative Director**	Enrico Bartens
Copywriter	Ulrik F. Juul	**Copywriter**	Steven Bodoux
Art Director	Rasmus Dunvad	**Art Director**	Jeroen de Snoo
Photographer	Christian Gravesen	**Photographer**	Andy Tan
Client	Hi-Fi Club	**Client**	PlayStation2

152 **Audiovisual Equipment & Accessories**

Agency	Sylva Ad Agency, Budapest		**Agency**	Åkestam Holst, Stockholm
Creative Director	Gabor Spielmann		**Copywriter**	Mark Ardelius
Copywriter	Gabor Spielmann		**Art Directors**	Andreas Ullenius
Art Director	Peter Nador			Johan Landin
Client	Nikon Coolpix L1		**Photographer**	Philip Karlberg
			Client	Pause Ljud & Bild

Agency	Leo Burnett, Milan	Agency	Åkestam Holst, Stockholm
Creative Directors	Sergio Rodriguez	Copywriter	Mark Ardelius
	Enrico Dorizza	Art Directors	Andreas Ullenius
Copywriter	Paolo Guglielmoni		Johan Landin
Art Director	Rosemary Collini Bosso	Photographer	Philip Karlberg
Photographers	Max & Douglas	Client	Pause Ljud & Bild
Client	Nintendo DS		

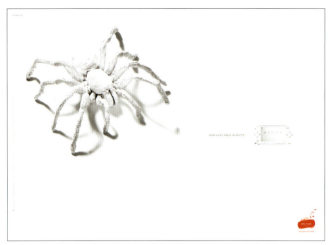

NOW AVAILABLE IN WHITE.

154   **Audiovisual Equipment & Accessories**

Agency	TBWA\Germany, Berlin
Copywriter	Dirk Henkelmann
Art Director	Philip Borchardt
Photographer	Alexander Gnädinger
Client	PlayStation2 Portable

Agency	TBWA\Merlin, Bucharest	**Agency**	TBWA\Vienna
Creative Director	Cristian Munteanu	**Creative Directors**	Elli Hummer
Copywriter	Cristian Munteanu		Gerd Turetschek
Art Director	Catalin Rucareanu		Robert Wohlgemuth
Photographer	Carioca	**Copywriter**	Tanja Trombitas
Illustrator	Alexandru Talamba	**Art Director**	Sabina Karasegh
Client	PlayStation2	**Photographer**	Gerhard Merzeder
		Client	PlayStation2 Portable

156   **Audiovisual Equipment & Accessories**

Agency	Advico Young & Rubicam, Zurich
Creative Directors	Urs Schrepfer
	Daniel Comte
Copywriter	Florian Birkner
Art Director	Roland Scotoni
Photographers	Stephan Schacher
	Steve Bloom
Client	Leica Ultravid Binoculars

Audiovisual Equipment & Accessories   **157**

Agency	FCB Kobza Werbeagentur, Vienna
Creative Director	Erich Falkner
Art Director	Andreas Gesierich
Photographer	Wolfgang Zajc
Client	Cosmos

158 Homes, Furnishings & Appliances

Agency	Leo Burnett, Milan
Creative Director	Enrico Dorizza
Copywriter	Francesco Simonetti
Art Director	Antonio Cortesi
Production	FilmMaster
Director	Dario Piana
Producers	Karim Bartoletti
	Renato Lamberti
Client	Ariston Aqualtis
	Washing Machines,
	"Underwater World"

This beautiful spot takes us inside a washing machine and transforms this humdrum environment into a tropical aquatic universe. A tie becomes an eel, socks play the role of darting tropical fish, a silk scarf is a jellyfish and shirt sleeves look like the waving fronds of seaweed. Even a humble bedcover is transformed into a stingray. The new Aqualtis is big inside.

The quietest vacuum cleaner in its class:
technopower sound & silence.

Siemens. The future moving in.

The quietest vacuum cleaner in its class:
technopower sound & silence.

Siemens. The future moving in.

The quietest vacuum cleaner in its class:
technopower sound & silence.

Siemens. The future moving in.

Homes, Furnishings & Appliances   **159**

Agency	Scholz & Friends Hamburg
Creative Directors	Stefan Setzkorn
	Gunnar Loeser
	Silke Schneider
Copywriter	Alexander Schierl
Art Directors	Axel Schilling
	Marc Ebenwaldner
Photographers	David Hiepler
	Fritz Brunier
Client	Siemens Technopower
	Sound & Silence
	Vacuum Cleaners

At times it's an illusion, just light playing tricks.

He trained his fingers to make all sorts of animals' shadows on the wall.

Enel

Agency	Saatchi & Saatchi, Milan
Creative Directors	Luca Albanese
	Francesco Taddeucci
Copywriter	Francesco Taddeucci
Art Director	Luca Albanese
Production	H Films
Director	Laurence Dunmore
Producers	Daniela Cattaneo
	Cecilia Barberis
	Manuela Fidenzi
Client	Enel, "Energy Goes Beyond What We See"

A gravel-voiced Italian actor recounts three folk tales. In the first, an old man uses his hands to make the shadows of animals on the wall of his grandson's bedroom. One day, a deer shape comes to life and bolts out the window. In the second tale, a chef finds that he grows wiser with each meal he makes, and that he is able to pass that wisdom on to those who eat his food. Finally, an inventor in a stuffy office switches on his electric fan, which blows his papers out of the window. Running down to the street to gather them, he rediscovers the world outside his office – and is inspired. Energy enhances our lives.

France doesn't move forward any more

Yes, the French are upset

They need comfortable and well designed bedrooms

They need comfortable and well designed bedrooms

IKEA
IKEA of Sweden
R≠AGISSEZ
Vote for IKEA

Nowadays French people don't debate any more

Generations don't understand each other any more

We need to re-establish communication

So with IKEA say yes to change

IKEA
IKEA of Sweden
R≠AGISSEZ
Vote for IKEA

160   **Homes, Furnishings & Appliances**

Agency	La Chose, Paris
Creative Director	Pascal Grégoire
Copywriter	Pascal Grégoire
Art Director	Alex Poulanges
Production	Quad
Director	Didier Barcelo
Producers	Isabelle Darroman
	Marie Massis
Client	Ikea, "Vote For Ikea"

With the French presidential elections on the way, Ikea mounts its own campaign in these two charming spots. In the first 'propaganda film', a politician explains that France lacks energy and dynamism. In order to wake up, it needs a decent night's sleep – so it requires comfortable bedroom furniture.

In the second spot, French people have forgotten how to communicate. That's because they need to get together in a nicely designed kitchen. For an improved France, vote Ikea!

Agency	Scholz & Friends Berlin
Creative Directors	Matthias Spaetgens
	Jan Leube
Copywriter	Michael Haeussler
Art Director	Kay Luebke
Photographer	Ralph Baiker
Client	Weru Windows

Agency	Publicis Conseil, Paris	In a cramped kitchen, a man seriously
Creative Director	Olivier Altmann	lacks storage space. He forces a
Copywriter	Bruno Delhomme	saucepan into a packed cupboard and
Art Director	Andrea Leupold	slams the door violently. Next door, the
Production	Première Heure,	handle of the man's saucepan rips right
	Paris	through the wall and emerges from a
		portrait of a boxer dog, giving the animal a
Director	Emmanuel Bellegarde	tail it didn't have before. Sitting beside his
Producers	Jérôme Rucki	mistress at the piano, the real dog – and
	Bertrand Ayache-	the subject of the portrait – glances at his
	Anguenot	own tail-less rear, intrigued. The new Tefal
Client	Tefal, "The Dog"	saucepans with removable handles save
		space.

162   Homes, Furnishings & Appliances

Agency	Taivasmainos, Helsinki
Copywriter	Markku Haapalehto
Art Director	Nestori Bruck
Production	Callboy
Director	Max Vitali
Producers	Johan Lindström
	Mary Lee Copeland Sjönell
Client	Oras Faucets,
	"Story of Mike"

"This is Mike," says the narrator, as we see a young man up to his knees in water in his apartment. The narrator explains that, at home, Mike uses 56,000 litres of water a year. At his local gym, Mike and the other guys get through 960,000 litres a year. We see them sloshing around in it. Mike and the other customers at an apparently flooded restaurant use more than 2.5 million litres of water a year. The new Oras tap with motion detector halves water consumption, which is good for both your bills and the environment.

Agency	Leo Burnett Brussels
Creative Directors	Jean-Paul Lefebvre
	Michel De Lauw
Copywriter	Gregory Ginterdaele
Art Director	Marie-Laure Cliquennois
Production	Caviar, Brussels
Director	Bram Van Riet
Producers	Kato Maes
	Brigitte Baudine
	Monique Sampermans
Client	Société Wallonne
	des Eaux, "Rain Dance"

In a series of urban environments, people perform an exotic African dance. Before them lie empty vessels: a glass, a cooking pot, a bath tub, a cleaners' bucket. Men dance beneath the dry shower heads at the gym. Unfortunately, even using an African rain dance, they can't conjure up water out of nowhere. Tap water is irreplaceable.

Homes, Furnishings & Appliances   **163**

Agency	Duval Guillaume Brussels
Creative Directors	Peter Ampe
	Katrien Bottez
Copywriter	Tom Berth
Art Director	Geert De Rocker
Photographer	Griet Dekoninck
Client	Top Interieur

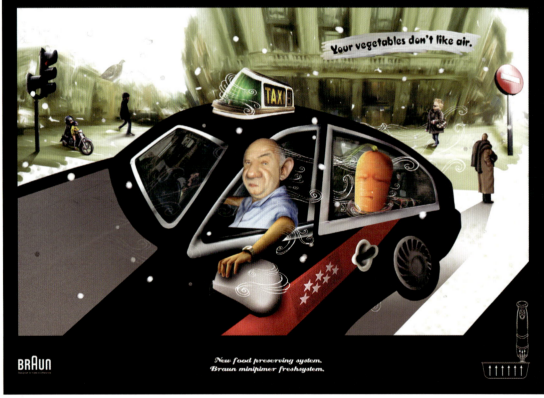

164   **Homes, Furnishings & Appliances**

Agency	Goss, Gothenburg	Agency	Tiempo BBDO Madrid
Copywriters	Michael Schultz	Creative Director	Carlos Alija
	Ulrika Good	Copywriter	Carlos Alija
	Richard Hallberg	Art Director	Ricardo Pastor
Art Directors	Gunnar Skarland	Client	Braun Minipimer
	Emil Jonsson		
	Jan Eneroth		
	Mattias Frendberg		
	Mimmi Andersson		
Photographer	Oscar Mattsson		
Illustrator	Fredrik Persson		
Client	Koll.se,		
	Online Home-Exchange		

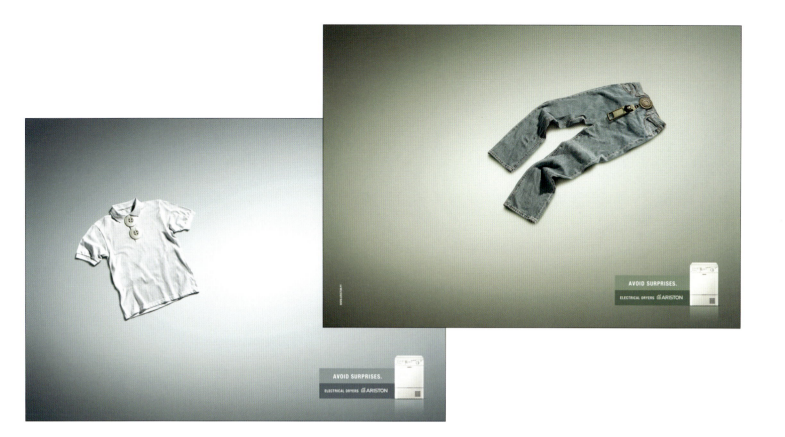

Agency	Leo Burnett, Lisbon	Agency	Leo Burnett Frankfurt
Creative Director	Fernando Bellotti	Creative Director	Andreas Pauli
Copywriter	Marilu Rodrigues	Copywriter	Andreas Stalder
Art Director	Paulo Areas	Art Director	Ulf Henniger von Wallersbrunn
Photographer	Marcelo Ribeiro	Client	Messer Roedter Knives
Client	Ariston Dryers		

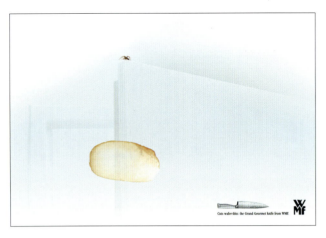

Cuts wafer-thin: the Grand Gourmet knife from WMF.

166   Homes, Furnishings & Appliances

Agency	KNSK Werbeagentur, Hamburg
Creative Directors	Anke Winschewski
	Vappu Singer
Copywriter	Daniela Schubert
Art Directors	Jan Blumentritt
	Christine Manger
Client	WMF Knives

Agency   KNSK Werbeagentur, Hamburg
Creative Directors Anke Winschewski
                        Vappu Singer
Copywriter   Daniela Schubert
Art Director   Jan Blumentritt
Client   WMF Knives

168 | **Household Maintenace**

Agency	Markom Leo Burnett, Istanbul
Creative Directors	Yasar Akbas
	Idil Akoglu
Copywriter	Ilkay Yildiz
Art Director	Bahadir Fenerci
Production	Soda Istanbul
Director	Ozer Feyzioglu
Producers	Yalcin Kilic
	Sevinc Oktem
Client	Polisan Elegans Paint, "Bedroom"

A man wakes bleary-eyed, last night's tie still around his neck. Obviously hung over, he looks around an unfamiliar bedroom. His clothes are scattered all over the place, mingled with those of a woman. Gasping, the man turns to see a woman sleeping with her back to him. Suddenly wide awake, he jumps out of bed, hauls on his trousers and autodials "Sweetheart" on his mobile phone, preparing his excuses. A phone rings beside the bed he's just left – and his wife answers it. Polisan paint will change your home so much, you might not recognise it.

Agency	TBWA\Paris
Creative Director	Erik Vervroegen
Copywriter	Benoit Leroux
Art Director	Philippe Taroux
Photographer	Achim Lippoth
Client	Spontex Sponges

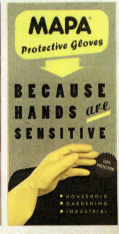

170   **Household Maintenace**

Agency	TBWA\Paris
Creative Director	Erik Vervroegen
Copywriter	Xander Smith
Art Directors	Bjoern Ruehmann
	Joakim Reveman
Production	Big Fish
Directors	The Vikings
Client	Mapa Protective Gloves, "The Bill Please"

Two hands are eating ice-creams in a café. The "female" hand turns to a poster advertising a performance by some hunky male stripper hands. She studies it with interest before turning back to her ice-cream. Her male companion says gloomily: "If you don't like me anymore, we should end it now." Hands are sensitive. Protect them, with Mapa rubber gloves.

Agency	TBWA\Paris
Creative Director	Erik Vervroegen
Copywriter	Xander Smith
Art Directors	Joakim Reveman
	Bjoern Ruehmann
Photographer	Hans Starck
Client	Mapa Protective Gloves

Agency	Leo Burnett, Dubai	Agency	TBWA\Vienna
Creative Director	Malek Ghorayeb	Creative Directors	Elli Hummer
Copywriter	Yayati Godbole		Gerd Turetschek
Art Director	Yayati Godbole		Robert Wohlgemuth
Client	Tide		Johannes Krammer
		Copywriter	Gerd Turetschek
		Art Directors	Elli Hummer
			Robert Wohlgemuth
		Photographer	Christian Maricic
		Client	Henkel Blue Star

PROTECTS
WOOD

PROTECTS
WOOD

172   **Household Maintenace**

Agency	DDB Amsterdam	**Agency**	JWT Paris
Copywriter	Niels Westra	**Creative Directors**	Andrea Stillacci
Art Director	Jakko Achterberg		Pascal Manry
Photographer	Jaap Vliegenthart	**Copywriter**	Luissandro Del Gobbo
Client	Pattex Superglue	**Art Director**	Giovanni Settesoldi
		Photographer	Riccardo Bagnoli
		Illustrator	Claudio Luparelli
		Client	O Cedar Liquid Wax

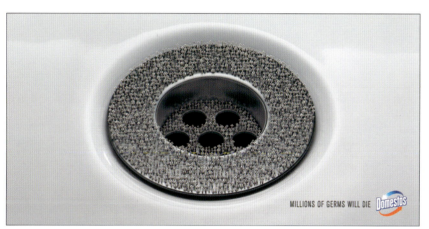

Agency	BBDO Düsseldorf	Agency	Lowe London
Creative Directors	Carsten Bolk	Creative Director	Ed Morris
	Sebastian Hardieck	Copywriter	George Prest
Copywriter	Marc Steinberg	Art Director	Johnny Leathers
Art Director	Bernd Faust	Photographer	Giles Revell
Photographer	Jost Hiller	Illustrator	Richard Green
Client	Persil Color	Client	Domestos

Craftsmen now for rent at Hornbach. 0180/44 55 660 24 ct/ call

For tough lime deposits

For tough lime deposits

174   **Household Maintenace**

Agency	Heimat, Berlin	**Agency**	Leo Burnett, Frankfurt
Creative Directors	Guido Heffels	**Creative Directors**	Andreas Heinzel
	Juergen Vossen		Peter Steger
Copywriter	Till Eckel	**Copywriter**	Florian Kroeber
Art Director	Tim Schneider	**Art Director**	Claudia Böckler
Photographer	Sven Schrader	**Photographer**	Frank Pichler
Illustrator	Michael Mackens	**Client**	Antikal
Client	Hornbach DIY Services		

Agency	Spillmann/Felser/Leo Burnett, Zurich	This magazine ad used both sides of the same page to show how Tela paper towels absorb grease.	**Agency** Saatchi & Saatchi, Dubai
Creative Director	Martin Spillmann		**Creative Director** Ed Jones
Copywriter	Stefan Ehrler		**Copywriters** Fadi Yaish
Art Director	Cornelia Wenk		Micky Larosse
Photographers	Walter und Spehr		**Art Director** Fadi Yaish
Client	Tela Paper Towels		**Photographer** David Bramley
			Illustrator Fadi Yaish
			Client Ariel

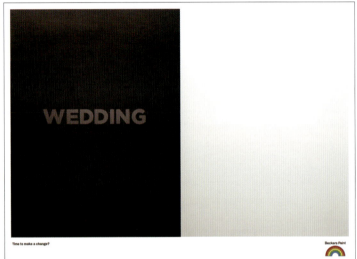

176 **Household Maintenace**

Agency	Åkestam Holst, Stockholm
Copywriter	Filip Laurent
Art Director	Jesper Holst
Photographer	Alexander Crispin
Client	Beckers Paint

An ecological fertiliser that respects nature. ECOstyle

bonsaimania.com

Agency	McCann Erickson Belgium, Hoeilaart		**Agency**	Saatchi & Saatchi, Madrid
Creative Director	Jean-Luc Walraff		**Creative Director**	Carlos Anuncibay
Copywriter	Grégory Defay		**Copywriters**	Miguel Roig
Art Director	Laurie Lacourt			Carmen Pacheco
Photographer	Bernard Blisin		**Art Directors**	Miguel Roig
Client	Ecostyle Fertiliser			Carmen Pacheco
			Photographer	Fernando Maselli
			Client	Bonsai Mania

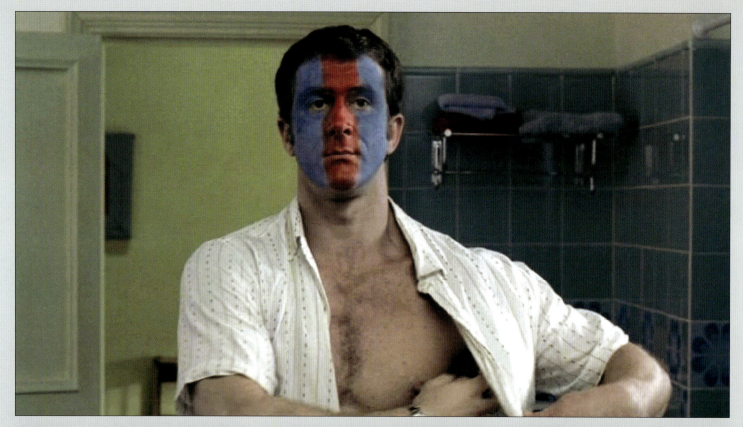

178 **Beauty Products & Services**

Agency	Lowe London
Creative Director	Ed Morris
Copywriter	Tom Hudson
Art Director	Lee Goulding
Production	Independent, London
	Biscuit Works, Los Angeles
Director	Noam Murro
Producers	Jay Veal
	Richard Packer
	Charles Crisp
Client	Sure for Men,
	"Go Wild"

In the run-up to a major soccer match, supporters and fans are transformed into wild animals. Monkeys dangle from streetlights and yell at opposing supporters from the windows of cars. Apes pick a fight with chimps in a café. On the metro, hyenas jeer at the fat seals on the platform. A group of penguins (could this be the media?) greets the soccer stars at the airport; one of the players obligingly provides a fish. Finally, in a pub, we see the apes turn back into humans. When you're wearing Sure Sport antiperspirant, you can go wild with confidence.

PHOENIXVILLE
POLICE DEPARTMENT
COMPOSITE DRAWING UNIT N° H 1300 5255
DATE 10/21 ARTIST DET. CLODAGH LEE

Set _____
Age _____
Height _____

Weight _____
Hair _____
Eyes _____

Unforgettable hair.

▲ Beauty Products & Services   179

Agency   JWT Paris
Creative Directors Andrea Stillacci
                    Pascal Manry
Copywriter   Luissandro Del Gobbo
Art Director   Giovanni Settesoldi
Photographer   Riccardo Bagnoli
Illustrator   Claudio Luparelli
Client   Sunsilk Shampoo

Agency	TBWA\Vienna
Creative Directors	Elli Hummer
	Gerd Turetschek
	Robert Wohlgemuth
	Johannes Krammer
Copywriter	Gerd Turetschek
Art Directors	Elli Hummer
	Robert Wohlgemuth
Production	Film Factory, Austria
Director	Florian Kehrer
Producer	Thomas Andreasch
Client	Atrix Hand Cream, "Cheese"

A woman is preparing a classic Italian meal. Amazingly, when it's time to add a sprinkling of parmesan, she uses the palm of her hand as a cheese-grater. Ouch! Rough hands! She needs Atrix cream.

180 **Beauty Products & Services**

Agency	Duval Guillaume Brussels
Creative Directors	Peter Ampe
	Katrien Bottez
Copywriter	Peter Ampe
Art Director	Katrien Bottez
Production	Ed Commercials
Director	Anne de Clercq
Producers	Marc Van Buggenhout
	Eric Daem
Client	Olivier Dachkin Shampoo, "Stronger Hair"

A woman washes her sumptuous dark hair in the shower. While she is drying it in front of the bedroom mirror, a man pads up behind her – he's obviously planning to kiss her tenderly on the neck. With a flick of her hair, she catches him in the face with her shiny tresses and knocks him out cold. Using Olivier Dachkin shampoo gives you stronger hair.

Agency	Lowe London
Creative Director	Ed Morris
Copywriter	Tom Hudson
Art Director	Lee Goulding
Production	Independent, London
	Biscuit Works, Los Angeles
Director	Noam Murro
Producers	Jay Veal
	Richard Packer
	Jane Rattle
Client	Sure for Women, "Super Heroine"

A Super Woman flies into the air and catches up with a speeding school bus in order to give her kids their forgotten packed lunches. Back at home, we see her levitating a bottle of Sure deodorant and whizzing it into her palm. Whether she's catching the tube, working, shopping, or at the gym, she uses her super powers to be faster and better than the average woman. That's why she uses Sure deodorant – super protection, for super women.

Agency	Scholz & Friends Hamburg	Agency	Saatchi & Saatchi, Frankfurt
Creative Directors	Gunnar Loeser	Creative Director	Eberhard Kirchhoff
	Silke Schneider	Copywriter	William John
Copywriter	Robert Herter	Art Director	Patrick Ackmann
Art Director	Stefan Schoembs	Client	Oil of Olaz
Photographer	Dennis Reher		
Client	Guhl Colorshine		
	Shampoo & Conditioner		

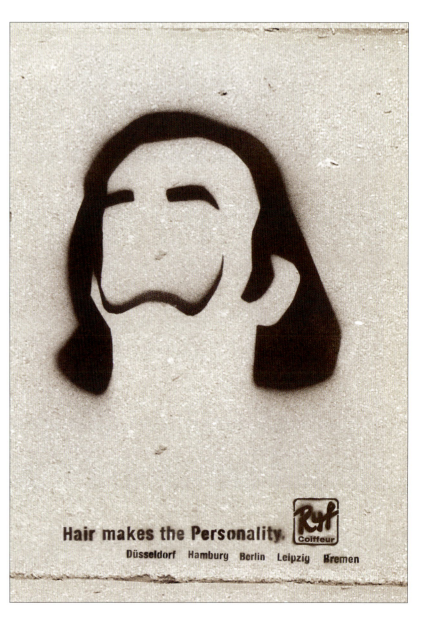

182 **Beauty Products & Services**

Agency	Navigator, Edinburgh		**Agency**	Scholz & Friends Hamburg
Creative Director	Tony Bibby		**Creative Directors**	Marcus Korell
Copywriter	Chris Miller			Gerrit Kleinfeld
Art Director	Malcolm Thompson		**Copywriter**	Bastian Otter
Photographer	Douglas Jones		**Art Directors**	Sina Maria Malosczik
Client	Demon Barber			Pamela Petersein
			Photographer	Lisa Port
			Illustrator	Sina Maria Malosczik
			Client	Ryf Coiffeur

Stops sweat.

Agency	Leo Burnett Frankfurt
Creative Directors	Andreas Pauli
	Kerrin Nausch
	Udo Leichauer
	Albert Schlierbach
Copywriter	Anatol Müller-Dumont
Art Director	Albert Schlierbach
Photographer	Till Melchior
Client	Sweat Off Deodorant

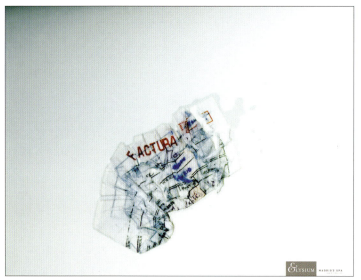

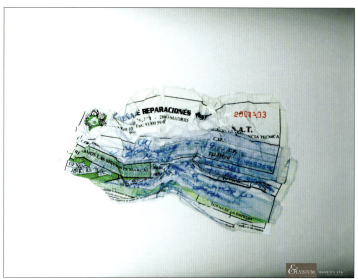

184   **Beauty Products & Services**

Agency	Zapping, Madrid	An electricity bill, a car repair invoice
Creative Directors	Uschi Henkes	and a parking fine after a visit to
	Manolo Moreno	Madrid's Elysium Spa.
	Urs Frick	
Copywriter	Manolo Moreno	
Art Director	Uschi Henkes	
Client	Elysium Spa	

Agency	JWT Warsaw	Agency	DraftFCB, Hamburg
Creative Director	Darek Zatorski	**Creative Director**	Bernd Bender-Asbeck
Copywriter	Monika Kaminska	**Copywriter**	Arne König
Art Director	Karolina Czarnota	**Art Director**	Mark Freiboth
Photographer	Darek Zatorski	**Photographer**	Moritz Nicolaus Schmid
Client	Sunsilk	**Client**	Nivea for Men
			Extra Soothing Moisturizer

Agency	Bob Helsinki	The narrator relates the amazing "true" story of
Copywriter	Kari Eilola	Vaclav, the man who can play his head like a
Art Directors	Zoubida Benkhellat	xylophone. Or is it a glockenspiel? Never mind:
	Jaakko Veijola	Vaclav is hailed as a maestro, playing with the
Production	Flodellfilm, Stockholm	greatest orchestras and moving in elite circles.
Director	Tomas Jonsgården	Until, that is, years of head-playing give him a
Producers	Magnus Åkerstedt	violent headache. Unable to play, he becomes
	Mary Lee Copeland Sjönell	a recluse. After consulting a Finnish doctor,
Client	Pamol F Painkillers,	however, he stages a miraculous comeback.
	"Headplayer"	His headache is gone and his playing is better
		than ever. Could it be thanks to Pamol F
		headache pills?

I ♥ INDIA

For stomachs on holiday.

Toiletries & Health Care   **187**

Agency   Saatchi & Saatchi, Stockholm
Creative Director Adam Kerj
Copywriter   Magnus Jakobsson
Art Director   Nima Stillerud
Client   Bifacid

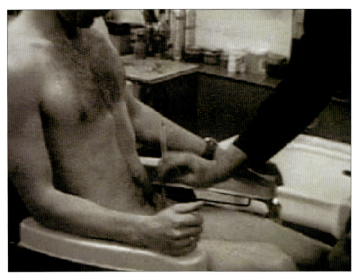

Agency	Grey London
Creative Director	David Alberts
Copywriters	Jay Marlow
	Jimmy Blom
Art Directors	Jay Marlow
	Jimmy Blom
Production	Lucky Films, London
Directors	Jay Marlow
	Jimmy Blom
Producer	Toby Horrocks
Client	Remington
	Body Hair Trimmer,
	"Barber"

We see an old-fashioned barber's shop – but nobody is having their hair cut. Instead, the barber uses cut-throat razors to remove chest, pubic, back and arse-crack hair. The customers look decidedly uncomfortable and, when they have gone, the barber doesn't look very happy with his lot either. The Remington Body Hair Trimmer: for all the places you don't want your barber to go.

188   **Toiletries & Health Care**

Agency	Garbergs Reklambyrå,
	Stockholm
Copywriter	Stefan Pagréus
Art Director	Lotta Mårlind
Production	Bacon, Copenhagen
Director	Martin Werner
Producers	Charlie Gaugler
	Jessica Thorelius
Client	Treo Painkillers,
	"Psscchhyy"

A man emerges from the delicatessen in the rain, to discover that his car is being towed away. Behind him, his little boy makes a strange hissing noise. Later, the man's computer screen goes blank. The boy, who's yanked the plug out, makes the hissing noise again. On a boating trip, in the garage or when guests arrive for a dinner, something always goes wrong – and the boy makes the same noise. Finally, we see that he's imitating the sound of a Treo pill dissolving. Headaches can suddenly happen, especially if you have kids.

Agency	McCann Erickson
	Romania, Bucharest
Creative Directors	Adrian Botan
	Alexandru Dumitrescu
Copywriter	Constantin Milu
Art Director	Andrei Tripsa
Production	Factor, Bucharest
Director	Octavian Segarceanu
Producer	Tiberiu Munteanu
Client	Entran, "Karate"

During a karate bout, one of the combatants kicks the other in the groin. But while the recipient of the blow remains unmoved, the kicker collapses to the ground clutching his foot, as if he's just kicked a wooden post. We see that the man still standing has an impressive – and obviously rock hard – erection. Entran: for long lasting erections.

FOR ALL THE PLACES YOU DON'T

WANT YOUR BARBER TO GO

THE NEW REMINGTON MEN'S BODY HAIR TRIMMER AND SHAVER

Toiletries & Health Care   **189**

Agency	Grey London
Creative Director	David Alberts
Copywriters	Jay Marlow
	Jimmy Blom
Art Directors	Jay Marlow
	Jimmy Blom
Photographer	Paul Reas
Client	Remington Body Hair Trimmer

Agency	McCann Erickson, Athens	Agency	Advico Young & Rubicam, Zurich
Creative Director	Anna Stilianaki	Creative Directors	Urs Schrepfer
Copywriter	Eleftheria Petropoulou		Daniel Comte
Art Directors	Sonia Haritidi	Copywriter	Martin Stulz
	Nikos Perialis	Art Director	Christian Bobst
Illustrator	Nikos Perialis	Photographer	Roger Schneider
Client	Durex	Client	Condomshop.ch

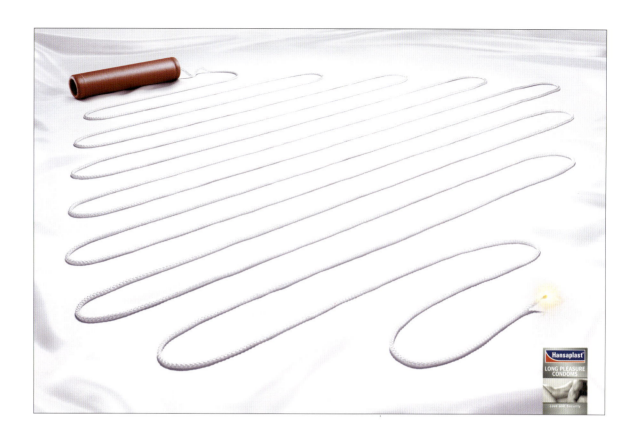

Agency	TBWA\Paris	Agency	King, Stockholm
Creative Director	Erik Vervroegen	Creative Director	Frank Hollingworth
Copywriter	Eve Rousssou	Copywriter	David Ljungberg
Art Director	Eve Roussou	Art Director	Eric Falk
Photographer	Serge Paulet	Client	RFSU Butt Plugs
Client	Hansaplast Condoms		

Agency	King, Helsinki		**Agency**	JWT Frankfurt
Copywriter	Olli Hietalahti		**Creative Director**	Mike Ries
Art Director	Kimmo Korhonen		**Copywriter**	Jan Koehler
Photographer	Paul Ruigrok		**Art Director**	Khai Doan
Client	Microlax		**Photographer**	Marc Wuchner
			Illustrator	Gerald Eskuche
			Client	Priorin Hair Strengthener

GEGEN ZAHNVERFÄRBUNGEN **Colgate**

GEGEN ZAHNVERFÄRBUNGEN **Colgate**

Sun.	Mon.	Tue.	Wed.	Thu.	Fri.	Sat.

For stomachs on holiday.

Agency — Young & Rubicam, Frankfurt
Creative Director — Uwe Marquardt
Copywriter — Christian Daul
Art Director — Monika Spirkl
Photographer — Michael Meisen
Client — Colgate Total Whitening Toothpaste

Agency — Saatchi & Saatchi, Stockholm
Creative Director — Adam Kerj
Copywriter — Magnus Jakobsson
Art Director — Nima Stillerud
Client — Bifacid

Agency	King, Stockholm	Agency	Instinct, Moscow
Creative Director	Frank Hollingworth	Creative Directors	Roman Firainer
Copywriter	Hanna Belaander		Yaroslav Orlov
Art Director	Patrik Reuterskiold	Copywriter	Igor Ivanov
Photographer	Carl-Johan Paulin	Art Directors	Daniil Ostrovskiy
Client	Royal Twisted Condoms		Viktor Zhizhin
		Client	Gardex Mosquito Repellent

Agency	Scholz & Friends Hamburg	Agency	Grey Worldwide,
Creative Director	Tobias Holland		Zagreb
Copywriter	Roman Jonsson	Creative Director	Mirka Modrinic
Art Director	Joche Saken	Art Director	Goran M Štimac
Photographer	René Clohse	Client	Šarić Optician
Illustrator	Liv Kristin Thiele		
Client	Euro Eyes		

196 Toiletries & Health Care

Agency	McCann Erickson Belgium, Hoeilaart	Agency	KNSK Werbeagentur, Hamburg
Creative Director	Jean-Luc Walraff	Creative Directors	Tim Krink
Copywriter	Philippe Thito		Niels Holle
Art Director	Sophie Norman	Copywriter	Berend Brüdgam
Illustrator	Alain Biltereyst	Art Director	Thomas Thiele
Client	Durex Sex Toys	Client	Livocab

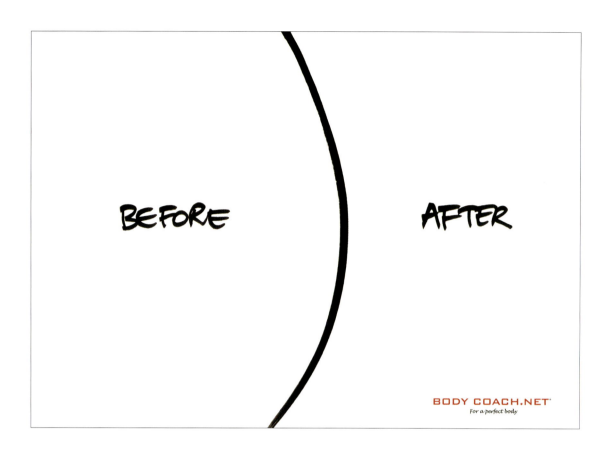

Agency	Duval Guillaume Brussels	Agency	McCann Erickson, Madrid
Creative Directors	Peter Ampe	**Creative Director**	David Moure
	Katrien Bottez	**Copywriter**	Pablo Castellano
Copywriter	Lies De Mol	**Art Director**	Ana Guillo
Art Director	Ilse Pierard	**Client**	Durex Lubricant
Client	Bodycoach		

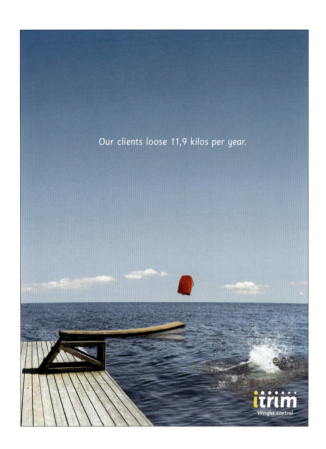

Our clients loose 11,9 kilos per year.

itrim
Weight control

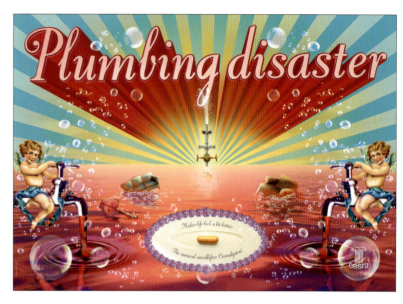

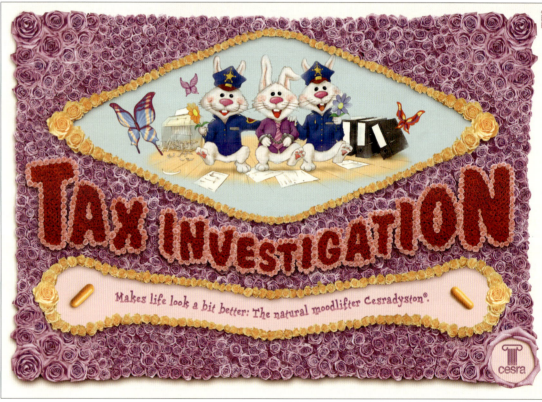

198   **Toiletries & Health Care**

Agency	WatersWidgren, Stockholm
Copywriter	Johan Nilsson
Art Director	Patrick Waters
Photographers	Therese Aldgård
	Mattias Nilsson
Client	Itrim Weight Control

Agency	Ogilvy & Mather, Frankfurt
Creative Directors	Helmut Himmler
	Lars Huvart
Copywriters	Ales Polcar
	Lars Huvart
Art Directors	Till Schaffarczyk
	Adam Figielski
	Ina Thedens
Photographer	Joachim Bacherl
Illustrators	Martin Popp
	Adam Figielski
Client	Cesradyston

When eating for two.

weightcoach.spray.com

Efficiently relieves fever

Agency	King, Stockholm	**Agency**	Ogilvy & Mather, Copenhagen
Creative Director	Frank Hollingworth		
Copywriters	Tommy Carlsson	**Copywriter**	Mads Ohrt
	Hedvig Bruckner	**Art Director**	Mads Ohrt
Art Director	Josephine Wallin	**Photographer**	Egon Gade
Photographer	Mattias Edwall	**Client**	Panodil
Client	Weightcoach		

Agency	BBH, New York
Creative Director	Thomas Hayo
Copywriter	Matt Ian
Art Director	Amee Shah
Production	Gorgeous Enterprises, London
Director	Frank Budgen
DOP	Benoit Delhomme
Producers	Flora Fernandez-Marengo
	Julian Katz
Client	Levi's, "News Story"

A police chase is being filmed by a TV news chopper. In an apartment nearby, a man is idly watching the chase live on TV, while his girlfriend reads. Suddenly he leans forward: the crook has abandoned his car – and escaped into the grounds of their building. The TV shows the criminal taking off his distinctive white trousers and grabbing a pair of jeans from the washing line. At this, the young man bounds out of the door. On the TV screen, we see him wrestle the criminal to the ground. No crook is going to make off with his Levi's!

wonderbra

Available soon in the United Arab Emirates

Agency	Tonic Communications, Dubai
Creative Directors	Vincent Raffray
	Khaled Gadallah
Copywriter	Vincent Raffray
Art Director	Peter Walker
Photographer	Dave Kennedy
Client	Wonderbra

Agency	1861United, Milan
Creative Directors	Pino Rozzi
	Roberto Battaglia
Copywriters	Stefania Siani
	Luca Beato
Art Directors	Federico Pepe
	Micol Talso
Production	H Films, Milan
Directors	Paolo Borgato
	Tommaso Bertè
Producers	Stella Orsini
	Consuelo Mauri
DOP	Sandro Bolzoni
Client	Freddy Sportswear, "Human Machine Man"

A trampoline, bicycle wheels, an old shopping trolley and an abandoned piano: these are some of the items used to make a giant mechanical construction in a warehouse. Once it gets going, the machine can play music, produce soap bubbles, blow up balloons; even make a cup of coffee or a glass of orange juice. But the secret of the machine is that it is powered only by human energy. It's a huge interactive exercise centre, and getting it to work requires seriously athletic moves – a task made easier by Freddy sportswear.

Deadly pass without a striker to receive it? Impossible!

Titan, titan...without your defense you're nothing.

There is no "I" – there is just "us"!

Agency	TBWA\Germany, Berlin
Creative Directors	Stefan Schmidt
	Kurt Georg Dieckert
Copywriter	Helge Blöck
Art Director	Boris Schwiedrzik
Production	Hager Moss, Munich
Director	Bruce St. Clair
Producers	Eric Moss
	Fabian Barz
Client	Adidas DFB Jersey, "+10"

Stars of the German soccer team demonstrate their skills. They're moving at lightning speed, but at the crucial moment the film slows right down so they can indulge in a bit of casual conversation with the audience. They explain that individual skills are all very well, but it's the team that counts: "There is no 'I' – there's just us." Or as we say in English, there's no "I" in "team".

Agency	BBH, New York
Creative Director	Thomas Hayo
Copywriter	Tom Kraemer
Art Director	Nick Klinkert
Production	Gorgeous Enterprises, London
Director	Tom Carty
DOP	Benoit Delhomme
Producers	Ciska Faulkner
	Julian Katz
Client	Levi's, "Straight Walking"

A man and a woman walk towards one another from opposite ends of the same city. They walk in a straight line, never deviating no matter what the obstacle. They're forced to climb fences, cross busy roads, even walk through crowded office buildings – but they always walk as the crow flies, straight ahead, no curves allowed. Finally they meet, face to face, in the middle of the street. "Because you're mine, I walk the line," in the words of the soundtrack. The ad is for Levi's straight jeans.

Agency	Publicis Conseil, Paris	Agency	Gossip, Paris
Creative Director	Olivier Altmann	**Creative Director**	Fréderic Temin
Copywriter	Olivier Camensuli	**Copywriter**	Fréderic Temin
Art Directors	Frédéric Royer	**Art Director**	Nicolas Chauvin
	Yves Sarhadian	**Photographer**	Terry Richardson
Photographer	Vincent Dixon	**Client**	Diesel
Client	Wonderbra		

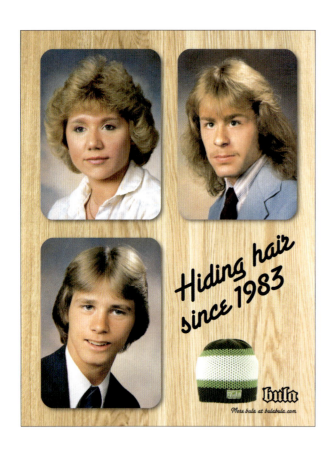

Agency	Goss, Gothenburg		**Agency**	Ogilvy & Mather Frankfurt
Copywriters	Michael Schultz		**Creative Directors**	Helmut Himmler
	Ulrika Good			Lars Huvart
Art Directors	Gunnar Skarland		**Copywriter**	Ales Polcar
	Emil Jonsson		**Art Director**	Till Schaffarczyk
	Jan Eneroth		**Photographer**	Jean-Yves Lemoigne
	Mattias Frendberg		**Client**	Nur Die Opaque Stockings
	Mimmi Andersson			
Illustrator	Fredrik Persson			
Client	Bula Hats			

Still freezing? Why? Stay warm with a base layer of fine merino wool in a terry knit. The terry loops trap air between the skin and the clothing to create a warm insulating layer. Wool also has a natural ability to carry away moisture and perspiration. Our base layers are used for work, sports and leisure, and by people who would simply rather not be freezing cold. Using the material Ullfrotté Original, Woolpower has been manufactured up in the Swedish town of Östersund since 1972.

www.woolpower.se

Woolpower
ÖSTERSUND

Agency	McBride, Stockholm
Creative Director	Lena McBride
Copywriter	Åke Larsson
Art Director	Lena McBride
Photographer	Jörgen Reimer
Client	Woolpower

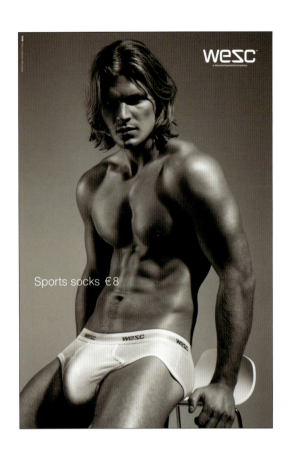

Sports socks € 8

CROSS AIR
CARVED FROM >

CORK 900 LEADING TAIL
CARVED FROM >

206   **Clothing & Fabrics**

Agency	King, Stockholm	**Agency**	Wieden+Kennedy, Amsterdam
Creative Director	Frank Hollingworth	**Creative Directors**	Mark Hunter
Copywriter	Peter Fjäll		Alvaro Sotomayor
Art Director	Pelle Sjönell	**Copywriter**	Oliver Frank
Photographer	Calle Stoltz	**Art Director**	Paulo Martins
Client	WESC Underwear	**Photographer**	Giles Revell
		Client	Nike ACG

HENNING MARTHINSEN / NORWAY /
TEAM NIKE ALL CONDITIONS GEAR /
RIDES IN: ALL MOUNTAIN JACKET & PANTS /
SIGNATURE MOVE: FRONTSIDE 900 MELON GRAB /

SIGNATURE.................

MATHIEU IMBERT / FRANCE /
TEAM NIKE ALL CONDITIONS GEAR /
RIDES IN: BARRIER RIDGE DOWN JACKET - CRUISER CARGO PANTS /
SIGNATURE MOVE: CORK 5 TRUE TAIL /

SIGNATURE.

ANDREAS HÅTVEIT / NORWAY /
TEAM NIKE ALL CONDITIONS GEAR /
RIDES IN: BARRIER RIDGE DOWN JACKET & CRUISER CARGO PANTS /
SIGNATURE MOVE: FAKEY CORK 720 MUTE GRAB /

SIGNATURE...................

Clothing & Fabrics   **207**

Agency	Wieden+Kennedy, Amsterdam
Creative Directors	Mark Hunter
	Al Moseley
	John Norman
Copywriters	Sezay Altinok
	Anders Stake
Art Director	Carlos Furnari
Photographer	Rick Guest
Client	Nike ACG

Agency	BETC Euro RSCG, Paris		Agency	Geller Nessis - Leo Burnett, Tel Aviv
Creative Directors	Rémi Babinet Safia Bouyahia		Creative Director	Rony Schneider
			Copywriter	Einat Eker
Art Directors	Volker Gehr Yuki Kani		Art Director	Shiri Man
Photographer	David Sims		Client	TNT Fashion
Client	Lacoste			

Agency	Leo Burnett, Beirut	Agency	SCP, Gothenburg
Creative Director	Bechara Mouzannar	Creative Director	Tommy Östberg
Copywriter	Raja Farah	Copywriter	Eva Östberg
Art Directors	Celine Khoury	Art Director	Oscar Plasidius
	Carma Andraos	Photographer	Marcel Pabst
Client	Aizone Youth Fashion Store	Client	Frank Dandy Superwear

Footwear & Personal Accessories

Agency	Wieden+Kennedy, Amsterdam
Creative Directors	Mark Hunter
	Alvaro Sotomayor
Copywriter	Oliver Frank
Art Director	Paulo Martins
Production	Park Pictures, New York
Directors	Lance Acord
	Joaquin Baca-Asay
Producers	Lalou Dammond
	Elissa Singstock
	Veronika Kaufmann
Client	Nike Air Max, "Endure"

In a series of scenes that are actually painful to watch, we see athletes giving their all for their sports. They strain, they sweat, they struggle and they fall, but they'll never give up. Although their expressions tell the whole story, the spot is made doubly effective by the mournful voice of Johnny Cash intoning: "I hurt myself today…to see if I still feel…" The spot ends with a runner cruising serenely down an empty road. Nike: a little less hurt.

IMPOSSIBLE IS NOTHING

Footwear & Personal Accessories   **211**

Agency	180 Amsterdam
Creative Director	Andy Fackrell
Copywriters	Lee Hempstock
	Richard Bullock
Art Directors	Chris Landy
	Andy Fackrell
Production	Stink Productions, London
Director	Ivan Zacharias
Executive Producer	Daniel Bergman
Producers	Nick Landon
	Cedric Gairard
	Sarah Billens
Client	Adidas Int'l, "Equipo" & "Partido"

Pedro and José, a couple of inner city kids, play fantasy football with real soccer stars. Miraculously they manage to conjure up the likes of Cissé, Beckham and Zidane, but Pedro laughs derisively when José nominates 60-year-old Franz Beckenbauer. As this is fantasy football, a 1970s Beckenbauer duly appears, still youthful. At the suggestion of Zidane, Pedro retaliates by recruiting Michel Platini. An amazing soccer game commences, until José's mother calls him in for tea… then the fantasy soccer stars vanish.

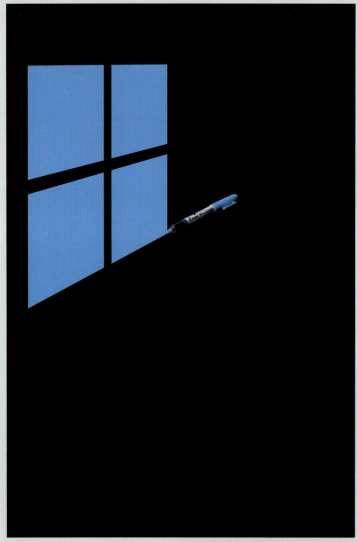

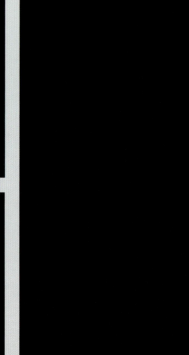
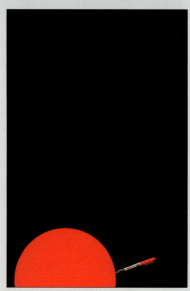

Agency Grey & Trace, Barcelona
Creative Directors Jürgen Krieger
Jose Miguel Tortajada
Copywriter Carla Olaortua
Art Directors Dani Páez
Saül Serradesanferm
Photographer Josep Maria Roca
Client Pilot V Liquid Light Markers

Carré *Ex Libris*
en twill de soie
gansé de zibeline
Gants en revre velours

HERMÈS EN ESCAPADE
HERMÈS
PARIS

An ILLUMINATING
FASHION AND CULTURE
HOME AND LEISURE
SWAROVSKI, DANIEL SWAROVSKI,
KRISTALLWELTEN, CRYSTAL PALACE,
CRYSTALLIZED, STRASS AND
SWAROVSKI OPTIK ARE REGISTERED
TRADEMARKS OF SWAROVSKI.

BY THE GRACE OF MIND
WITH THE GRACE OF HEART
IN THE GRACE OF LIGHT

SWAROVSKI

Agency	Publicis Et Nous, Paris	Agency	Select Communications, New York
Creative Director	Philippe Chanet	Creative Director	Olivier van Doorne
Photographer	Camilla Akrans	Copywriter	Sylviane Louzoun
Client	Hermès	Art Director	Rike Kaufmann
		Photographer	Craig McDean
		Client	Swarovski

Agency	Publicis Conseil, Paris
Creative Director	Olivier Altmann
Copywriter	Nicolas Schmitt
Art Director	David Ariyel
Production	The Gang Films, Paris
Director	Jan Wentz
Producers	Christine Clerc
	Pierre Marcus
Client	Pilot Frixion Pens,
	"Confidence"

A cop pulls over a young couple in a beat-up car. "You're missing a tail-light, kid," says the cop. When he starts to write out the fine, his pen isn't working, so the young man offers his own. He adds: "You might want to check the tyres, they're worn out." The cop checks them. "We're missing a windscreen wiper too," says the young guy. "One hundred bucks," sneers the cop. "Sign here." As the young woman distracts the cop with a display of cleavage, the guy erases his own registration number and substitutes it for that of the cop car. The Pilot Frixion pen comes with erasable ink.

Agency	Wieden+Kennedy,
	Amsterdam
Creative Directors	Mark Hunter
	Alvaro Sotomayor
Copywriter	Oliver Frank
Art Director	Paulo Martins
Production	Park Pictures, New York
Director	Joaquin Baca-Asay
Producers	Lalou Dammond
	Elissa Singstock
	Veronika Kaufmann
Client	Nike Air Max, "Defy"

In this beautiful spot, a series of athletes perform incredible aerial feats. A basketball player, a pole-vaulter, a skateboarder, martial arts experts, gymnasts and a high-jumper are among those who seem to leave the tethers of the earth behind. Are they not subject to the normal laws? The tagline reveals their secret. Nike: a little less gravity.

Agency	Åkestam Holst, Stockholm
Copywriters	Maria Fredriksson
	Sara Kolbäck
Art Director	Andreas Ullenius
Production	Flodell Film, Stockholm
Director	Jörn Haagen
Producers	Mikael Flodell
	Mary Lee Copeland Sjönell
Client	Puma,
	"Gets You There Faster"

In Mozambique, a kid called Leon is given a pair of Puma football boots for his birthday. He goes out for a kick-around in the yard – and then, in the space of one day, his fortunes totally change. He is signed up by a manger, recruited for the national team, becomes a local hero, plays in a major match, scores the winning goal, and gets to hold the trophy aloft. The Puma V1.06 soccer boot gets you there faster! In a brief epilogue, Leon is already discussing retirement with his manager.

Footwear & Personal Accessories   **215**

Agency	JWT Paris
Creative Directors	Andrea Stillacci
	Pascal Manry
Copywriter	Luissandro Del Gobbo
Art Director	Giovanni Settesoldi
Photographer	Riccardo Bagnoli
Illustrator	Claudio Luparelli
Client	Buttero Boots & Shoes

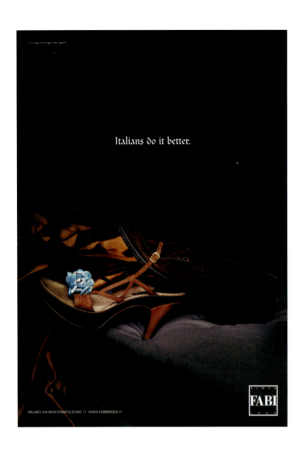

Agency	D'Adda Lorenzini Vigorelli BBDO, Milan	Agency	Jung von Matt, Berlin
Creative Director	Gianpietro Vigorelli	Creative Directors	Mathias Stiller
			Wolfgang Schneider
Copywriter	Bruno Vohwinkel	Copywriter	Michael Haeussler
Art Director	Luca Menozzi	Art Director	Michael Janke
Photographer	Brigitte Niedermair	Photographer	Daniel Zoubek
Client	Fabi Shoes	Client	Bic Cristal

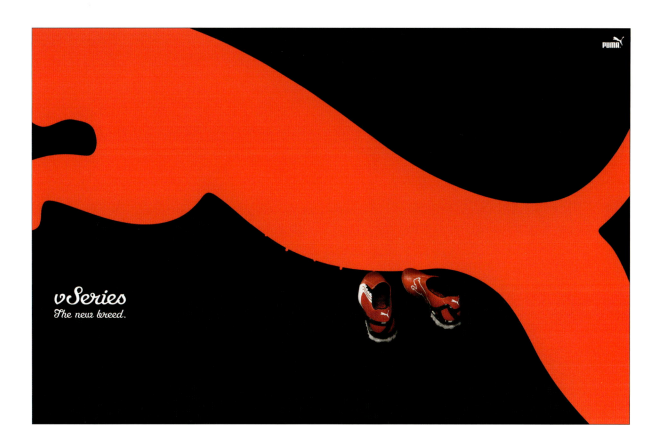

Agency	Åkestam Holst, Stockholm	Agency	King, Stockholm
Copywriter	Maria Fredriksson	Creative Director	Frank Hollingworth
Art Directors	Andreas Ullenius	Copywriter	Patrick Herold
	Johan Söderberg	Art Director	Tim Zastera
	Lars Holthe	Photographer	Carl-Johan Paulin
Client	Puma	Client	Cricket Lighters

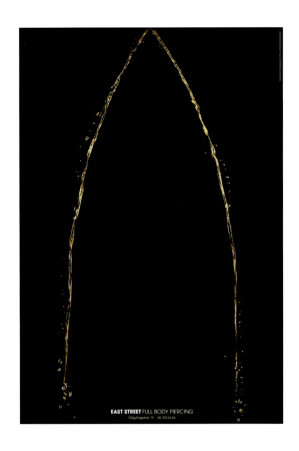

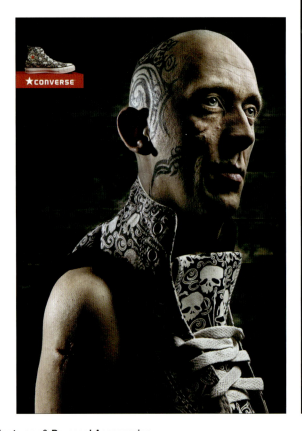

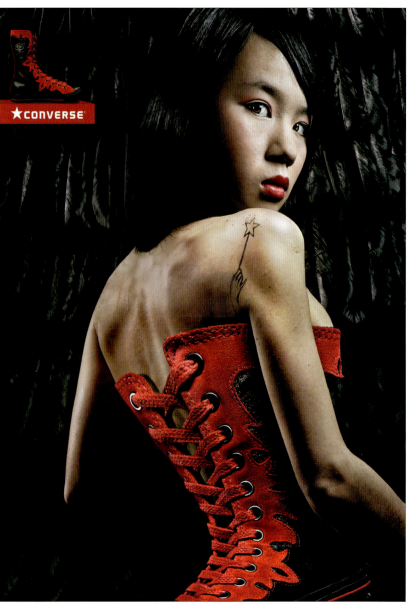

218   Footwear & Personal Accessories

Agency	Saatchi & Saatchi, Stockholm	Agency	JWT Warsaw
Creative Director	Adam Kerj	Creative Director	Darek Zatorski
Copywriter	Magnus Jakobsson	Copywriter	Kamil Nazarewicz
Art Directors	Gustav Egerstedt	Art Director	Katarzyna Macharz
	Nima Stillerud	Photographer	Andrzej Dragan
Photographer	Henrik Bonnevier	Client	Converse Shoes
Client	East Street Piercing		

Agency	Devarrieuxvillaret, Paris	**Agency**	TBWA\Paris
Creative Director	Nicolas Verdeau	**Creative Director**	Erik Vervroegen
Copywriter	Benjamin Seff	**Copywriter**	Veronique Sels
Art Director	Agnes Emonet	**Art Directors**	Stéphanie Thomasson
Photographer	Nicolas Verdeau		Caroline Khelif
Client	Bocage Shoes		Nicolas Hurez
		Photographer	Roger Turqueti
		Client	Naturoptic

220 **Automobiles**

Agency	Wieden+Kennedy, London
Creative Directors	Tony Davidson
	Kim Papworth
Copy/Art Directors	Michael Russoff
	Ben Walker
	Matt Gooden
Production	Partizan, London
Director	Antoine Bardou-Jacquet
Producers	David Stewart
	Helen Whiteley
Client	Honda Civic, "Choir"

"This is what a Honda feels like," says the narrator, as we see a choir standing in the unlikely surroundings of a multi-storey car park. Then, inter-cut with images of the speeding car, the choir begins to impersonate the sounds made by a Honda: tyres crunching over gravel or over cobbles; acceleration; deceleration; the swishing windscreen wipers or the smooth operation of electric windows. It seems that with a little imagination, the human voice is able to evoke mental images of a memorable car journey. Honda: the power of dreams.

Automobiles   **221**

Agency	TBWA\Istanbul
Creative Director	H. Oner Sahin
Copywriter	Gokhan Yucel
Art Director	Boran Erem
Illustrator	Erol Gunes
Client	BMW 1 Series

Agency	CLM BBDO, Paris
Creative Directors	Gilles Fichteberg
	Jean-François Sacco
Copywriters	David Bertram
	Leo Berne
Art Directors	David Bertram
	Leo Berne
Production	CLM BBDO, Paris
Directors	David Bertram
	Leo Berne
Producer	Marie Massis
Client	Mercedes-Benz E-Class, "Freeze Frame"

A split screen shows us, on the left, a poised and beautiful woman talking, and on the right, a speeding Mercedes E-Class. The film of she woman keeps freezing, always capturing an unflattering expression, her face distorted into a grimace. At these moments, the woman suddenly seems a great deal less sophisticated. The Mercedes, however, remains implacably impeccable. The Mercedes E-Class is elegant, all the time.

222 Automobiles

Agency	BTS United, Oslo
Creative Director	Thorbjørn Naug
Copywriter	Ingvil Ladehuag
Art Director	Thorbjørn Naug
Production	Askild Action & Fredrik Fiction
Director	Thorbjørn Naug
Producer	Fredrik Pryser
Client	Audi A4 Quattro, "The Dog"

An Audi A4 Quattro glides through a snowy landscape. In a house beside the road, a dog waits patiently. When the car passes, the dog bounds out the house and chases the car, barking. The dog is doing a pretty good job of catching the vehicle, but as the car rounds a corner, the dog skids on a patch of ice, loses its footing and tumbles into a snowdrift. Animals may have four legs, but when it comes to road-holding they're no match for the Quattro.

Agency	Try Advertising Agency, Oslo
Copywriter	Petter Bryde
Art Director	Thorbjørn Ruud
Production	Trøbbel Film
Director	Ubbe Haavind
Producers	Hugo Hagemann Føsker
	Morten Polmar
	Cathrine Wennersten
Client	VW Touran, "Birthday"

A man is organising a garden party for his kids and their friends. But where are the fizzy drinks? Just in time, his wife arrives in the Volkswagen Touran, its spacious rear stuffed with bottles of soda. As the kids open the pop bottles they practically explode, showering everyone at the table with sticky stuff. The man looks inquiringly at the wife: how did she manage to shake up the bottles like that? She smiles knowingly. The Touran – sometimes it's a family car, sometimes not.

Agency	D'Adda Lorenzini Vigorelli BBDO, Milan
Creative Director	Giuseppe Mastromatteo
Copywriters	Nicola Lampugnani
	Lorenzo Crespi
Art Directors	Anselmo Tumpic
	Puccio Gonni
Production	The Family
	Anonymous Content
Director	John Dolan
Producers	Lorenzo Ulivieri
	Lorenzo Damiani
Client	Mini, "Zig Zag" & "Bikers"

These two spots illustrate the fun and manoeuvrability of the Mini. In the first, a guy zigzags at speed down an empty highway, while his passenger looks anxious. Suddenly, a fly splatters on the windscreen. "Game over!" says the passenger, gleefully taking the keys. Now it's his turn to dodge the flies. In the second spot, a black motorcycle appears to be following a Mini, staying on its tail even through extreme hairpin bends. As they both glide to a halt, we see that the Mini has actually been towing the bike to give the motorcyclist an unaccustomed thrill.

Agency	BBDO, Vienna
Creative Director	Dr. Markus Enzi
Copywriter	Michael Grill
Art Director	Emanuela Sarac
Production	Sabotage Films, Vienna
Director	Michael Kaufmann
Client	Jeep Cherokee, "Garage"

We see a Jeep Cherokee apparently parked in a garage. After a long moment, the garage door opens – revealing that the Jeep is just an image pasted onto the door. Behind lurks a much less desirable vehicle. Always wanted to drive a Jeep? The Cherokee is surprisingly affordable.

Agency	Leo Burnett Warsaw
Creative Director	Martin Winther
Copywriter	Lukasz Witkiewicz
Art Director	Leszek Ziniewicz
Production	Opus Film, Warsaw
Directors	Nic & Sune
Producer	Janusz Wlodarski
Client	Fiat Panda, "Feet"

At the dead of night, a young man returns his dad's car, which he has borrowed for the evening. He carefully cleans the vehicle, removing all traces of takeaway food and finding his missing Zippo lighter. In the morning, he bounds downstairs and climbs once again into the car – this time as a passenger. In the driving seat, his father looks at him sternly. Suddenly, the young man notices the imprint of bare feet on the windscreen, in a compromising pattern. Isn't it time you had your own car? A Fiat Panda isn't so expensive.

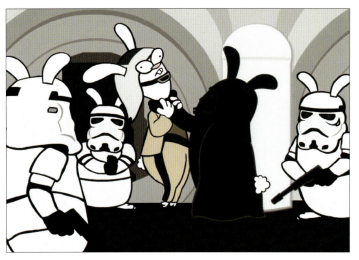

The new Fox.

Agency	DDB Germany, Berlin
Creative Directors	Amir Kassaei
	Eric Schoeffler
	Tim Jacobs
Copywriter	Sandra Illes
Art Directors	Jennifer Shiman
	Christian Brenner
Production	Angry Alien Productions, Los Angeles
	VCC Perfect Pictures, Düsseldorf
Director	Jennifer Shiman
Producers	James Strader
	Marion Lange
Client	VW Fox, "Short Cuts"

In the latest selection from the 'short but fun' series, ultra-summarized versions of classic films prove that, like the VW Fox, things that are small can also be cool. Animated rabbits act out the key lines and scenes from Star Wars, The Rocky Horror Picture Show, and Highlander. As well as being hilarious, these mini marvels save hours of DVD-watching time.

Makes anyone look strong.
The new Polo GTI®.

The new Golf GT with TSI®.

Agency	DDB Germany, Berlin
Creative Directors	Amir Kassaei
	Wolfgang Schneider
	Mathias Stiller
	Bert Peulecke
	Stefan Schulte
Copywriter	Ludwig Berndl
Art Director	Kristoffer Heilemann
Production	Radical Media, LA
Director	Sebastian Strasser
Producers	Christiane Lochte
	Marion Lange
Client	VW Polo GTI, "Basketball"

On a basketball court, two strapping young guys are arguing about who's going to recruit "Pete" for their team. Pete is obviously a star player. But when Pete appears in the scene, we see that he's a short, nerdy middle-aged white bloke. As the two team captains continue to argue about who's going to have Pete on their team, he goes to put his sunglasses in his Polo GTI. Someone throws him the ball, which he fluffs. But they still seem to think he's a genius. The Polo GTI makes anyone look good.

Agency	DDB Germany, Berlin
Creative Directors	Ami Kassaei
	Mathias Stiller
	Wolfgang Schneider
Copywriter	Ludwig Berndl
Art Director	Kristoffer Heilemann
Production	Markenfilm, Hamburg
	Outsider, London
Director	Henry Littlechild
Producers	Simona Daniel
	Nele Schilling
	Marion Lange
Client	VW Golf GT, "Fly"

A frog's long tongue lashes out to catch a fly. But to the frog's surprise the fly resists, hauling the frog out of the pond and dragging it into the air. Just like the fly, the new Golf GT is small, but surprisingly powerful. Relenting, the fly drops the frog into the water with a 'plop'.

Automobiles   **225**

Agency	DDB Germany, Berlin
Creative Directors	Amir Kasssaei
	Eric Schoeffler
	Raphael Milczarek
	Heiko Freyland
Copywriters	Heiko Freyland
	Felix Lemcke
Art Directors	Raphael Milczarek
	Fabian Kirner
Photographer	Uwe Düttmann
Illustrator	Stefan Kranefeld
Client	VW Golf R32

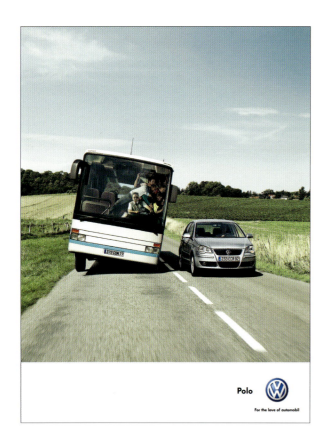

Automobiles

Agency	Agence V, Paris	Agency	DDB London
Creative Director	Christian Vince	**Creative Director**	Jeremy Craigen
Copywriter	Jocelyn Devaux	**Copywriter**	Matt Lee
Art Director	Sylvain Guyomard	**Art Director**	Peter Heyes
Photographer	Cédric Delsaux	**Client**	VW Golf & Polo
Client	VW Polo		

Agency	DDB Germany, Berlin
Creative Directors	Amir Kassaei
	Mathias Stiller
	Wolfgang Schneider
Copywriter	Ludwig Berndl
Art Director	Kristoffer Heilemann
Photographer	Jan Steinhilber
Client	VW TSI Engines

Agency	DDB London
Creative Director	Jeremy Craigen
Copywriter	Matt Lee
Art Director	Peter Heyes
Production	Partizan, London
Director	Eric Lynne
Producers	David Stewart
	Lucinda Ker
Client	VW Golf,
	"Hidden Camera"

A man wearing a hidden camera approaches the manager of a VW dealership. "I was just wondering," the man asks, with studied casualness. "How much is that Golf?" The manager replies: "It's 11,995." "That's pounds, yes?" The manager confirms this. The man seeks further assurances that he will become the legal owner of the car in exchange for a cheque for £11.995. The fact is that there's nothing dodgy about the car's low price. It may be incredible, but it's true.

228 Automobiles

Agency	DDB London
Creative Director	Jeremy Craigen
Copywriter	Matt Lee
Art Director	Peter Heyes
Production	Partizan, London
Director	Eric Lynne
Producers	David Stewart
	Lucinda Ker
Client	VW Golf, "Tea"

A young couple, both sipping from takeaway cups of tea, approach a VW salesman. His hair is damp and he has a nasty brown stain on his shirtfront. The couple inquire about the price of the new Golf. The salesman looks hesitant. "Can you just tell us the price?" urges the woman gently. Finally, the salesman admits that it's just £11,995. As the screen goes black, we hear the sound of the man accidentally spitting his tea over the salesman as he snorts with surprise. Incredibly, the Golf really is that cheap.

Agency	DDB London
Creative Director	Jeremy Craigen
Copywriter	Thierry Albert
Art Director	Damien Bellon
Production	RSA, London
Director	Brett Foraker
Producers	Casper Delaney
	Natalie Powell
Client	VW Golf Plus,
	"Wrap"

We see a VW Golf parked against the backdrop of a city street under the words: "The Golf Plus. A clever use of space." The director calls, "And...CUT." Technicians wander in to the shot. They take down the backdrop, pack up the lights and the camera equipment, stow the whole lot in the back of the Golf, and drive away. Then they come back for the slogan, fold that up and sling it into the back of the car, too. The VW Golf Plus really is spacious.

Closer to the road. The Golf Sportline.

Closer to the road. The Golf Sportline.

Closer to the road. The Golf Sportline.

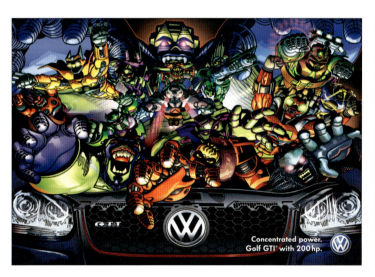

Concentrated power.
Golf GTI with 200 hp.

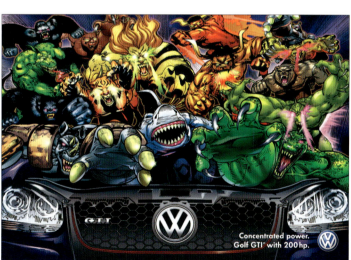

Concentrated power.
Golf GTI with 200 hp.

Agency	DDB Germany, Berlin	Agency	DDB Germany, Berlin
Creative Directors	Amir Kassaei	Creative Directors	Amir Kassaei
	Stefan Schulte		Stefan Schulte
	Bert Peulecke		Bert Peulecke
Copywriter	Marian Goetz	Copywriter	Kai Abd El-Salam
Art Director	Christian Jakimowitsch	Art Director	Andreas Böhm
Illustrator	Tom Ungemach	Illustrator	Alberto Saichann
Client	VW Golf Sportsline	Client	VW Golf GTI

The Polo. Just a bit wilder.
The CrossPolo.

Agency	DDB Germany, Berlin
Creative Directors	Amir Kassaei
	Bastian Kuhn
	Alexander Weber-Grün
Copywriters	Daniel Ernsting
	Lina Jachmann
Art Directors	Tino Heuter
	Björn Löper
Client	VW CrossPolo

You won't save money this summer.

In June, save up to 3,500 € at your local Volkswagen dealer.

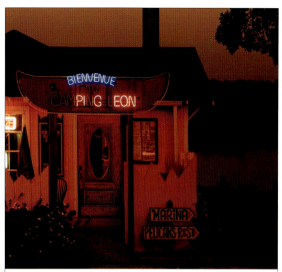

You won't save money this summer.

In June, save up to 3,500 € at your local Volkswagen dealer.

Your life.

Your life according to your parents.

Fox 7990 €. Make your parents proud.

Agency	Agence V, Paris	These broken neon signs transform	Agency	Agence V, Paris
Creative Director	Christian Vince	the French names of the Sailing Boat	Creative Director	Christian Vince
Copywriter	Pierre Riess	Restaurant and Leon's Campsite into	Copywriter	Fabien Teichner
Art Director	Romain Guillon	"It's a Rip-off" and "Welcome Sucker".	Art Director	Faustin Claverie
Photographer	Adolfo Fiori		Photographer	Franck Goldbronn
Client	VW Range		Client	VW Fox

Agency	Nordpol+ Hamburg
Creative Director	Lars Ruehmann
Copywriter	Ingmar Bartels
Art Directors	Gunther Schreiber
	Bertrand Kirschenhofer
	Christoph Bielefeldt
	Dominik Anweiler
Production	Element e
Director	Silvio Helbig
Producer	Juergen Joppen
Client	Renault Cars,
	"Crashtest"

Foodstuffs from around the world are exposed to the kind of crash test normally reserved for automobiles. A German sausage, a Japanese sushi, a Swedish crisp-bread and a French baguette are all put through their paces. While the sausage, the sushi and the crisp-bread explode, the baguette springs neatly back into shape. The safest cars are French: Renault.

232   Automobiles

Agency	TBWA\Paris
Creative Directors	Erik Vervroegen
	Chris Garbutt
Copywriter	Xander Smith
Art Directors	Joakim Reveman
	Bjoern Ruehmann
Production	La Pac
Director	Lieven Van Balen
Client	Nissan Murano,
	"4x4"

Confronted by a rockslide on a dirt road, the Nissan proves its versatility by morphing into a metallic four-legged animal and traversing the mountain range. With each challenge it encounters, the vehicle transforms into another wild creature: an agile spider, a slithering snake, a scaly amphibian. Finally, it reaches a clear stretch of road and assumes its habitual form: that of a classy mode of transport.

Agency	Agence V, Paris
Creative Director	Christian Vince
Copywriter	Fabien Teichner
Art Director	Faustin Claverie
Production	Addict, Paris
	H5, Paris
Producer	Corinne Persch
Client	VW Touran,
	"Roller Coaster"

We're off on the rollercoaster of life as we plunge through a nightclub filled with sexy ladies, only to find ourselves walking up the aisle, getting married and having kids. The rollercoaster plunges us into the "joys" of fatherhood: screaming babies, messy toddlers and incomprehensible adolescents. At last, we emerge into a quiet glade, where we find the new Volkswagen Touran, a classy family car. Finally, it's great to be a dad.

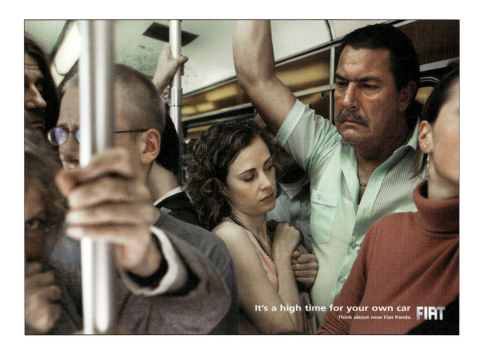

Agency	Leo Burnett Warsaw	Agency	Vitruvio Leo Burnett, Madrid
Creative Director	Martin Winther	Creative Directors	Rafa Antón
Copywriter	Lukasz Witkiewicz		Javier Álvarez
Art Director	Leszek Ziniewicz		Fernando Martín
Photographer	Sebastian Hanel	Copywriter	Fernando Martín
Client	Fiat Panda	Art Director	Javier Álvarez
		Photographers	Bela Adler
			Salva Fresneda
		Client	Fiat Panda Cross

234 Automobiles

Agency	Forsman & Bodenfors, Gothenburg	Agency	Kempertrautmann, Hamburg
Copywriter	Jacob Nelson	Copywriter	Lennart Witting
Art Directors	Johan Eghammer Mikko Timonen	Art Director	Florian Kitzing
Photographers	Henrik Halvarsson Lund Lund	Photographer	Anatol Kotte
Client	Volvo Cars	Client	Audi Q7

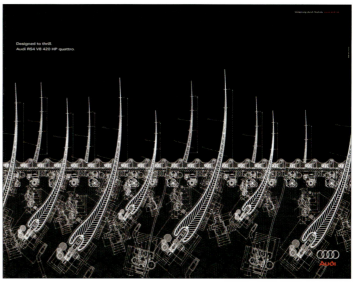

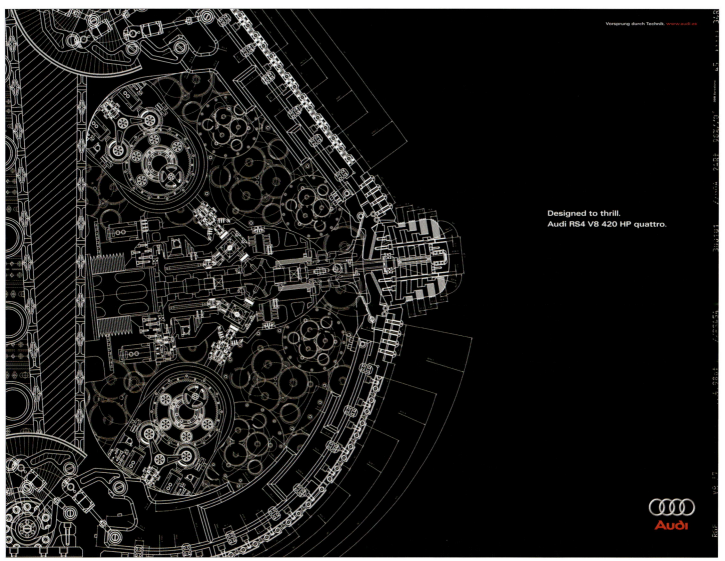

Agency	DDB Spain, Madrid
Creative Director	Alberto Astorga
Copywriter	Alfredo Binefa
Art Director	Jaume Badia
Illustrator	David Ruiz
Client	Audi RS4 Quattro

Twenty years of innovating hairstyles.

236 Automobiles

Agency	Lowe Brindfors, Stockholm	**Agency**	Contrapunto, Madrid
Creative Director	Magnus Wretblad	**Creative Director**	Antonio Montero
Copywriters	Henrik Häger	**Copywriter**	Mikel Etxeberria
	Anders Dalenius	**Art Director**	Leandro Cacioli
Art Directors	Pelle Lundquist	**Photographer**	Xabi Pastor
	Lova Bratt	**Client**	Smart
Photographer	Andreas Kock		
Client	Saab 93 Convertible		

Agency	Contrapunto, Madrid
Creative Directors	Antonio Montero
	José Mª Cornejo
	Fernando Galindo
Copywriter	Mikel Etxeberria
Art Director	Leandro Cacioli
Client	Smart

Agency	BETC Euro RSCG, Paris
Creative Director	Stéphane Xiberras
Copywriter	Olivier Apers
Art Director	Hugues Pinguet
Production	Wanda Productions
Director	Wilfrid Brimo
Producer	Sebastien Lintingre
Client	Peugeot 307 HDI, "Pigeon"

A gleaming Peugeot 307 HDI is parked innocently in a suburban street. Suddenly, a spatter of pigeon shit falls on its roof. A couple of seconds later, the pigeon alights on the car and fastidiously wipes away the mess with its wing. Because the HDI uses clean technology that is less harmful to the environment, nature respects it.

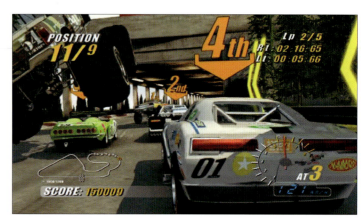

Agency	Euro RSCG London
Creative Director	Justin Hooper
Copywriters	Steve Nicholls
	Matthew Anderson
Art Directors	Steve Nicholls
	Matthew Anderson
Production	H5, Paris
Directors	Antoine Bardou-Jacquet
	Ludovic Houplain
	Hervé De Crecy
Producers	Robin Accard
	Caroine Guillard
Client	Citroen C4, "Ice Skater"

A group of geologists arrive at a lonely, frozen lake. As they set up their gear, their car decides to have a bit of fun. After transforming into a humanoid figure, the Citroen C4 skates off across the ice. It performs loops and whirls and even jumps a jetty. Then it skids to a halt in front of the scientists, its skates kicking up a shower of ice crystals. They look astonished – but they shouldn't be. The Citroen C4 is alive with technology.

Agency	BETC Euro RSCG, Paris
Creative Director	Rémi Babinet
Copywriter	Rémi Noel
Art Director	Eric Holden
Production	Partizan
Director	Antoine Bardou-Jacquet
Producers	Damien Fournier-Perret
	Simon Chater Robinson
Client	Peugeot 407, "End of Game"

We're in the middle of a fast and furious video game, with cars jostling for position on a racetrack. As the camera pulls back, we see a boy playing the game. When the doorbell rings, he freeze-frames the action. The camera then re-enters the video game, where the virtual drivers leave their garish racing cars and change into civilian clothes. One of them gets into his Peugeot 407 to enjoy a smooth ride home. He even stops to let another video game character cross the street. The Peugeot 407 – playtime is over.

Agency	Philipp und Keuntje, Hamburg
Creative Director	Diether Kerner
Copywriter	Oliver Ramm
Art Director	Johannes Hofmann
Photographer	Juergen Berderow
Client	Lamborghini

THE NEW ECO FRIENDLY CARS FROM VOLVO   VOLVO for life

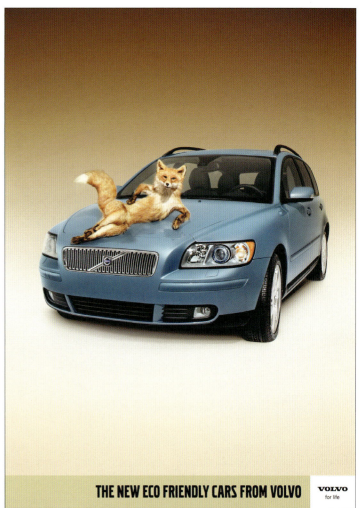

THE NEW ECO FRIENDLY CARS FROM VOLVO   VOLVO for life

240 Automobiles

Agency	Forsman & Bodenfors, Gothenburg
Creative Director	Mathias Appelblad
Copywriter	Jacob Nelson
Art Directors	Johan Eghammer
	Mikko Timonen
Photographer	Lasse Kärkääinen
Client	Volvo Cars

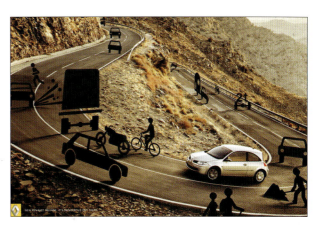

Automobiles   **241**

Agency	Publicis Conseil, Paris
Creative Directors	Olivier Altmann Hervé Plumet
Copywriter	Eric Helias
Art Director	Jorge Carreno
Photographer	Andy Glass
Client	Renault Mégane

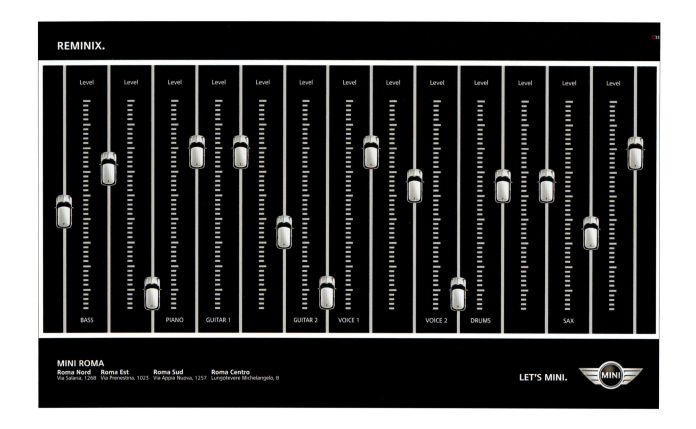

Agency	ON, Milan	Agency	JWT/PPGH, Amsterdam
Creative Directors	Francesco Emiliani	Creative Directors	Bart Kooij
Copywriter	Elsa Tomassetti		Nico Akkerman
Art Director	Alice Pozzi	Copywriters	Wouter Kiewiet de Jong
Client	Mini		Jan Pieter Nieuwerkerk
		Art Directors	Daan Kramp
			Jan Willem Baggerman
		Client	Mini

AT LEAST ONE THING IN YOUR DREAMS THAT REALLY EXISTS.

NEW SANTA FE HYUNDAI Drive your way

Agency	Duval Guillaume Brussels	**Agency**	Duval Guillaume Brussels
Creative Directors	Peter Ampe	**Creative Directors**	Peter Ampe
	Katrien Bottez		Katrien Bottez
Copywriter	Virginie Lepère	**Copywriter**	Virginie Lepère
Art Director	Frédéric Van Hoof	**Art Director**	Frédéric Van Hoof
Photographer	Christophe Gilbert	**Photographer**	Filip Vanzieleghem
Client	Hyundai Santa Fe	**Client**	Hyundai

244 Automobiles

Agency	Atletico International, Barcelona
Creative Directors	Arndt Dallmann
	Roland Vanoni
	Pepe Colomer
	José María Basora
Copywriter	Aleix Bou
Art Director	David García
Illustrator	Lucas Pigliacampo
Client	Seat Alhambra

ADVENTURE IS EVERYWHERE.

Jeep
THERE'S ONLY ONE

SIMPLY CLEVER

Agency	KNSK Werbeagentur, Hamburg	Agency	DDB Stockholm
Creative Directors	Tim Krink	Creative Director	Andreas Dahlqvist
	Niels Holle	Copywriter	Martin Lundgren
Copywriter	Berend Brüdgam	Art Director	Lennart Claesson
Art Director	Oliver Fermer	Photographer	Magnus Klackenstam
Client	Jeep	Client	Skoda

246 **Automotive & Accessories**

Agency	Wieden+Kennedy, London
Creative Directors	Kim Papworth
	Tony Davidson
Copywriters	Kim Papworth
	Sean Thompson
Art Directors	Tony Davidson
	Chris Groom
Production	Stink
Director	Ivan Zacharias
Producers	Nick Landon
	Julia Methold
Client	Honda,
	"Impossible Dream"

As the soundtrack of Andy Williams singing The Impossible Dream kicks in, a Honda test driver leaves his caravan beside the sea and rides off on a mini motorcycle. A quick cut later, and it's been transformed into a bigger bike. With each seamless change of scene the man's mode of transport evolves – from quad bikes to sports cars, racing bikes to sleek convertibles – describing practically the entire history of Honda products. Finally, when the man's speedboat races over the lip of a waterfall, he rises again in a hot air balloon. The music swells for the big finish.

We have to leave some proof
to convince you it's used.

Audi First Choice.
The best used cars guaranteed, selected and checked by Audi.

We have to leave some proof
to convince you it's used.

Audi First Choice.
The best used cars guaranteed, selected and checked by Audi.

Automotive & Accessories   **247**

Agency	DDB, Milan
Creative Director	Vicky Gitto
Copywriter	Davide Valenti
Art Director	Francesco Vigorelli
Photographer	Pierpaolo Ferrari
Client	Audi First Choice
	Used Cars

Agency   Publicis, Zurich
Copywriter   Roland Wetzel
Art Director   Florian Beck
Client   Ducati Motorcycles

248   **Automotive & Accessories**

Agency   MKK Werbeagentur, Hamburg
Creative Directors   Andreas Kant / Tobias Wasmuth
Copywriters   Tobias Wasmuth / Sebastian Witte
Art Director   Mariusz Roclawski
Production   Bakery Films, Hamburg
Director   Ralf Huettner
Producers   Stefan Schuh / Johannes Farenholtz
Client   VW Crafter, "Hot Dog"

A couple of delivery men get into a new white VW Crafter van. The passenger taunts his colleague with the fact that he's just bought a hot dog. The driver gets his own back by braking and then rapidly accelerating. This causes the sausage in the hotdog to slide back and forth in the bun, eluding the man's mouth. The van obviously has impressive acceleration and braking.

Agency   CLM BBDO, Paris
Creative Director   Gilles Fichteberg
Production   The Gang Films, Paris
Director   Joachim Back
Producers   Jean Villiers / Geuillaume Delmas
Client   Total Excellium Petrol, "843 Km"

A car drives through a forest. We cut to a Total station. A customer stirs coffee; the guy at the cash register looks anxious. Cut back to the road, where night has fallen and the car enters a foggy vale. It promptly runs out of petrol. But instead of looking perturbed, the driver punches the air in triumph. He phones the service station. "Patrick?" he says to the cashier, "843!" The men in the Total station look at one another. "843 kilometres?" they repeat. Then they too begin to celebrate. At Total, you get further on a full tank.

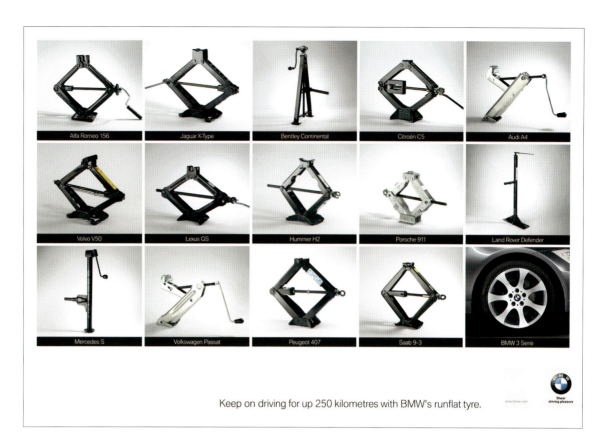

Keep on driving for up 250 kilometres with BMW's runflat tyre.

EVERY COMPANY FITS IN A CITROËN JUMPER

Agency	JWT/PPGH, Amsterdam		**Agency**	EURO RSCG Amsterdam
Creative Directors	Bart Kooij		**Creative Directors**	Joost van Praag Sigaar
	Nico Akkerman			Laurens Boschman
Copywriter	Wouter Kiewiet de Jong		**Copywriter**	Ivar van den Hove
Art Director	Daan Kramp		**Art Director**	Bert Kerkhof
Photographer	Nico Gartsman		**Photographer**	Jaap Vliegenthart
Client	BMW Runflat Tyres		**Client**	Citroën Jumper

250 **Automotive & Accessories**

Agency	JWT Paris	Agency	DDB, Milan
Creative Directors	Andrea Stillacci	Creative Director	Vicky Gitto
	Pascal Manry	Copywriter	Michelangelo Cianciosi
Copywriter	Luissandro Del Gobbo	Art Director	Francesco Fallisi
Art Director	Giovanni Settesoldi	Photographers	Winkler & Noah
Photographer	Ilario-Magali	Client	Garmin GPS
Client	Galileo GPS		

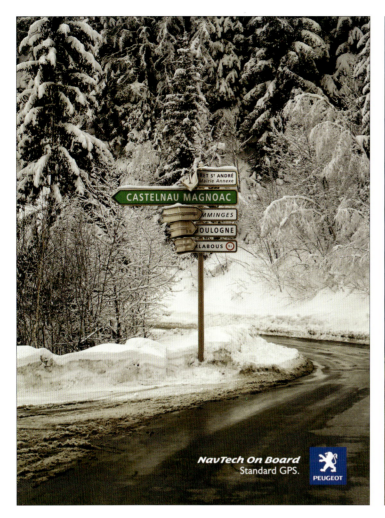

Agency	BETC Euro RSCG, Paris	Agency	BBDO Düsseldorf
Creative Director	Stéphane Xiberras	Creative Director	Sebastian Hardieck
Copywriter	Olivier Apers	Copywriter	Dietmar Neumann
Art Director	Hugues Pinguet	Art Director	Patrick Hahne
Illustrator	Baptiste Massé	Client	Falk Navigation Systems
Client	Peugeot NavTech GPS		

Agency	DDB Paris
Creative Directors	Alexandre Hervé
	Sylvain Thirache
Copywriter	Edouard Pérarnaud
Art Director	Martin Darfeuille
Photographer	Jean-Yves Lemoigne
Client	VW Commercial Vehicules

Agency   DDB Paris
Creative Directors Alexandre Hervé
                    Sylvain Thirache
Copywriter   Edouard Pérarnaud
Art Director   Martin Darfeuille
Photographer   Nick Meek
Client   VW Combi Transporter

Agency   DDB Paris
Creative Directors Alexandre Hervé
                    Sylvain Thirache
Copywriter   Matthieu Elkaim
Art Director   Pierrette Diaz
Photographer   Stephan Ruiz
Client   VW Transporter

I saw this brilliant film on Canal Plus :

"March of the Emperor" ?

Yes, it all takes place in Antarctica.

Like when they pass their eggs to each other.

CANAL+
THE CINEMA CHANNEL

254 Media

Agency	BETC Euro RSCG, Paris
Creative Director	Stéphane Xiberras
Copywriters	Pierre Riess
	Luc Rouzier
Art Directors	Romain Guillon
	Eric Astorgue
Production	Radical Media, New York
Director	Glue Society
Producer	David Green
Client	Canal+,
	"March of the Emperor"

In a canteen, a woman gets the wrong end of the stick while a colleague describes the plot of a film called March of the Emperor. The film is actually about emperor penguins, but the woman doesn't know that, so she imagines Napoleon trekking through the wilderness. When the man tells her that the film takes place in the Antarctic, her mind fine-tunes the setting. "There are hundreds of emperors… sliding on their bellies," the man says. The film running in the woman's imagination becomes ever more surreal, especially when the man adds: "Before that they were all having sex together…for hours." Movies were meant to be seen, not described.

That girl just caught you staring so now you're trying to pretend you're fascinated with this poster. Soon you're going to have to go back to staring out of the window or reading the small print on the back of your ticket. Don't you wish you'd bought a paper?

Don't you just wish you'd bought a paper to read instead of reading this over and over again? Don't you just wish you'd bought a paper to read instead of reading this over and over again? Don't you just wish you'd bought a paper to read instead of reading this over and over again?

Agency	The Bridge, Glasgow
Creative Director	Jonathan d'Aguilar
Copywriters	Jonathan d'Aguilar
	Doug Cook
Art Directors	Doug Cook
	Liz O'Connor
Typographer	Andy Mulvenna
Client	Scottish Daily
	Newspaper Society

Agency	GMP Advertising, Bucharest
Creative Director	Emilian Arsenoaiei
Copywriters	Emilian Arsenoaiei
	Mihai Botarel
Art Director	Theodor Sandu
Production	Tandem Film
Director	Maurus vom Scheidt
Client	Boom Comedy, "Pig"

A man hypnotises a pig until it falls asleep. As the camera pulls back, we see that the man is a chef, and that the pig is sleeping on a silver platter. He bastes the pig and surrounds it with salad. Cut to the man, now dressed as a waiter, bearing the platter through a busy restaurant. He lays it before a table of slavering guests. Has he cooked the pig? Nope. At a word from the man, the pig jumps up and runs off, sending diners scattering in terror. Need more comedy? You're better off with Boom, the comedy channel.

Agency	Vasata Schröder Werbeagentur, Hamburg
Creative Directors	Daniel Rieck
	Sönke Busch
	Jürgen Florenz
Copywriter	Petra Schotten
Production	Final Touch, Hamburg
Directors	Anne Hirschmann
	Tom Schlösser
Client	Cinema Magazine, "Action"

An amateur film fanatic recreates a disaster movie with cardboard sets and…his fingers. Drawing little faces on them turns them into convincing actors, more or less. One of these 'characters' is wearing a salami hat. A dog's snout moves into frame and eats the salami, providing a moment of high drama. From home cinema to Hollywood, Cinema magazine covers the lot.

Agency	BETC Euro RSCG, Paris
Creative Director	Stéphane Xiberras
Copywriter	Olivier Couradjut
Art Director	Rémy Tricot
Production	Hamster
	Spy Films
Director	Trevor Cornish
Producer	Virginie Chalard
Client	13éme Rue, "Biathlon"

We're watching winter sports coverage, as a Swedish competitor takes part in the biathlon. He pauses to raise his rifle, but instead of shooting at the target, he shoots a French rival. The commentator seems entirely unfazed by this incident. "Yes, very good move from the Swede," he approves. Next up is a Russian, who shoots back. And appearing out of nowhere is a German, "with his singular technique", which involves blowing up the Swede with a rocket launcher. If the crime channel 13 éme Rue made sports shows, they'd look like this.

Agency	Devilfish, London	We see smoking factory chimneys and
Creative Director	Richard Holman	then, incongruously, the exterior of a
Copywriter	Nik Stewart	school. As the camera moves in through
Art Director	Jonny Parker	a classroom window, familiar music alerts
Production	Gorgeous Enterprises,	us to what is going on. Over the next few
	London	seconds we see a "live action" replica of
Director	Chris Palmer	the credits sequence of The Simpsons, as
Producers	Rupert Smythe	a look-alike Simpsons family rush home to
	Audrey Hawkins	catch the beginning of the show. Sky One
Client	Sky One,	is the home of The Simpsons.
	"Come Home	
	to the Simpsons"	

Agency	1861United, Milan	On the streets of Rio, a small boy is
Creative Directors	Pino Rozzi	attracted to the sound of German oompah
	Roberto Battaglia	music filtering through a window. He
Copywriters	Pino Rozzi	stands on tiptoes to get a look. Improbably,
	Vincenzo Celli	he sees Brazilian soccer star Kakà dressed
Art Directors	Roberto Battaglia	in lederhosen and practising a German folk
	Peppe Cirillo	dance. Kakà is clearly preparing for the
Production	H Films	World Cup in Germany. His antics soon
Director	Owen Harris	attract a crowd. Kakà looks embarrassed,
Producers	Stella Orsini	but the lederhosen trend catches on…
	Carla Beltrami	
Client	Sky Satellite TV,	
	"Training for Germany "	

Agency	TBWA\PHS, Helsinki	In an idyllic park, a cute sparrow on a
Copywriters	Tommy Makinen	tree opens its beak and starts singing in a
	Erkko Mannila	raucous, tobacco-and-whisky tinged voice.
Art Director	Mikko Torvinen	An elderly woman runs away in horror. A
Production	Kaivopuiston Grilli, Helsinki	rock concert has been held in Helsinki's
Director	Pete Riski	Central Park every summer since 1969.
Producer	Hanna Salminen	
Client	Radio Nova,	
	"Rockin' Sparrow"	

Agency   DDB Paris
Creative Directors Alexandre Hervé
                        Sylvain Thirache
Copywriter   Thomas Marmol
Art Director   Julien Syrigos
Production   DDB Atelier, Paris
Producer   Agathe Michaux Terrier
Client   MTV Unplugged,
                        "Hip Hop"

A hip-hop musician is "scratching" at his mixing desk. The results are less than spectacular as the thing isn't switched on. All we hear is a faint shushing noise. It's an ad for MTV Unplugged, which is devoted to acoustic music.

Agency   BTS United, Oslo
Creative Director Thorbjørn Haug
Copywriter   Ingvil Ladehaug
Art Director   Thorbjørn Naug
Production   Radio Film Company
Director   Thorbjørn Naug
Producer   Steve St. Peter
Client   Nettavisen,
                       "The President"

In a classroom at Sarasota, Florida, on September 11 2001, we see a couple of presidential aides looking at a laptop screen. On the screen are the first pictures of a plane slamming into one of the Twin Towers. One of the aides quickly goes in to the neighbouring classroom – where we cut to the famous footage of George W. Bush being told about the disaster (and his baffled expression). Get news first on the web, with Nettavisen.

Agency   Jung von Matt, Berlin
Creative Directors Wolfgang Schneider
                        Mathias Stiller
                        David Mously
                        Jan Harbeck
Copywriter   Christopher Ruckwied
Art Director   Marius Lohmann
Production   Jo!Schmid, Berlin
Director   Martin Schmid
Producers   Johannes Schmid
                        Nadja Catana
Client   Welt Kompakt,
                        "Montana on Fire"

A TV news reporter is interviewing a fire chief about the blaze that is ravaging woodland in Montana. The chief reveals that the fire was probably started by a cigarette. Then he starts to go into improbable detail about the incident. "The cigarette was flicked with the left hand… Using the middle finger, which has more power…" The TV reporter looks bemused. You're better off with Welt Kompakt, the new compact newspaper that only covers the important stuff.

Hotande svältkatastrof

I en nyligen publicerad rapport utmålas en mycket dyster bild av situationen i NordKorea. De mänskliga rättigheterna är grovt åsidosatta och miljontals människor befaras drabbas av svält under den kommande vintern. Andra sidan av floden är grå och livlös och kullarna kalhuggna. Inte en rökstrimma från fabrikerna eller de små rucklen i byarna. En ensam oxkärra på vägen och på en station blockeras spåret sen månader av ett strandat tågsätt. Kontrasten mot grönskan på vår sida – det mest förbjudna – kunde inte vara större. Tumen är gränsflod mellan Nordkorea och Kina och obetydligt större än en skänsk å. Inget hinder för desperata nordkoreaner som flyr undan tyranniet i hopp om en bättre framtid. Det är Kinas sårbaraste gräns. Beijing fruktar en gigantisk flyktinginvasion över floden när sanktionerna efter kärnvapentestet börjar bita eller om det forna »arbetarparadiset« skulle kollapsa. En lika stor risk är att Den käre ledaren Kim Jong Il dumpar miljontals utmärglade trashankar på andra sidan. Skälet till att Kina tvekar om ekonomiska sanktioner och isolering av Nordkorea är att man själv kan tvingas betala priset. Rapporterna inifrån »Hermit Kingdom« är entydigt mörka, men har länge behandlats nästan som vittnesutsagorna en gång från »Killing Fields« i Pol Pots Kampuchea: fruktansvärt hemskt men har inte flyktingar alla skäl att överdriva? Fakta är en stor bristvara: Var det 500 som dog i skyfallen i juli i år eller 54 000? Har hunger och svält krävt en halv miljon liv eller 2,5 miljoner – en tiondel av befolkningen?

FN och internationella hjälporganisationer tillåts bara en nästintill symbolisk närvaro. Att stå upp för mänskliga rättigheter är helt otänkbart. Nordkorea är en polisstat med total social kontroll – också barnen tvingas delta i angiverisystemet – och de som klagar eller »sprider rykten« förpassas till gulager i de mest otillgängliga bergsområdena som är stängda för alla utomstående. Mer än 200 000 tros vara internerade i dessa arbetsläger som i många fall är rena dödsläger. Klassindelningen är strikt men baseras inte på ekonomisk status utan på lojalitet. »Kimilsungismen« är mer religion och Maranata än ideologi. Enbart troende ges tillstånd att flytta till Pyongyang. De som ifrågasätts får sin höjd lägre poster och mer än en miljon ses som parias. En generations försyndelser drabbar nästa.

Hela landet är fullt av Potemkin-kulisser. De flesta utländska besökare lämnar landet med intryck av en vacker huvudstad med en välmående befolkning. Men bakom idyllen döljs skjul, armod och undernärda barn.

När jag första gången besökte Nordkorea 1979 så visade regimen stolt upp modernt mekaniserade kollektivfarmer och rabblade produktionssiffror. I dag finns det tre gånger fler oxkärror än traktorer – som i de flesta fall är oanvändbara till följd av brist på bränsle. Skördarna har halverats. Det är lätt att skylla eländet på en rad naturkatastrofer. Men det är i stället gigantiska kostnader för militären som knäcker diktaturen. »Juche« – en slogan om självtillit som levde i 30 år – har kompletterats med »Songun« som betyder militären först och blivit en ny statsideologi. Indoktrinering pågår från kindergarten till fabriksgolv och alla lär sig tänka som soldater för att möta det »amerikanska hotet«.

Den stora frågan nu är hur många människoliv som svält och hunger kommer att kräva i vinter. Livsmedelsbiståndet kommer tvekslöst att sina. EU och FN:s livsmedelsprogram fortsätter att ge marthjälp. Men vart tredje barn är redan kroniskt undernärt och hämmat i växten och bara två miljoner av de 6,5 miljoner desperat behövande kan i bästa fall nås av hjälp. De utländska hjälporganen kan inte längre dela ut mat till de mest utsatta eftersom staten tagit över distributionen. Är då inte den »Den käre ledaren« oroad inför vintern? Svaret är nej. Såvitt känt så har Kim Jong Il aldrig besökt något katastrofområde eller med ord berört lidandet. I stället har staten försvårat leveranserna, stoppat tonvis av kläder och krävt mat i förpackningar utan utländska ord och logos. De senaste två åren har Kim enbart besökt militärförband för att »peppa« nationens hjältar i händelse av krig. Det är en form av långsamt folkmord som pågår i propagandans arbetarparadis. Ur Fokus nr 33, 2006. www.fokus.se

**Get the context
in Sweden's news magazine.**

Agency	Bungalow25, Madrid	Agency	RBK Communication,
Creative Directors	Julio Gálvez		Stockholm
	Pablo Pérez Solero	Creative Director	Fredrik Dahlberg
Copywriter	Pablo Pérez Solero	Copywriter	Fredrik Dahlberg
Art Director	Julio Gálvez	Art Director	Erik Larsson
Photographers	Pablo Díez	Client	Fokus News Magazine
	Carlos Yebra		
Client	Fox TV		

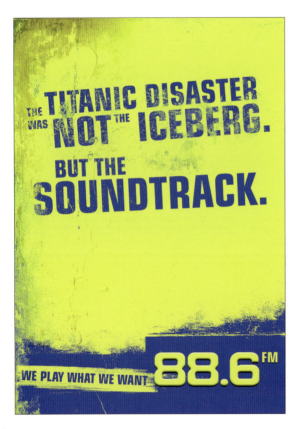

Agency	CLM BBDO, Paris		**Agency**	FCB Kobza, Vienna
Creative Directors	Gilles Fichteberg		**Creative Director**	Joachim Glawion
	Jean-Francois Sacco		**Copywriter**	Florian Ludwig
Copywriters	Axel Orliac		**Art Director**	Michael Köditz
	Laurent Dravet		**Illustrator**	Tanja Bug
Art Directors	Laurent Dravet		**Client**	Radio 88,6 FM
	Axel Orliac			
Photographer	Pascal Hirsch			
Client	Playboy.fr			

IS FRANCE ALLERGIC TO REFORM?

LET'S TALK · 104.7 FM

IS THE WAR OF THE SEXES REALLY OVER?

LET'S TALK · 104.7 FM

HOW FAR WILL WE LET THING GO BEFORE MONEY TAKES OVER SPORT?

LET'S TALK · 104.7 FM

IS RELIGION THE ONLY THING WE CAN'T JOKE ABOUT?

LET'S TALK · 104.7 FM

HOW CAN POLITICIANS MAKE YOUNG PEOPLE BELIEVE IN POLITICS AGAIN?

LET'S TALK · 104.7 FM

Agency	Publicis Conseil, Paris
Creative Director	Olivier Altmann
Copywriter	Eric Helias
Art Directors	Jorge Carreno
	Benoît Blumberger
Photographer	Oliver Rheindorf
Client	Europe 1

Movie: Terminator Tonight Channel 6

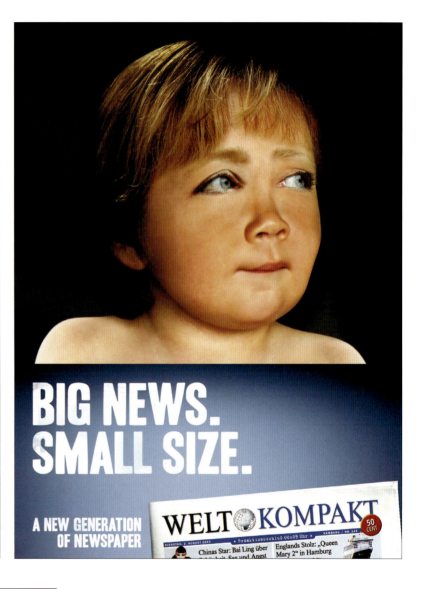

BIG NEWS. SMALL SIZE.

A NEW GENERATION OF NEWSPAPER

WELT KOMPAKT

Agency	Leo Burnett Associates, Dublin		Agency	Jung von Matt, Berlin
Creative Director	John Flynn		Creative Directors	Burkhart von Scheven
Copywriter	Eoin Ryan			David Mously
Art Director	Fergal Hurley			Jan Harbeck
Photographer	Donal Maloney		Copywriter	Jan Harbeck
Client	Channel 6		Art Director	David Mously
			Client	Welt Kompakt

Agency	DDB Germany, Berlin	Each portrait in the series is made up of tiny icons that typify the personality in question.
Creative Directors	Amir Kassaei	
	Eric Schoeffler	
	Thomas Schwarz	
	Tim Jacobs	
Copywriters	Tim Jacobs	
	Sandra Illes	
	Georgios Kalfopoulos	
Art Directors	Thomas Schwarz	
	Christian Brenner	
Illustrator	Peter Klanke	
Client	Spiegel News Magazine	

Four long weeks of **WORLD CUP FOOTBALL**. From the 9th of June.

NEED ENTERTAINMENT?
CHANNELTWO

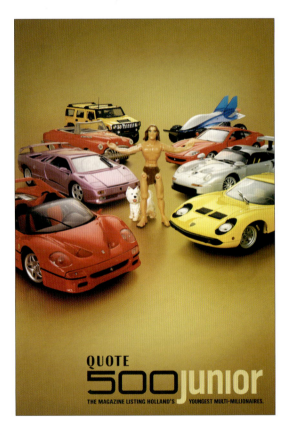

Agency	Duval Guillaume Antwerp	**Agency**	Selmore, Amsterdam
Creative Directors	Geoffrey Hantson	**Photographer**	Carlfried Verwaayen
	Dirk Domen	**Illustrator**	Magic
Copywriter	Geoffrey Hantson	**Client**	Quote 500 Junior
Art Director	Dirk Domen		
Photographers	Stan Huaux		
	Studio Habousha		
Client	Channel Two		

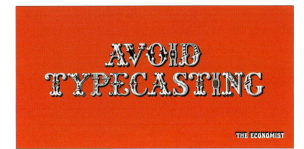

AVOID TYPECASTING

THE ECONOMIST

Sparks & Mensa.

The Economist

Is your
indecision final?

The Economist

Makes white
collars brighter.

The Economist

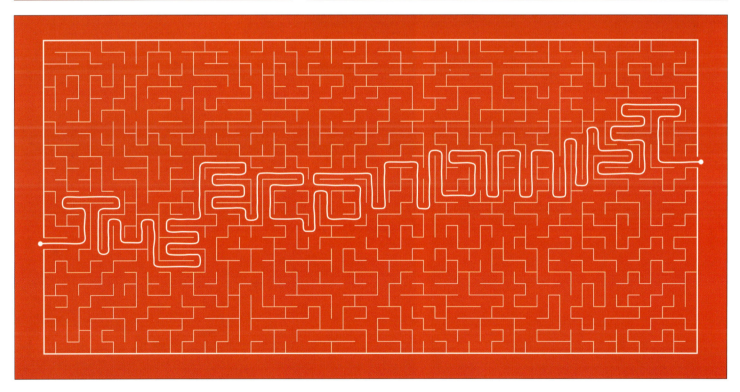

Agency	Abbott Mead Vickers BBDO, London
Creative Director	Paul Brazier
Copywriters	Tim Riley
	Mark Fairbanks
	Stephen Moss
Art Directors	Paul Brazier
	Tim Riley
	Jolyon Finch
Client	The Economist

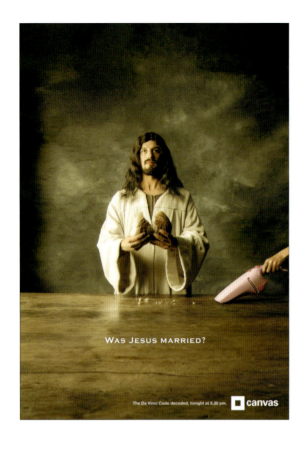

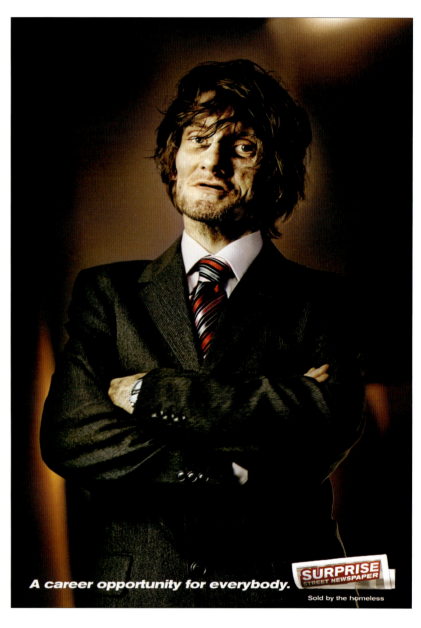

Agency	Duval Guillaume Brussels	Agency	Publicis, Zurich
Creative Directors	Peter Ampe	Creative Director	Markus Gut
	Katrien Bottez	Copywriter	Roy Spring
	Xavier Bouillon	Art Director	Simon Staub
Copywriters	Eva De Jonckheere	Photographer	Alberto Venzago
	Catheline Leroy	Client	Surprise Street Newspaper
Art Directors	Eva De Jonckheere		
	Catheline Leroy		
Photographer	Koen Demuynck		
Client	Canvas		

Agency	Publicis, Zurich	Agency	BBDO Portugal, Lisbon	Publico offers its readers a complete
Creative Director	Philipp Skrabal	**Creative Director**	Nuno Jerónimo	collection of Woody Allen DVDs;
Copywriter	Johannes Jost	**Copywriter**	Hellington Vieira	promising that the subtitles alone are
Art Director	Simon Staub	**Art Director**	Juliano Bertoldi	worth it.
Photographer	Felix Streuli	**Client**	Público	
Client	Gault Millau Restaurant Guide			

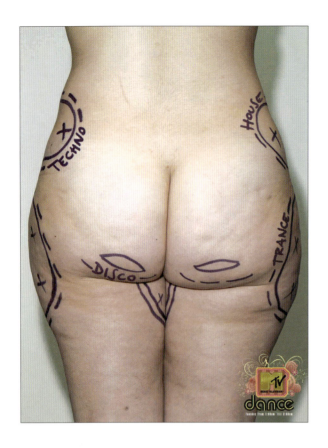

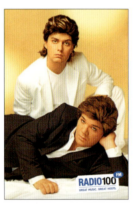

268 **Media**

Agency	Tiempo BBDO, Madrid		**Agency**	Wibroe, Duckert & Partners, Copenhagen	Radio 100FM plays pop music. The people featured in this campaign host the stations morning show and have become Danish celebrities in their own right.
Executive CD	Andrés Martínez Echeverría		**Creative Directors**	Henrik Juul	
Creative Director	Jorge Candeal			Thomas Torp	
Copywriter	Jorge Candeal		**Copywriter**	Peter Boye	
Art Director	Gemma Guio		**Photographer**	Simon Ladefoged	
Photographer	Miguel Toledano		**Client**	Radio 100FM	
Client	MTV				

Agency	KNSK Werbeagentur, Hamburg
Creative Directors	Tim Krink
	Niels Holle
Copywriter	Berend Brüdgam
Art Director	Oliver Fermer
Client	Capital Magazine

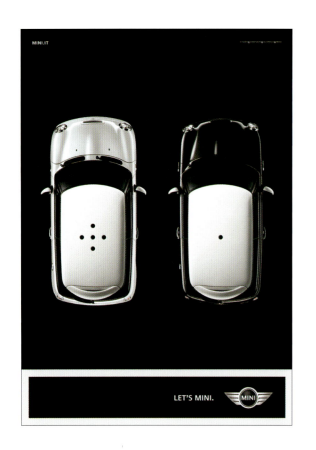

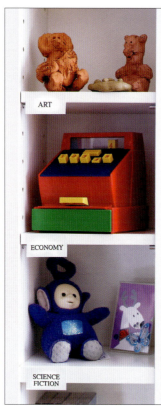

Agency	D'Adda Lorenzini Vigorelli BBDO, Milan		**Agency**	Mayer McCann, Ljubljana
Creative Directors	Giuseppe Mastromatteo		**Creative Director**	Vera Stankovic
	Luca Scotto di Carlo		**Copywriter**	Andrej Basa
Copywriters	Federico Bonenti		**Art Director**	Tina Brezovnik
	Alessandra Bergamaschi		**Photographer**	Riccardo Callin
Art Directors	Luis Toniutti		**Client**	Vale Novak Bookstore
	Luca Zamboni			
Photographer	Piero Perfetto			
Client	Mini Eat-Out Guide			

How long will we have to work in the future?

Sharpen your view. **n-tv** The newsstation

How is America reacting to global warming?

Sharpen your view. **n-tv** The newsstation

Shameless
New series starts 3 January 10pm

Agency	Euro RSCG Düsseldorf		**Agency**	4Creative, London
Creative Directors	Felix Glauner		**Creative Director**	Brett Foraker
	Martin Breuer		**Copywriter**	Tom Tagholm
Copywriters	Martin Venn		**Art Director**	Tom Tagholm
	Kajo Titus Strauch		**Photographer**	Peter Rad
Art Director	Ingmar Krannich		**Illustrator**	Darren Perry
Client	N-TV News Chanel		**Client**	Chanel 4 - Shameless Series

272 **Recreation & Leisure**

Agency	Abbott Mead Vickers BBDO, London	In this charming animated spot, a leather bag unexpectedly drops through a skylight and lands on the bed of a sleeping couple. Waking up, the man opens the bag and sees that it contains beaming smiles. Quickly we realise that the couple live in a town without smiles – but having remedied that situation at home, the man putters about distributing smiles to all and sundry. It's all a metaphor for a lottery win. What would you do if you won?
Creative Director	Paul Brazier	
Copywriters	Phil Cockrell	
	Peter Souter	
Art Director	Graham Storey	
Client	Camelot Lottery, "Bag of Smiles"	

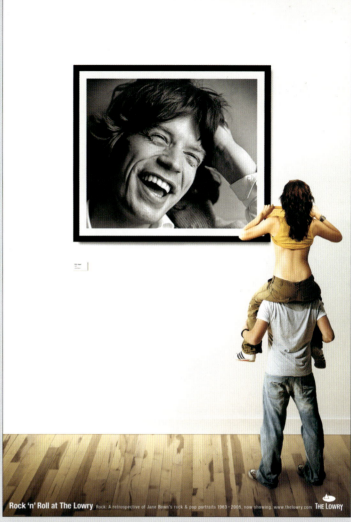

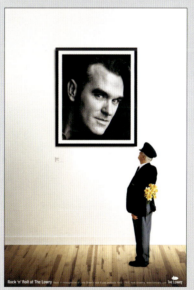

Agency	BJL, Manchester
Copywriter	Lisa Nichols
Art Director	Gary Fawcett
Photographer	Paul Moffat
Client	The Lowry Gallery

16th International Akbank Jazz Festival

Agency	Publicis Yorum, Istanbul
Creative Director	Cevdet Kizilay
Copywriter	Ebru Ataman Firat
Art Director	Adnan Elmasoglu
Production	E-Motion Istanbul
Director	Walky Talky
Producers	Ali Sengel
	Arzu Koksal
Client	Akbank Jazz Festival, "Sound of the City"

Thanks to some neat special effects, Istanbul's buildings, bridges and monuments pulse and jump to the sound of a hot jazz band. The Jazz Festival, sponsored by Akbank, is coming to the city.

Here I am in Steide, Norway,

Lotto-millionaires are not like ordinary millionaires

The Pay Per View Channel now with subtitles and Dolby Digital 5.1 quality audio.

Recreation & Leisure

Agency	Try Advertising Agency, Oslo
Creative Director	Kjetil Try
Copywriter	Øystein Halvorsen
Art Directors	Einar Fjøsne
	Karin Lund
Production	Motion Blur, Oslo
Director	Harald Zwart
Producers	Espen Horn
	Morten Polmar
	Cathrine Wennersten
Client	Norsk Tipping Lotto, "Klondyke"

In the backwater town of Steide, Norway, a TV news reporter interviews an unlucky man who has lost his million dollar winning lottery ticket. Almost as soon as the interview has been broadcast, busloads of strangers descend on the town, all intent on finding the valuable scrap of paper. Meanwhile, the man gets home and takes his hat off. The ticket flutters to the ground. When the man goes to cash it in, he sees that the influx of strangers is boosting the town's economy – so he decides to keep it for a while longer.

Agency	Saffirio Tortelli Vigoriti, Turin
Creative Director	Aurelio Tortelli
Copywriter	Michela Grasso
Art Director	Daniele Ricci
Production	Movie Magic Int'l, Milan
Director	Angel Gracia
Producer	Guido Borghi
Client	Mediaset Premium, "Grande Cinema"

A series of tongue-tied Italian actors stumble over the classic final lines of the film Gone with the Wind. As far as their English is concerned, their accents and pronunciation leave a lot to be desired. Listening to them mangling the dialogue is painful. "Frankie, my deal, I don' give damn." Improve your English with great movies on Mediaset Premium.

Agency	BITA Advertising, Kiev
Creative Director	Spector Svjatoslav
Copywriter	Spector Svjatoslav
Art Director	Maxim Ksenda
Production	BeePlaneFilms
Director	Spector Svjatoslav
Producer	Syrjatskaja Elena
Client	Kiev Int'l Advertising Festival, "Advertisement is Useful!"

A man performs a strange half-crouching dance while keeping one eye on the television. He edges towards the door, but the film's dialogue seems to have him in its grip: "Let me finish him, boss." "No. We'll be killing him slowly…very slowly." The man clutches at his private parts in agony, and we realise that he is desperate for a pee. Advertising breaks can be useful in other ways, too. Come to the 7th Kiev International Advertising Festival to see why.

Agency	Livingbrands, Copenhagen
Copywriter	Finn Balleby
Art Director	Nicolas Rafn
Production	STV, Odense
Director	Thomas Villum
Producer	Leon Nørgaard
Client	Varelotteriet, "Bubblebath"

Three women are bathing together at a spa. Suddenly, bubbles rise to the surface, indicating that one of them has broken wind. At first she looks embarrassed, but then they all laugh. Joining in, the second woman farts too, causing a slightly larger eruption of bubbles. Finally, the third woman lets loose a veritable underwater explosion that makes the waters boil. She looks pleased with herself. Do you like to win? Play the lottery.

Agency	New Moment New Ideas Company, Skopje
Creative Director	Dusan Drakalski
Copywriter	Marko Stojanovic
Art Director	Nikola Vojnov
Production	SIA, Sofia
Client	Skopje Film Festival, "Skopje Film Festival"

This ad for the Skopje Film Festival was also a competition – viewers were challenged to identify as many of the film titles hidden in the spot, in return for tickets to the event. As a camera moves around a room, we see visual clues that recall the titles and characters of films such as Silence of the Lambs, Kill Bill, The Deer Hunter, Star Wars, Blow Up, Basic Instinct, Taxi Driver, the Indiana Jones movies…and more. The music is from Jaws.

Agency	Storåkers McCann, Stockholm
Copywriters	Mia Cederberg
	Monica Hulten
Art Director	Henrik Almquist
Production	Esteban
Director	Markus Ernerot
Client	The Polar Music Prize, "The Groupie"

A middle-aged woman in some disarray emerges from a hotel room. She is wearing a leather jacket and her hair is a mess. As a chambermaid looks on disapprovingly, she adjusts a stocking. Pausing, she presses her body against the hotel room door, as if trying to cling to the bliss she's just experienced. Then, with a serene smile on her face, she leaves. The rock band Led Zeppelin is back in town after 30 years – and still capable of pulling the birds.

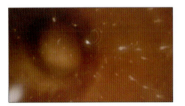

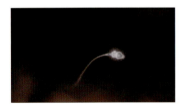

276 Recreation & Leisure

Agency	Leo Burnett, Oslo
Creative Directors	Kristoffer Carlin
	Martin Thorsen
	Morten Borgestad
	Martin Lund
Production	Toxic
Client	Europride, "The Sperm"

Sperm begin their incredible journey. One of them streaks ahead of the pack, as if confident that its mission to fertilise will be successful. But suddenly it hesitates, looking a bit lost. Where's the egg? Why is there just a black void ahead? What's going on? The words that now appear on the screen explain everything: Oslo Gay Festival.

Agency	Grey Worldwide Middle East, Beirut
Creative Director	Philippe Skaff
Copywriter	Philippe Skaff
Art Director	Serge Zahar
Production	Wanda Productions, Paris
Director	Louis Leterrier
Producers	Nancy Gabriel
	Rania Khoury
	Serge Zahar
Client	Doha Asian Games, "Torch Relay"

On their way to deliver the torch to the Doha Asian Games, a succession of athletes take on the form of animals that help them in their quest: an elephant to move a heavy load, a tiger to part the crowds, a fish to swim the ocean, even a dragon to traverse the Great Wall of China. And each of these creatures, of course, symbolise an aspect of Asia.

Agency	Doom & Dickson, Amsterdam	Agency	Euro RSCG Switzerland, Zurich
		Creative Director	Petra Bottignole
Copywriter	Joeri van Oostwaard	Copywriter	Serge Deville
Art Director	Heinrich Vejlgaard	Art Directors	Dominik Oberwiler
Photographer	Frieke Janssens		Sebastian Krayer
Illustrator	Heinrich Vejlgaard	Photographer	Andrea Vedovo
Client	The Naturist Camping Guide	Client	ZKO – Zurich Chamber Orchestra

LED ZEPPELIN IS BACK IN TOWN
FOR THE FIRST TIME IN 30 YEARS.
Watch them and Valery Gergiev receive the polar price on the 22 of May.

POLAR MUSIC PRIZE
THE ROYAL SWEDISH ACADEMY OF MUSIC AWARD

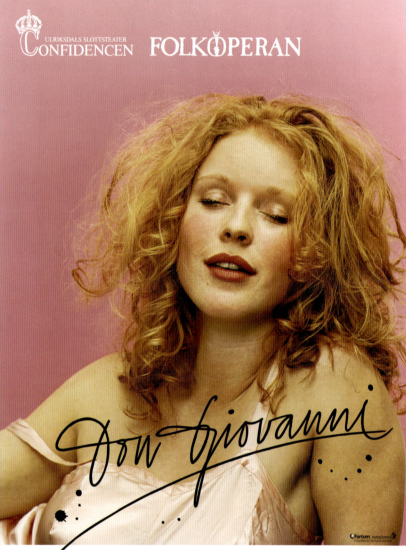

Don Giovanni by Mozart. **Confidencen July 30 – August 26, 2006**
Tickets: Ticnet 077-170 70 70, ticnet.se, folkoperan.se, confidencen.se

Don Giovanni by Mozart. **Confidencen July 30 – August 26, 2006**
Tickets: Ticnet 077-170 70 70, ticnet.se, folkoperan.se, confidencen.se

Agency	Storåkers McCann, Stockholm		**Agency**	Lowe Brindfors, Stockholm
Copywriters	Mia Cederberg Monica Hulten		**Creative Director**	Håkan Engler
			Copywriter	Olle Langseth
Art Director	Henric Almquist		**Art Directors**	Rickard Villard Kalle dos Santos
Client	The Polar Music Prize		**Photographer**	Gösta Reiland
			Client	Folkoperan

The **I'VE JUST SPLIT UP** Collection

We know how it feels. You don't even want to wake up in the morning. Your confidence has taken a bit of a knock and we understand. So much so we've prepared a little Collection to cheer you up. Especially, since you have a little more time on your hands now. (Sorry). Ready to feel better? First, stand in front of the Pre-Raphaelite masterpiece *Ophelia from Hamlet* by Millais. See? Someone else went through that too. Her loneliness should make you feel... less lonely, strangely enough. Maybe it's not the end of the world for you. Actually, you should look at the monumental *The Last Judgement* by John Martin in Room 9. Now, that is the end of the world, quite literally. This painting will help you put things in perspective, so no more sobbing, alright? Now we should talk about your future. Think about it, you're facing a moment of endless possibilities, a bit like Simon Patterson's contemporary work *The Great Bear* in Room 26. (You know, the one with the underground map.) It means that anything can happen. So comb your hair because you never know who's around. Now, you're ready for a Turner Stand in front of *Sunrise, with a Boat between Headlands*. Its highlights represent the idea of a bright new beginning. Everything will be okay. And remember, we're always here for you (10.00 – 17.50 daily).

Create your own Collection

Admission Free   ⊖ Pimlico
www.tate.org.uk   ⛴ Millbank Pier

British Art Displays 1500 – 2006
Supported by BP

BRITAIN
TATE

The **I HAVE A BIG MEETING** Collection

Meetings, meetings, meetings... all of them important, all of them crucial. How crazy is today's world? Anyway, if you need a hand with a meeting, this Tate Britain Collection is designed to help you look good and ooze confidence. Lesson number one: important matters should be treated as small matters. In Room 6, *Harvest Home* by John Linnell should help you achieve this state of mind. You can almost breathe the fresh air from a stunning golden afternoon. Fill your lungs with its greatness, and always remember to make yourself bigger before entering a room. Now it's time to take a look at a champion. *Teucer* by Sir Hamo Thornycroft, near the Millbank entrance, portrays one of the heroes of Homer's Trojan War. This monumental bronze archer teaches us to never lose focus on what we're aiming for. Now we need to work on your look. Eyes are the most powerful weapons in meetings. Stare at the portrait of *Queen Elizabeth I* in Room 2. Study her eyes and her pose because she's the model to follow. Don't even dare leave the room until you've nailed that look. Finally, spend some time in front of *The Battle of Camperdown* by Philip De Loutherbourg. This breathtaking sea battle dominates Room 9 completely. Meetings are often a lot like this, but take heart from the fact that this painting still depicts the precise moment of victory. So off you pop bravery's the name of the game, and remember, for maximum effect, we suggest you experience this Collection twenty-four hours prior to your meeting.

Create your own Collection

Admission Free   ⊖ Pimlico
www.tate.org.uk   ⛴ Millbank Pier

British Art Displays 1500 – 2006
Supported by BP

BRITAIN
TATE

MUSEUM OF CONTEMPORARY ART DonnaREgina NAPLES

Agency	Fallon London	**Agency**	Ambrosio Maoloni, Rome
Executive CDs	Richard Flintham	**Creative Directors**	Luca Maoloni
	Andy McLeod		Gabriella Ambrosio
Creative Director	Richard Flintham	**Copywriter**	Daniele Botti
Copywriter	Juan Cabral	**Art Director**	Giulia Maoloni
Art Director	Juan Cabral	**Photographer**	Ottavio Celestino
Typographer	Ginny Carrel	**Client**	Madre Art Museum
Client	Tate Britain		

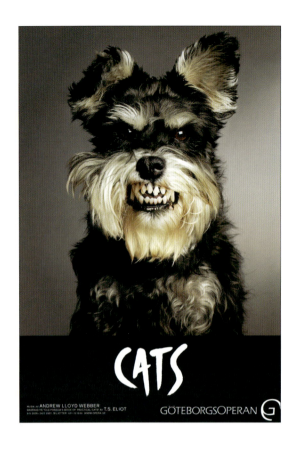

Recreation & Leisure

Agency	Forsman & Bodenfors, Gothenburg		Agency	Publicis, Zurich
Creative Director	Martin Cedergren		Creative Director	Markus Gut
Copywriter	Anders Hegerfors		Copywriter	Florian Beck
Art Directors	Pål Eneroth		Art Director	Florian Beck
	Lars Johansson		Client	Zurich Zoo
Photographer	Lucia Kangur Röed			
Client	Gothenburg Opera			

Agency	New Moment New Ideas Company, Skopje	Agency	Ogilvy & Mather, Copenhagen
Creative Director	Dusan Drakalski	Copywriter	Mikkel Elung-Jensen
Copywriter	Marko Stojanovic	Art Director	Claus Collstrup
Art Director	Nikola Vojnov	Photographer	Martin Soeby
Client	Skopje Jazz Festival	Client	Scrabble

Recreation & Leisure

Agency	Publicis Conseil, Paris
Creative Directors	Olivier Altmann
	Hervé Plumet
Copywriter	Olivier Camensuli
Art Directors	Frédéric Royer
	Yves Sarhadian
Photographer	Arnaud Pyvka
Client	Stihl Garden Tools

THINK BIGGER. STIHL

VIKING
THE NEW 6 SERIES LAWN-MOWER
COMPLETE WITH FRONT BUMPER.

Agency	Publicis Conseil, Paris	Agency	Publicis Conseil, Paris
Creative Directors	Olivier Altmann	Creative Directors	Olivier Altmann
	Hervé Plumet		Hervé Plumet
Copywriter	Patrice Lucet	Copywriter	Marc Rosier
Art Director	Charles Guillemant	Art Director	Jean-Marc Tramoni
Photographer	Jean-Yves Lemoigne	Photographer	Michael Lewis
Client	Stihl Chain Saws	Client	Viking Lawn Mowers

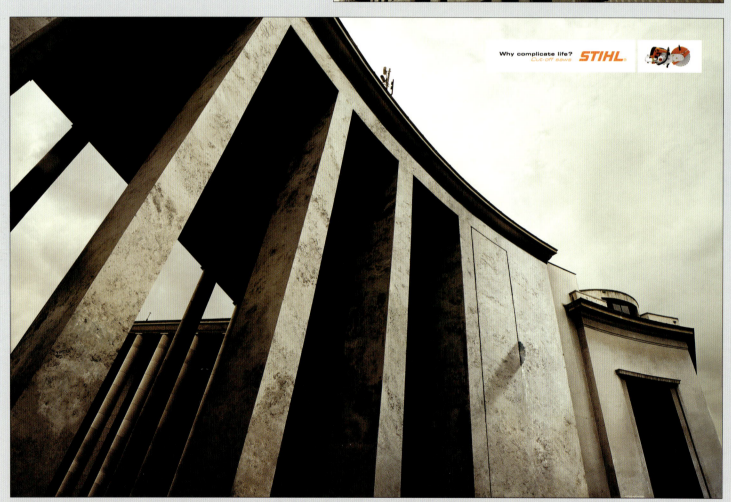

Agency	Publicis Conseil, Paris
Creative Directors	Olivier Altmann
	Hervé Plumet
Copywriter	Eric Helias
Art Directors	Jorge Carreno
	Benoît Blumberger
Photographer	Hervé Plumet
Client	Stihl Saws

Agency	JWT Italia, Milan	Agency	Heye & Partner, Unterhaching
Creative Director	Pietro Maestri	Creative Directors	Jan Okusluk
Copywriter	Rachele Proli		Oliver Diehr
Art Director	Hugo Gallardo	Copywriter	Gunnar Immisch
Photographer	Riccardo Bagnoli	Art Director	Hannes Ciatti
Client	Scatto Cement	Client	Pattex Power Tape

APRIL 28th - SAFETY AT WORK DAY

KROMASIL. IT JUST GOES ON AND ON.

Kromasil® HPLC columns are based on high purity Kromasil silica. They give you symmetrical peaks even for basic compounds, just as you would expect from other top performing analytical columns. The difference is that Kromasil columns last much longer.

During the past ten years, Kromasil has been the leading brand for large-scale HPLC, where long lifetime and thereby high chemical stability are crucial for minimizing costs.

Want to know how Kromasil gives you more analyses from every column? You can find everything from detailed product descriptions to order information on our website. Or why not contact your nearest Kromasil distributor directly? It could be the beginning of a relationship that just goes on and on.

Kromasil is available in particle sizes of 3.5, 5, 7,10, 13 and 16µm, pore sizes of 60, 100 and 300Å and several surface modifications.

Eka Chemicals AB, Separation Products, SE-445 80 Bohus, Sweden. Tel. +46 31 58 70 00
For NAFTA countries: Eka Chemicals, 7 Livingstone Avenue, Dobbs Ferry, NY 10522-3401, U.S.A. Tel.+1 914 674 5019.
kromasil@eka.com - www.kromasil.com

AKZO NOBEL

KROMASIL. KEEPS ON RUNNING WHEN OTHERS GIVE UP.

Kromasil® HPLC columns are based on high purity Kromasil silica. They generate symmetrical peaks even for basic compounds, just as you would expect from other top performing analytical columns. The difference is that Kromasil columns last longer.

That's because Kromasil has been developed to produce high chemical stability, which leads to long column lifetimes and lower costs. In large-scale HPLC, where cost-efficiency is crucial for company survival, Kromasil has been the leading brand for the past ten years.

Want to know more about how Kromasil gives you additional analyses from every column? You can find everything from detailed product descriptions to order information on our website. Or why not contact your nearest distributor directly? You'll be up and running in just a few days.

Eka Chemicals AB, Separation Products, SE-445 80 Bohus, Sweden. Tel. +46 31 58 70 00
For NAFTA countries: Eka Chemicals, 7 Livingstone Avenue, Dobbs Ferry, NY 10522-3401, U.S.A. Tel.+1 914 674 5019.
kromasil@eka.com - www.kromasil.com

AKZO NOBEL

---

286   **Industrial & Agricultural Products**

Agency	New Moment New Ideas Company, Belgrade		**Agency**	Sandberg Trygg, Gothenburg
Creative Director	Dragan Sakan		**Copywriter**	Fredrik Hansson
Copywriter	Svetlana Copic		**Art Director**	Ola Carlberg
Art Director	Ivana Veljkovic		**Photographer**	Johan Wedenström
Client	Lafarge Cement		**Client**	Kromasil HPLC Columns

From CO₂ and NH₃ to fresh-baked bread

On the road to a better environment

Turning your future into reality
think in paper

VOITH
Engineered reliability.

Industrial & Agricultural Products 287

Agency	Ehrenstråhle BBDO, Stockholm
Copywriter	Per Ehrenstråhle
Art Director	Lotta Hjalmarson
Client	Sandvik

Agency	RTS Rieger Team Business-to-Business Communication, Leinfelden-Echterdingen
Creative Director	Boris Pollig
Copywriter	Siegfried Schaal
Art Director	Ute Witzmann
Photographer	Pim Vuik
Client	Voith Paper

Communication bundles, 360°...

CRM, here comes CRM...

Award-winning commercials... Interactive, digital...

We've got wicked headlines...

... and killer layouts...

Fucking great ads with tiny logos...

MESERIE, MANCA-V-AS!

Scala JWT. It's the real shit, man!

Agency	Scala JWT, Bucharest	A self-promotion ad for the agency
Creative Director	Mark Walton	Scala JWT, which is located in a part of
Copywriter	Mihai Cojocaru	Bucharest noted for its gypsy saleswomen,
Production	Chainsaw Europe,	who walk the streets crying out the wares
	Bucharest	they have on offer. In this version, however,
Director	Mark Walton	the gypsy woman shouts about the wares
Client	Scala JWT,	of the agency: "Concepts! CRM! Award
	"Taking it to the Streets"	winning commercials! Wicked headlines!

Killer layouts!" And so on. As the agency
puts it, "It's better than a boring credentials
presentation."

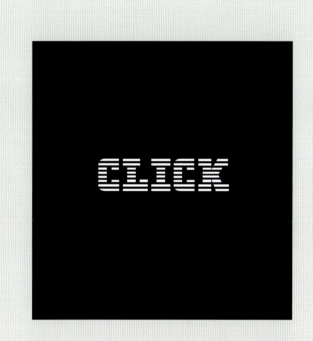

Professional Equipment & Services   **289**

Agency	Grabarz & Partner, Hamburg
Creative Directors	Ralf Heuel
	Ralf Nolting
Copywriter	Markus Ewertz
Art Director	Tomas Tulinius
Graphic artist	Julia Elbers
Client	Studio Funk

Berlitz®
Language for life

Agency	BTS United, Oslo
Creative Director	Thorbjørn Naug
Copywriter	Pål Sparre-Enger
Art Director	Thorbjørn Naug
Production	Motion Blur
Directors	Nic & Sune
Producer	Espen Horn
Client	Berlitz Language School, "The German Coastguard"

At a German coastguard station, a new recruit is given a run-down of the equipment. Seconds after the senior officer left the control room, a mayday comes in from an English ship. "We are sinking!" says the voice, desperately, "We are sinking!" The German recruit considers this, then answers in heavily accented English: "Vot…are you…sinking…about?" He needs Berlitz language school.

Pal, rub my lard lump
I'm bum!

Hi, I really buy a rib-eye!

Pour tea, Sir ray!

Foreign languages sound like a bumble?

Berlitz
Language School

A.R.T. STUDIOS
AUDIOPRODUCTION FOR ADVERTISING

290   **Professional Equipment & Services**

Agency	ACW-Grey, Tel Aviv
Creative Directors	Yonatan Stirin
	Nir Livni
Copywriter	Shani Gershi
Art Director	Tal Ben Ari
Production	ACW Grey Israel
Producers	Rinat Keinan
	Maya Salant
Client	Berlitz Language School, "La Bamba"

This ad plays out to the famous song La Bamba. It depicts the English words a person might substitute for the original Spanish lyrics if they didn't understand that language. As a result, the song becomes totally nonsensical. Altogether now: "Pal rub my lard lump, I'm bum! You're dragon shit. I really buy a rib-eye! bumble, bumble." If languages are a bumble, try the Berlitz language school.

Agency	Saatchi & Saatchi, Frankfurt
Creative Directors	Eberhard Kirchhoff
	Thomas Kanofsky
Copywriter	Alex Priebs-Macpherson
Art Director	Nicole Groezinger
Production	Schulten Film, Frankfurt
Director	Alex Feil
Client	A.R.T. Sound Studios, "The Jump"

In a recording studio, we see a sound engineer gaffer-taping his willing colleague to the floor. He then places one leg of a chair against the guy's teeth. He takes a run-up, jumps, and is about to land hard on the chair when…we cut to a woman noisily biting into a crunchy crisp-bread. A.R.T Studios: they give their all for the best sound effects.

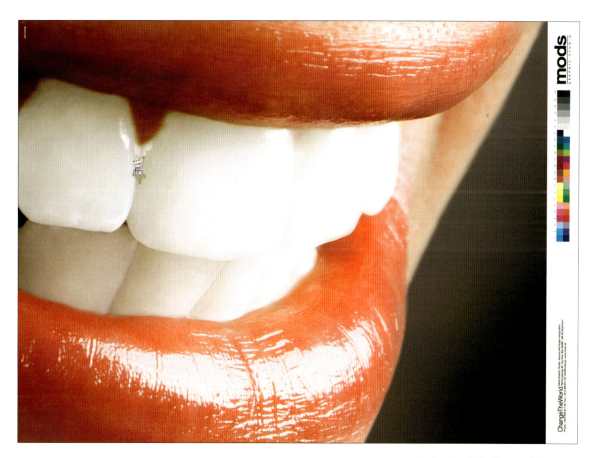

Agency	DDB Oslo	**Agency**	Åkestam Holst, Stockholm
Copywriter	Torbjørn K Madsen	**Art Directors**	Jesper Holst
Art Directors	Joachim Bjørndahl		Lars Holthe
	Jan Erik Nilsen		Johan Baettig
	Rune Markhus	**Photographer**	Alexander Pihl
Photographer	Sebastian Ludvigsen	**Client**	Mods Graphic Studio
Client	Hydro Engineering		

Agency	Scher Lafarge, Paris
Creative Director	Gilbert Scher
Copywriter	Olivia Aubert
Art Director	Elisa Gilbert
Production	Première Heure, Paris
Director	Emmanuel Bellegard
Producers	Jérôme Rucki
	Ingrid Vasseur
	Agathe Naffag
Client	BVP, "The Dinner"

It's a romantic dinner…for the moment. A young woman confides to her date: "What I like about you is that you're obviously not obsessed by sex." The man confesses that, when he was younger, he was violently bitten by a dog, "you can imagine where". His sex life is non existent. But he remains full of hope, he adds. "Soon I am going to try a new transplant of pig genital glands." The woman looks thoroughly turned off. It's not always wise to tell the truth…except in advertising. The spot is for the French advertising standards authority.

292 Professional Equipment & Services

Agency	Zebra Werbeagentur, Chemnitz
Creative Director	Joerg G. Fieback
Copywriter	Stefka Meyer
Art Director	Romek Müller
Photographer	Thomas Herbrich
Client	Senso Alarm

Agency	Kolle Rebbe, Hamburg
Creative Directors	Ulrich Zuenkeler
	Sven Klohk
	Christoph Hildebrand
Copywriter	Sebastian Oehme
Art Directors	Alexander Hesslein
	René Gebhardt
	Antje Gerwien
	Bjoern Kernspeckt
Photographer	Bernd Westphal
Graphics	Kerstin Berk
Client	Bisley Office Furnishings

WHAT OUR STAFF GET UP TO AFTER-HOURS.

WHAT OUR STAFF GET UP TO AFTER-HOURS.

Professional Equipment & Services

Agency	TBWA\PHS, Helsinki		Agency	Publicis, Zurich
Copywriter	Markku Ronkko		Creative Director	Markus Gut
Art Director	Minna Lavola		Copywriter	Johannes Jost
Photographer	Elina Moriya		Art Director	Ralph Halder
Illustrators	Pia Pitkanen		Client	Straumann Retouching
	Tommi Rapeli			
	Fake Graphics			
Client	CFP-E/Shots			
	Young Director Award			

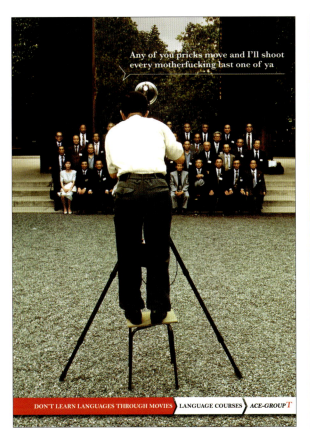

Agency	Duval Guillaume Brussels	**Agency**	Vitruvio Leo Burnett, Madrid
Creative Directors	Peter Ampe	**Creative Director**	Rafa Antón
	Katrien Bottez	**Copywriters**	Pablo Burgués
Copywriter	Tom Berth		Roberto De La Cruz
Art Director	Geert De Rocker	**Art Directors**	Pablo Burgués
Client	Ace-Group T		Roberto De La Cruz
	Language School	**Client**	EOI Language School

THE WEATHER FORECAST SAID RAIN.
IN TOKYO.

SOMETIMES THE BEST INTENTIONS
ARE NOT GOOD ENOUGH.

The best of maps are useless, if you ignore the signs. Native tongues still won't communicate, if you address the wrong people. And thousands of words cannot relate the writing that's already on the wall.
All the good will in the world won't save a homework poorly done. Nor will it make up for lax attention to details. Especially in post conflict areas, where you just might not get a second chance. Are you ready to take that risk? If not, contact us now.

Reconstruction assistance in post-conflict areas - www.raints.com

Agency	Peer Communication, Malmö	The complex legal and corporate jargon associated with intellectual property rights is crossed out; leaving only the phrase "patent attorneys who take a stand."	Agency	Glenn Reklambyrå, Malmö
Creative Director	Peer Eriksson		Creative Director	Patrik Lundberg
Copywriter	Henric Lindqvist		Copywriter	Ivan Matanovic
Art Director	Peer Eriksson		Art Director	Patrik Lundberg
Photographer	Peer Eriksson		Photographer	Johan Berglund
Client	Awapatent, Patent Attorneys		Client	RA International

Agency	Heye & Partner, Unterhaching
Art Director	Andi Stenzel
Client	Text-College München

Agency	Scholz & Friends Hamburg
Creative Directors	Matthias Schmidt
	Suze Barrett
	Tobias Holland
Copywriter	Dennis Lueck
Art Director	Christine Rose
Photographer	Ralph Baiker
Client	NHB Sound Studios

DEATH TO UGLINESS   **LAUS'06**

The most passionate kiss ever.

(HEARING IS BELIEVING ON RADIO.)

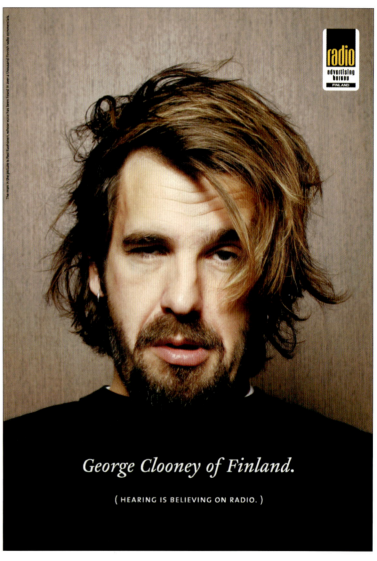

George Clooney of Finland.

(HEARING IS BELIEVING ON RADIO.)

Agency	Zapping, Madrid
Creative Directors	Uschi Henkes
	Manolo Moreno
	Urs Frick
Copywriter	Manolo Moreno
Art Director	Uschi Henkes
Client	Laus Graphic Design
	& Visual Communication Awards

Agency	Dynamo Advertising,
	Helsinki
Copywriter	Vesa Kujala
Art Director	Jyrki Poutanen
Photographer	Juuso Westerlund
Client	Radio Advertising Bureau

ache?

 hit the fan?

Grinding ?

Hit the ?

Let  do the work!

Agency	Åkestam Holst, Stockholm		**Agency**	1576, Edinburgh
Copywriters	Calle Lewenhaupt		**Creative Director**	Adrian Jeffery
	Göran Åkestam		**Copywriter**	Chris Muir
Art Director	Olle Matsson		**Art Director**	Simon Phillips
Illustrator	John Jacobsson		**Photographer**	Robbie Smith
Client	Posten – Swedish Post Office		**Client**	Denholm Associates

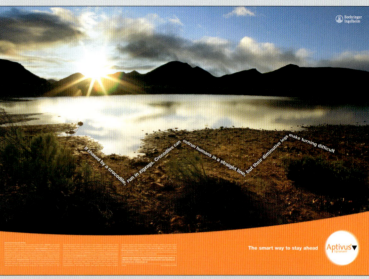

300 Prescription Products

Agency	Huntsworth Health, Marlow
Creative Director	Andy Bell
Copywriter	Sophie Johnson
Art Director	Martin Gaul
Photographer	Stuart McClymont
Client	Aptivus, HIV Treatment

REQUIP ropinirole

PUT THEIR LIVES BACK IN THEIR HANDS

Prescribe early, because what he loses, he could lose forever.

Help stop the spiral of decline

Risperdal CONSTA risperidone LONG-ACTING INJECTION

Agency	Junction 11, London		**Agency**	Torre Lazur McCann, London
Creative Directors	Richard Rayment		**Creative Director**	Don Nicolson
	John Timney		**Copywriter**	Matt Macland
Copywriter	Richard Rayment		**Art Director**	Craig Chester
Art Director	John Timney		**Photographer**	Chris Frazer Smith
Photographer	Bob Wing		**Client**	Risperdal Consta,
Client	ReQuip,			Antipsychotic Medication
	Parkinson's Disease Treatment			

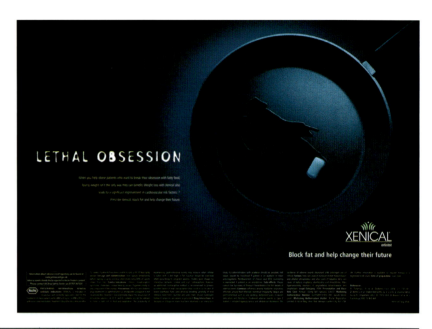

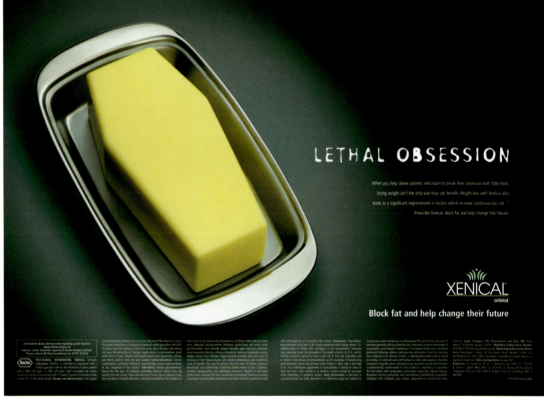

302   **Prescription Products**

Agency	Adventis Healthcare, London
Creative Director	Dave Wyatt
Copywriters	Dave Wyatt
	Kevin McGetrick
Art Director	Kevin McGetrick
Illustrator	Dave Wyatt
Client	Benzamycin,
	Acne Medication

Agency	Paling Walters, London
Creative Director	Frank Walters
Copywriter	Carmel Thompson
Art Director	Adrian Parr
Photographer	Johnathan Knowles
Client	Xenical,
	Weight Loss Treatment

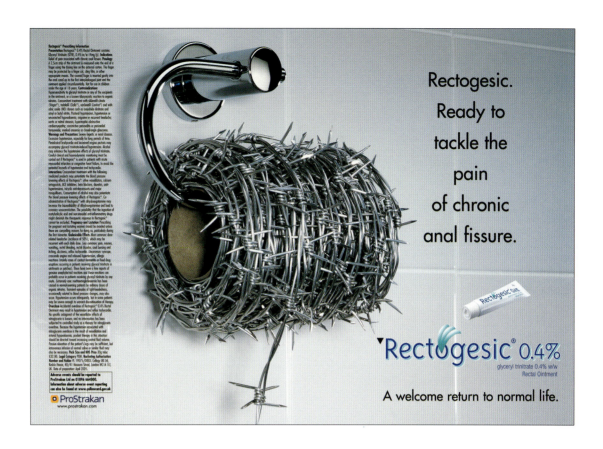

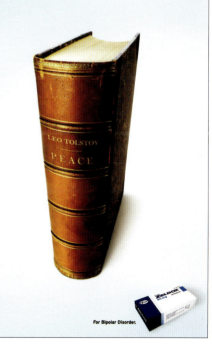

Agency	Huntsworth Health, Marlow	Agency	TBWA\PHS, Helsinki
Creative Director	Liz Maclaren	Copywriter	Erkko Mannila
Copywriter	Linda Dunn	Art Director	Mikko Torvinen
Art Director	Pete Brown	Illustrator	Minna Toivonen
Photographer	Adrian Lyon	Client	Zeldox, Antidepressant
Client	Rectogesic, Rectal Ointment		

DAS GRAUEN IST NÄHER, ALS DU DENKST.

FORBIDDEN
SIREN 2

PlayStation.2

304　**Consumer Direct**

Agency	TBWA\Germany, Berlin
Creative Directors	Philip Borchardt
	Dirk Henkelmann
Copywriter	Friedrich Tromm
Art Director	Leila El-Kayem
Design	Arnaud Loix Van Hooff
Producer	Katrin Dettmann
Client	Sony PlayStation2 - Forbidden Siren 2

To promote the horror video game Forbidden Siren 2, the agency handed out free cameras at a games convention in Leipzig. When the recipients developed the film, scary, ghoulish-looking ghosts appeared on their photos. The last photo in the pile was an ad: "The horror is closer than you think: Forbidden Siren 2."

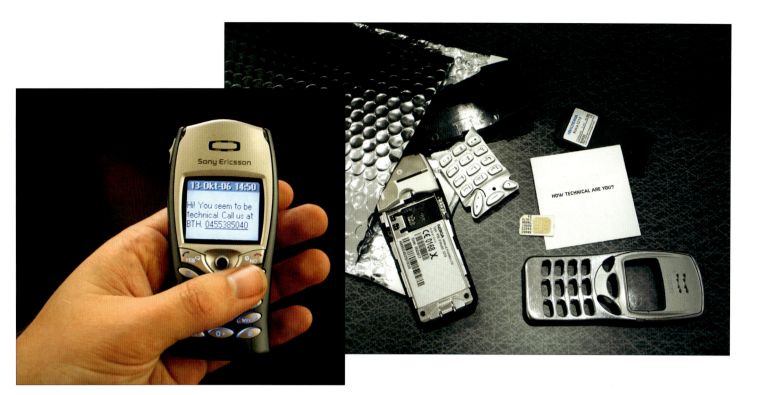

Agency	The Fan Club, Malmö	Technical university BTH wanted to recruit new students. This mailing of cell phone parts was sent to the campuses of competing technical schools. When the recipient successfully assembled the parts and switched on the phone, they got an SMS saying: "Hi! You seem to be technical. Call us at BTH."
Creative Directors	Christian Barrett	
	Ola Obrant Andreasson	
Copywriter	Ola Obrant Andreasson	
Art Director	Christian Barrett	
Client	BTH - University of Technology	

Agency	TBWA\Germany, Berlin	In order to promote the exotic flavours of Haagen Dazs ice cream and support the slogan "let your tongue travel", the agency created its own postage stamps. When customers licked the backs of the stamps, they tasted of chocolate chips, cookies & cream, macadamia nut brittle and so on. Customers could literally send their favourite flavour on a journey to a friend or loved one.
Creative Director	Dietrich Zastrow	
Copywriters	Susanne Thomé	
	Sigrun Abel	
Art Director	Kirsten Frenz	
Client	Häagen-Dazs	

INSTANT RESPECT KIT

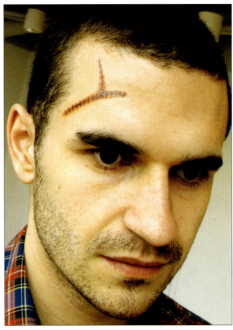

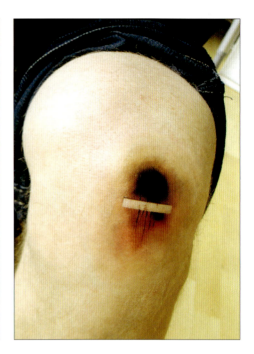

Agency	Goss, Gothenburg
Copywriters	Michael Schultz
	Ulrika Good
Art Directors	Gunnar Skarland
	Emil Jonsson
	Mattias Frendberg
	Mimmi Andersson
	Jan Eneroth
Illustrator	Fredrik Persson
Client	Langley Travel

Tour operator Langley wanted to make its winter sports clients travel with the company in the summer, too. This kit was sent to people who usually travelled with Langley on really tough ski trips, like off-piste skiing in Iran. The purpose was to tell the target group that Langley had a huge program of activities on its resorts. But by wearing the fake tattoos, the guest could also choose to relax by the pool while maintaining a daredevil image.

Agency	Wunderman Germany,
	Frankfurt
Executive CD	Bernd Fliesser
Creative Director	Erik Backes
Copywriter	Uwe Schatz
Art Director	Viola Laeufer
Client	Frankfurter Allgemeine
	Zeitung

This promotion for a series of collectible comic books used nostalgia to appeal to adults. In the mailing, only the speech-bubbles in the comic strips were visible. To see the images, you had to use a torch – just as you may have done when you secretly read comic books under the bedcovers late into the night as a child.

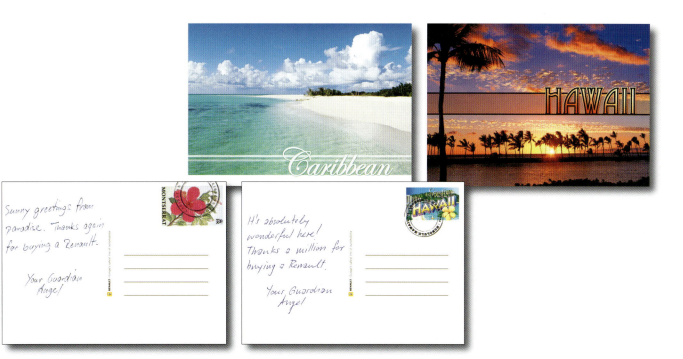

Agency	Publicis, Zurich	To promote the safety of Renault
Creative Director	Philipp Skrabal	cars, "guardian angels" who now find
Copywriter	Claude Ramme	themselves out of jobs send postcards
Art Director	Isabelle Hauser	from vacation destinations to Renault
Client	Renault Switzerland	owners, congratulating them on their
		choice.

Agency	McCann-Erickson	Every Christmas, the premature baby unit
	Belgium, Hoeilaart	at Edith Cavell hospital sends cards to
Creative Director	Jean-Luc Walraff	the other departments and to ex-patients.
Copywriter	Gregory Defay	This year, the unit sent out the card in mid-
Art Director	Gregory Defay	October. When recipients opened it they
Photographer	Thierry Siebrand	saw the message, "It's a little premature, but
Client	Edith Cavell Hospital	Happy Christmas."

All my clients are morons, they don't see how great I am
I said, all my clients are morons, they don't see how great I am

That old deadline is killin' me
I've got the Adman's blues

My account director is only good at kissin' ass
I said, my account director is only good at kissin' ass

That old burnout is comin'
I've got the Adman's blues

All the awards have gone to the judges
I said, all the awards have gone to the judges

That old envy is killin' me
I've got the Adman's blues

Woke up this morning, and found my client gone
I said, I woke up this morning, and found my client gone

I'm going out drinkin'
I've got the Adman's blues

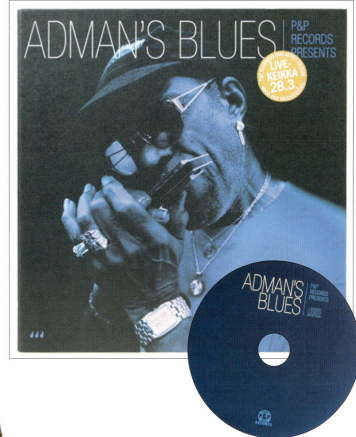

Agency	Hasan & Partners, Helsinki	Finnish newspaper Helsingin Sanomat wanted to inspire creatives to make better print advertising and revive interest in this "old-fashioned" medium. So it arranged a seminar for Finnish creatives featuring a talk by award-winning adman Lorenzo de Rita. The direct mail invitation challenged creatives to ask themselves whether agencies moaned too much rather than looking for solutions. The mailing looked like a classic blues LP cover. Inside it there was a concert poster and a CD featuring "The Adman's Blues".
Copywriter	Mick Scheinin	
Art Director	Mega Maunula	
	Jarno Luotonen	
Client	Helsingin Sanomat	

Agency	Scholz & Friends, Hamburg	The task was to develop a mailing that generated donations for children in need. To make a donation, you needed to remove a form from this cardboard slipcase. When you slid out the form, the image on the cover changed: a child was magically removed from the street and placed in a safe home.
Creative Directors	Richard Jung	
	Matthias Schmidt	
Copywriter	Dennis Lueck	
Art Director	Martin Dlugosch	
Client	Help for Children in Need	

Agency	Kolle Rebbe, Hamburg	Vivil means fresh breath – in any situation. To illustrate this claim the agency produced a "fresh breath flip book". Although it depicted someone who had just eaten a large kebab, their breath did not smell of kebab meat and chilli sauce, because the pages of the book had been impregnated with a peppermint scent.
Creative Director	Katrin Oeding	
Copywriter	Alexander Baron	
Art Director	Erik Hart	
Photographer	Erik Hart	
Graphics	Reginald Wagner Florian Schmucker	
Client	Vivil Breath Fresheners	

Agency	Maxzwo, Munich	How do you convey the feeling of test driving an extremely sporty car? The mailing does this by pulling the reader through 60 seconds of speed and performance. A horizontal brochure unfolds in five time slots. You reach 100 km/h after 5.7 seconds, full power after 15 seconds, take the first corner after 30 seconds, hit the brakes and come to a halt at 60 seconds. Now you can start breathing again. A giveaway stop watch underlines the intensity of the test-drive experience.
Creative Directors	Kerstin Antony Holger Kalvelage	
Copywriter	Uta Tescari	
Art Directors	Kilian Neddermeyer Birgit Nadler	
Client	Audi S3	

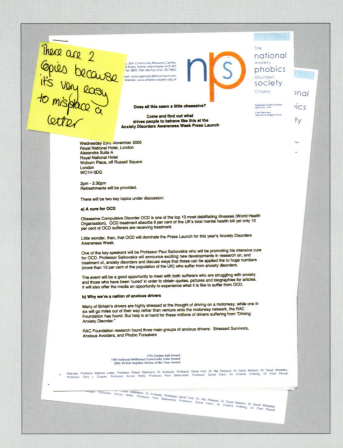

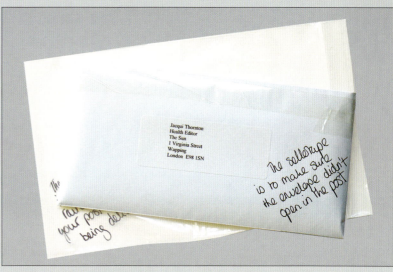

Agency	Harrison Troughton Wunderman, London	The National Phobics Society wanted the media to attend the press launch of National Anxiety Awareness Week. So it sent journalists a series of mailings focusing on common forms of Obsessive Compulsive Disorder. Mailing 1 focused upon the obsessive person's need to take precautions against all eventualities. Mailing 2 focused upon an obsessive need for neatness (see the keys re-arranged in alphabetical order). Mailing 3 was a copy of the last article written by the journalist who received it. But every single letter "o" in the article had been filled in – another common form of compulsive behaviour.
Creative Director	Steve Harrison	
Copywriters	Nigel Webb	
	Mike Poole	
	Stephen Timms	
Art Directors	Richard Kenyon	
	Alan Mackie	
	Matt Williams	
Client	National Phobics Society	

Het effect van direct mail

"Case File" Brochure

Agency	JWT/PPGH, Amsterdam
Creative Directors	Bart Kooij Nico Akkerman
Copywriter	Robin Kemme
Art Director	John de Vries
Client	TPG Post

The mailing was designed to convince business clients that they would achieve a better response to their mail-outs by working with TPG (Royal Dutch Mail). In Dutch the "spons" in the word "response" also means "sponge"; so targets received a mailing containing a dry sponge in the shape of the letters RE and the text: "The effect of direct mail". When placed in water the sponge will grow – just like your response when you use Royal Dutch Mail.

Agency	Lowe, Zurich
Creative Director	Keith Loell
Copywriter	Livio Dainese
Art Director	Fernando Perez
Client	Independant Wrestling Association

To help the Independant Wrestling Association generate corporate sponsorship opportunities the agency bravely positioned it as an entertainment alternative that was "barely legal" and probably "should be banned". A series of increasingly threatening (and funny) reply cards were sent to prospects. Those who replied were sent an "evidence" bag outlining wrestling's history, its fan base and sponsorship possibilities. The package also included three "get-out-of-jail-free" vouchers for the next event and a "subpoena" to schedule a presentation.

Agency	McCann Erickson, Belgrade
Creative Director	Christophe Muesser
Copywriters	Bogdan Spanjevic
	Milena Kvapil
	Vladimir Cosić
Art Directors	Marko Svirčević
	Vladimir Radišić
Photographer	Marko Savic
Client	Ekonomist Magazine

The readers of Serbian magazine Ekonomist are able to spot business opportunities in everything they touch. Even this devalued bank note from the period of high inflation in Serbia could be a valuable object – to a collector.

Agency	Harrison Troughton Wunderman, London
Creative Director	Steve Harrison
Copywriter	Vaughan Townsend
Art Director	Matt Williams
Client	Microsoft Windows Mobile 5.0

Windows Mobile 5.0 is the software behind a Pocket PC that allows workers remote access to company networks as well as their emails and programmes like Office, Excel and PowerPoint. This mailer explained that, with a Windows Mobile Pocket PC, everywhere is your office. The cover said simply: "A sample of your new office carpet is enclosed." Inside was a real square of grass – an eye-catching way to say that this summer, you'd be free to kick off your shoes and work in the park.

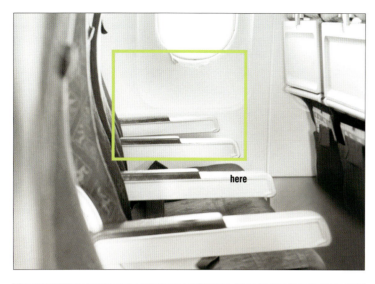

here

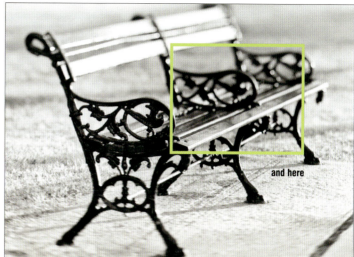

and here

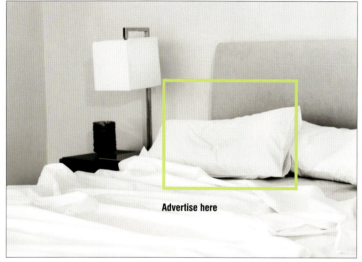

Advertise here

A newspaper reaches places other forms of advertising can't.

To find out more about the way people use newspapers, contact Jim Raeburn on 0131 240 3276.

YOU GET MORE OUT OF A PAPER

Guten Appetit *

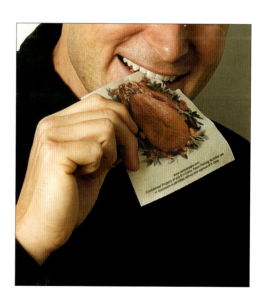

Agency	The Bridge, Glasgow	Research commissioned by the Scottish
Creative Director	Jonathan d'Aguilar	Daily Newspaper Society showed that
Copywriters	Jonathan d'Aguilar	people have a more intimate relationship
	Doug Cook	with their paper than any other media.
Art Directors	Doug Cook	They keep it with them throughout their
	Liz O'Connor	day, come back to it during their work
Typographer	Andy Mulvenna	breaks and use it to shut out the world
Client	Scottish Daily	in busy situations. This also implied that
	Newspaper Society	newspapers could reach people where

Research commissioned by the Scottish Daily Newspaper Society showed that people have a more intimate relationship with their paper than any other media. They keep it with them throughout their day, come back to it during their work breaks and use it to shut out the world in busy situations. This also implied that newspapers could reach people where other media simply couldn't. The point is clearly made by this trade mailer, aimed to ensure that newspapers featured more prominently on media schedules.

Agency Wunderman, Frankfurt
Creative Director Bernd Fliesser
Copywriter Wolf Mandl
Art Director Melissa Seelig
Client Wunderman

Direct marketing firm Wunderman invited its clients to Christmas dinner – by sending out an edible mailing that actually tasted of turkey. The agency used a new patented method that "prints" the taste of different dishes onto paper. The mailing supported the positioning of Wunderman as an innovative agency.

314   **Business to Business Direct**

Agency	OgilvyOne Worldwide, Frankfurt	The Evangelical Church in Frankfurt commissioned an advertising campaign to encourage people to come back to the church. As a first step, all of the ministers in Frankfurt were invited to an informational meeting at which the campaign would be explained. A simple mailing illustrated the reality of the situation with excruciating clarity: the invitation was as empty as most churches in Frankfurt. Many ministers were unhappy to be confronted with the truth. Despite that, 90 per cent of the ministers showed up at the meeting.
Creative Director	Michael Koch	
Copywriter	Ramon Daehne	
Art Director	Regina Placzek	
Client	Evangelical Church Frankfurt	

Agency	OgilvyOne Worldwide, London	Historically, small and medium businesses have not been a focus for Cisco. Cisco set out to change this perception and show that they provide solutions for the more independent worker. To emphasise the message that Cisco solutions are designed for YOU, the agency created personalised letters in the form of mirrors.
Creative Director	Cordell Burke	
Copywriter	Peter Mabbott	
Art Director	Gary Willis	
Client	Cisco Systems	

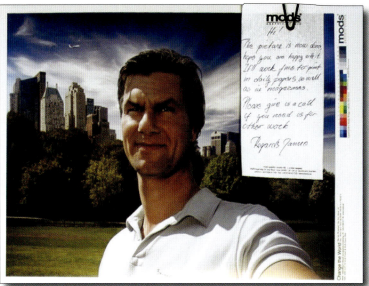

Agency	Åkestam Holst, Stockholm	Mods is the Swedish market leader in retouch and graphics processing. It wanted to remind advertising agencies of its existence. It sent art directors photos of account managers at their agencies, accompanied by lists of faults that the account manager needed correcting in order to ensure a more handsome image. The cleaned-up photos, courtesy of Mods, were also attached. The art directors assumed that they had been sent the images by mistake and were delighted to have "proof" of their account managers' vanity. The pictures were tailor-made for each agency and became hot topics of conversation.
Copywriter	Maria Fredriksson	
Art Directors	Jesper Holst Andreas Ullenius	
Illustrator	Torbjörn Krantz	
Client	Mods Graphic Studio	

Agency	Scholz & Friends, Berlin	A well-known toy dramatizes the power and easy handling of a Bosch chainsaw. When the button on the bottom is pressed, the trees are cut down and a "proud" lumberjack is revealed, holding up a Bosch Chainsaw. A sticker reads: "High performance. Easy to use."
Creative Directors	Mario Gamper Michael Winterhagen	
Copywriter	Alexander Schierl	
Art Director	Marc Ebenwaldner	
Client	Bosch Chain Saw	

Media Innovation

Agency	Scholz & Friends, Berlin
Creative Directors	Matthias Spaetgens
	Jan Leube
Copywriter	Axel Tischer
Art Director	David Fischer
Photographer	Hans Starck
Graphics	Artist Inga Schulze
	Sara dos Santos Vieira
Client	Jobsintown.de

Agency	Duval Guillaume Antwerp	Let us keep dreaming of a better world.	**Agency**	Family Advertising, Edinburgh
Creative Directors	Geoffrey Hantson		**Creative Directors**	Kevin Bird
	Dirk Domen			David Isaac
Copywriter	Eric Becker		**Copywriter**	David Isaac
Art Director	Gilles de Boncourt		**Art Director**	Kevin Bird
Photographer	Geert De Wolf		**Production**	Baillie Signs
Client	Ché Men's Magazine		**Producer**	Bill White
			Client	Scottish Slimmers

Agency	Hallelujah, Amsterdam	In this pro-environment action, trees were planted illegally in city streets as a protest against the illegal felling of trees around the world.	
Creative Directors	Peter van der Helm Matthieu Elvers		
Copywriter	Matthieu Elvers		
Art Director	Peter van der Helm		
Illustrator	Sander Slager		
Client	Friends of the Earth		

Agency Grey Worldwide, Düsseldorf
Creative Directors Florian Meimberg
Torsten Pollmann
Copywriters Torsten Pollmann
Claudia Meimberg
Art Director Florian Meimberg
Client Toys "R" Us

Agency	Uncle Grey, Oslo	Radio Tango is Oslo's rock 'n' roll radio station. In order to dramatise its positioning, stickers in the shape of loudspeaker diaphragms (along with the text "Radio Tango brings the sound of rock 'n' roll to the city") were made and slapped on everything that resembled the shape of a loudspeaker in the streets of Oslo.
Creative Director	Frank Nystuen	
Copywriters	Christian Hygen	
	Frank Nystuen	
Art Director	Per Erik Jarl	
Illustrator	Kenneth Hverven	
Client	Radio Tango	

Agency	Lowe, Hoeilaart
Creative Director	Véronique Hermans
Copywriter	Julie Bosteels
Art Director	Ad van Ongeval
Illustrator	Ad Van Ongeval
Client	Axe

Agency	Publicis, Frankfurt
Creative Directors	Stephan Ganser
	Nico Juenger
	Peter Kaim
Copywriter	Konstantinos Manikas
Art Director	Nico Juenger
Client	Rowenta VU 1010

Agency	TBWA\Germany,
	Berlin
Creative Directors	Stefan Schmidt
	Kurt Georg Dieckert
Copywriter	Helge Blöck
Illustrator	Felix Reidenbach
Art Director	Boris Schwiedrzik
Photographer	Joerg Reichardt
Producer	Katrin Dettmann
Client	Adidas

Two larger than life installations that greeted visitors to Germany's soccer World Cup in the summer of 2006. The world's largest football fresco covered the ceiling of Cologne's central train station; elevating stars like Beckham, Zidane and Raul into a Renaissance–style football heaven. Meanwhile, a 65-metre, Oliver Kahn panel crossed the busy four-lane highway near Munich international Airport.

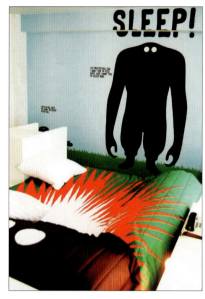

Agency	Agenda Group, Copenhagen
Creative Directors	Laust Chr. Poulsen
	Cedric Ebener
Client	Volkswagen Fox

Project Fox was the blanket term for the Copenhagen launch of the new VW Fox. During Project Fox a large group of young creative talent from all over the world developed and displayed new ideas in the fields of design, illustration, urban art, music, gastronomy, and hotel management. The event included a hotel, nightclub and studio. Hotel Fox was a traditional 61–room 3–star establishment that young graphic artists refurbished with complete freedom. Club Fox served as a nightclub and restaurant where top chef's served innovative new dishes every night. Finally, at Studio Fox, cars were transformed into works of art.

Agency	D'Adda Lorenzini Vigorelli BBDO, Milan
Creative Directors	Giuseppe Mastromatteo
	Luca Scotto di Carlo
Copywriter	Cristinia Battista
Art Director	Dario Agnello
Photographer	Armando Rebatto
Client	Mini

Agency	Jung von Matt, Zurich
Creative Directors	Michael Rottmann
	Alexander Jaggy
Copywriters	Lars Haensell
	Ole Kleinhans
Art Directors	David Hanselmann
	Hendrik Schweder
Client	Mini

Agency	Demner, Merlicek & Bergmann, Vienna	In order to reinforce the claim "Looks better, doesn't it?" used by the Mömax chain of furniture stores, special Citylight displays were developed featuring an ugly man standing naked in the shower. But passers-by did not have to endure this unpleasant sight for long: all they had to do was cover him with a Mömax shower curtain.
Creative Director	Gerda Reichl-Schebesta	
Copywriter	Alistair Thompson	
Art Director	Bernhard Grafl	
Photographer	Georg Schlosser	
Producer	Norbert Rabenseifner	
Client	Mömax Furniture Stores	

Agency	Nitro, London	To launch the Nike Air Max 360 – the ultimate air-cushioned shoe – the agency created an animated projection of running shoes and beamed it around the streets of London from a special van. The result was a pair of shoes that literally ran on air around the city.
Creative Director	Paul Shearer	
Copywriters	Olly Farrington	
	Neil Richardson	
Art Directors	Neil Richardson	
	Olly Farrington	
Illustrator	Adam Brewster	
Client	Nike Air Max 360	

This is just a duplicate.
The original hangs in a prison cell somewhere in China, Indonesia or the Middle East. Without witnesses. Without hope. Help us to stop this happening: www.amnesty-international.de

Agency	Ogilvy & Mather, Frankfurt	**Agency**	Venividi, Forst an der Weinstrasse
Creative Directors	Stephan Vogel	**Creative Directors**	Benito Babuscio
	Christian Mommertz		Steffen Hofmann
Copywriter	Stephan Vogel		Konstantinos Manikas
Art Director	Christian Mommertz		Daniela Hook
Artist	Christian Schönwälder	**Copywriters**	Benito Babuscio
Client	Amnesty International		Konstantinos Manikas
		Art Director	Steffen Hofmann
		Client	Frankfurt Roedelheim
			Volunteer Fire Department

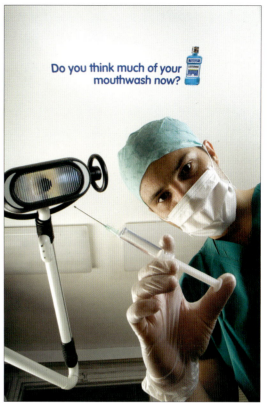

Agency	EURO RSCG, Prague
Creative Director	Dejan Stajnberger
Copywriter	Stepan Zalesak
Art Director	Michal Gabriz
Client	Listerine Mouthwash

Listerine mouthwash can prevent tooth decay. To remind people of this while they visited the dentist, messages were placed on the ceiling just above the patient's head. Maybe it will keep them out of the dreaded chair a little longer!

Agency	Ogilvy Amsterdam
Creative Director	Carl Le Blond
Copywriter	Edsard Schutte
Art Director	Jan-Willem Smits
Client	DHL

This gigantic three-dimensional billboard was installed directly in front of Schiphol Airport's main entrance. A small ball rolls from point A to point B via the shortest route. At the end of its journey, the ball is transported via an invisible conveyor belt back to the top of the billboard, where it begins the same journey again. Like a DHL parcel, it always arrives at its destination via the quickest route.

Agency	Leo Burnett, Lisbon	The agency created and placed huge packets of Friskies bird food on billboards. Strategically located in the city's main squares, the packages had a tray full of bird food on top of them (invisible to onlookers), which attracted lots of pigeons and other birds to the billboards.
Creative Director	Fernando Bellotti	
Copywriter	Miguel Brito	
Art Director	João Roque	
Producer	António Junior	
Client	Friskies Bird Food	

Agency	Saatchi & Saatchi Poland, Warsaw	This campaign for Amnesty International "censored" the front pages of Poland's biggest daily newspapers, Gazeta Wyborcza and Rzeczpospolita. Sections of articles were blacked out with markers, changing their meaning. Beneath the pages was the headline "This is what freedom of speech looks like in Belarus" and a call to action.
Creative Director	Jacek Szulecki	
Copywriter	Jakub Korolczuk	
Art Director	Ryszard Sroka	
Client	Amnesty International	

Agency	Abbott Mead Vickers BBDO, London	In 2005 Guinness revived its "Good things come to those who wait" endline. To carry this through from the commercial to the pub, a beer mat was created that seemed like a meaningless collection of curvy backwards lettering on a black background. However, once you had waited for the pint to be poured, the writing and message became clear, but only for a Guinness drinker.
Creative Director	Paul Brazier	
Copywriter	Ben Kay	
Art Director	Daryl Corps	
Client	Guinness	

Agency	Mikado-Publicis, Luxembourg
Creative Director	Didier Leclercq
Copywriter	Frédéric Thill
Art Director	Didier Leclercq
Client	Optique Moitzheim

Agency	Duval Guillaume Antwerp
Creative Directors	Geoffrey Hantson
	Dirk Domen
Copywriter	Eric Becker
Art Director	Gilles de Boncourt
Producers	Christ Lannoy
	Carole Michels
Client	Schweppes

Agency	Street Life, Madrid
Creative Director	Angel Gonzalez
Copywriter	Angel Gonzalez
Art Directors	Paco Luque
	Diego Guirao
Client	Schweppes

Every time the referee asked for "Quiet, please" during a tennis match, the first letters of the Schweppes brand (Schhhh...) appeared on the score screens of the Masters Arena Stadium in Madrid.

Agency	King, Stockholm	How should you travel between Stockholm
Creative Director	Frank Hollingworth	and Gothenburg, the two largest cities in
Copywriter	Niclas Carlsson	Sweden: fly, drive, or take the train? This
Art Directors	Alexander Elers	campaign for Sweden's SJ rail service
	Josephine Wallin	teased those who'd taken the daftest
Client	SJ Swedish Railways	option and chosen to drive – a journey

of five hours. After three hours, they see
the message: "With SJ you would have
already arrived."

Agency	Kolle Rebbe, Hamburg	Top model Eva Padberg personally
Creative Directors	Ulrich Zuenkeler	presented the new Otto mail order
	Sven Klohk	catalogue to thousands of homes across
Copywriter	Stefan Wuebbe	Germany. Whoever looked through their
Art Director	Rolf Leger	spy-hole to see who was there saw Eva
Photographer	Leif Schmodde	brandishing the catalogue. Unfortunately
Client	Otto Mail Order	for many men (and – who knows? – some

women) it was an optical illusion obtained
by nothing more curvaceous than a piece
of folded cardboard.

330 Media Innovation

Agency	BBDO, Berlin
Creative Directors	Johannes Krempl
	Patrick They
Copywriter	Patrick They
Art Director	Johannes Krempl
Photographer	Matthias Koslik
Client	Blush Dessous

Blush is a lingerie boutique in the heart of Berlin. Ugly and inconvenient fencing around a construction project made it hard to see and access the store. Turning an eyesore into an advantage, the fence became the backdrop for a series of directional posters that started 300 metres from the store. Those who followed them saw a woman strip-teasing right down to her Blush lingerie...and right up to the store's entrance!

Agency	McCann-Erickson Belgium, Hoeilaart
Creative Director	Jean-Luc Walraff
Copywriters	Marleen Galle
	Kwint De Meyer
Art Directors	Marleen Galle
	Kwint De Meyer
Client	Durex Condoms

Agency	Saatchi & Saatchi, Budapest	Agency	Grey Worldwide, Düsseldorf
Creative Director	János Debreceni	**Creative Director**	Lars Riebartsch
Copywriter	László Nagy	**Copywriter**	Marlo Horn
Art Director	Sándor Haszon	**Art Director**	Jochen Heimann
Photographer	István Lábady	**Producer**	Kerstin Novak
Client	Ariel	**Client**	Meister Proper

Agency	MindShare, Stockholm
Creative Director	Lars Bönnelyche
Client	Magnum Ice Cream
	Product Placement

Magnum wanted to associate its ice creams with luxury, pleasure, sensuality and celebrities. As well as sponsoring Top Model Scandinavia, it also managed to get the ice-creams into the editorial content of the TV programme. During a photo shoot depicted in the show, the ice creams were used as props and several models spontaneously expressed their appreciation of them.

Agency	DDB London
Creative Director	Jeremy Craigen
Copywriters	Feargal Balance
	Dylan Harrison
Art Directors	Dylan Harrison
	Feargal Ballance
Client	Philips Bikini Trimmer

To promote the new Philips Bikini Trimmer, trimmed bushes were placed in venues visited by body-conscious women - gyms, health clubs and swimming pools.

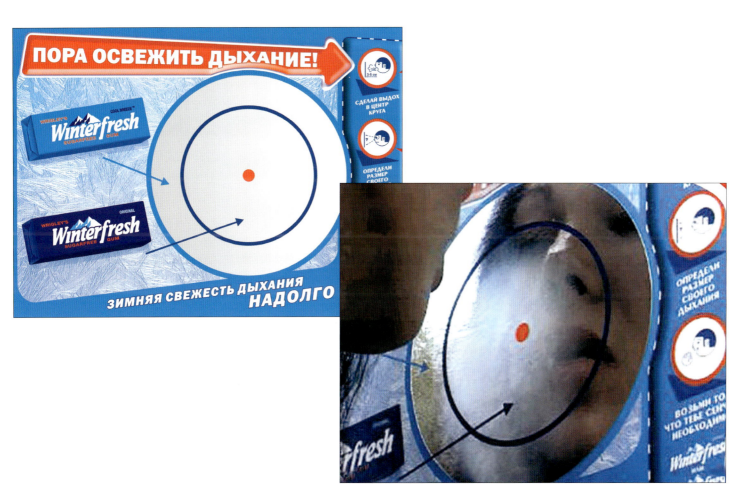

Agency	Ogilvy & Mather, Copenhagen	
Copywriter	Tobias Aggergaard	
Art Director	Bo Bernichow	
Client	Copenhagen Jazz Festival	

Agency	Kryn/Starcom, Minsk
Creative Director	Alexander Shevelevich
Copywriter	Alexander Shevelevich
Art Director	Yulia Holovina
Illustrator	Vladimir Pirogoff
Client	Winterfresh Chewing Gum

"Measure your breath": this interactive device invited consumers to breath onto a metallic disc to determine which variety of Winterfresh gum was right for them.

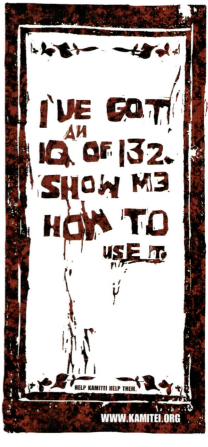

Agency	BBDO, Stuttgart
Creative Directors	Armin Jochum
	Andreas Rell
Copywriters	Andreas Rell
	Achim Szymanski
	Ono Mothwurf
Art Director	Armin Jochum
Photographer	Aernout Overbeeke
Illustrators	Marcus Widmann
	Julia Stackmann
Client	Kamitei Foundation

Advertising Photography 335

Agency	Gossip, Paris
Creative Director	Frédéric Temin
Copywriter	Frédéric Temin
Art Director	Nicolas Chauvin
Photographer	Terry Richardson
Client	Diesel

336 **Advertising Photography**

Agency	Publicis Et Nous, Paris		**Agency**	Euro RSCG, London
Creative Director	Philippe Chanet		**Creative Director**	Gerry Moira
Photographer	Camilla Akrans		**Copywriters**	George Leaney
Client	Hermes			Ben Parton
			Art Directors	George Leaney
				Ben Parton
			Photographer	David LaChapelle
			Client	Evian

Agency	Armando Testa, Milan
Creative Director	German Silva
Art Directors	Andrea Lantelme
	Haitz Mendibil
	Riccardo Pagani
Photographer	Erwin Olaf
Client	Lavazza Coffee

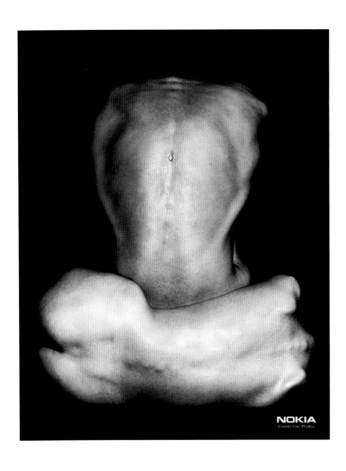

Advertising Photography

Agency	Alabama Art Buying & Production, Warsaw		**Agency**	Saatchi & Saatchi, Amsterdam
Creative Director	Adam Wlazly		**Copywriter**	Menno Schipper
Art Director	Adam Wlazly		**Art Director**	Nils Taildeman
Photographer	Adam Wlazly		**Photographer**	Edo Kars
Client	Nokia		**Client**	Mercedes-Benz E-Class

We invented quattro for more driving pleasure.
Now we've invented a car for more quattro® – the Audi Q7.

Coming soon.

Sticks in your mind.
The new Audi A6 allroad quattro.

Agency	Kempertrautmann, Hamburg		**Agency**	Kempertrautmann, Hamburg
Copywriter	Lennart Witting		**Creative Directors**	Gerrit Zinke
Art Director	Florian Kitzing			Jens Theil
Photographer	Anatol Kotte		**Copywriter**	Jens Theil
Client	Audi Q7			Filiz Tasdan
			Art Directors	Gerrit Zinke
				Tim Belser
			Photographer	Uwe Düttmann
			Client	Audi A6 Allroad Quattro

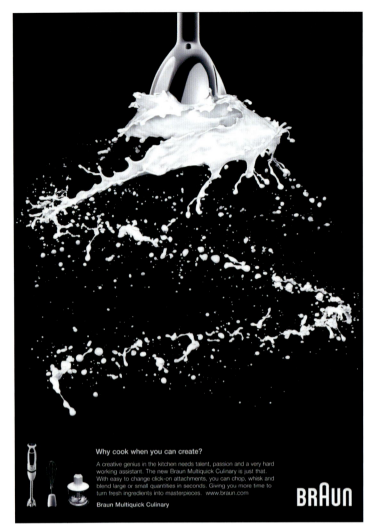

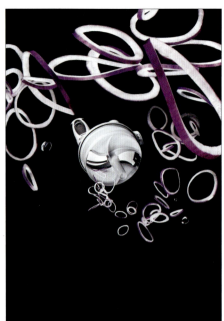

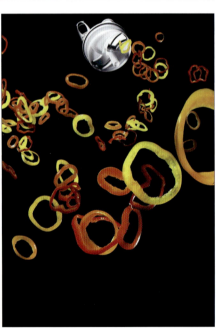

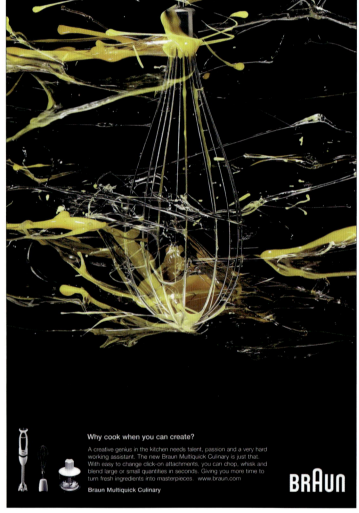

Why cook when you can create?

A creative genius in the kitchen needs talent, passion and a very hard working assistant. The new Braun Multiquick Culinary is just that. With easy to change click-on attachments, you can chop, whisk and blend large or small quantities in seconds. Giving you more time to turn fresh ingredients into masterpieces. www.braun.com

Braun Multiquick Culinary

BRAUN

Agency	BBDO, Düsseldorf
Creative Directors	Stefan Vonderstein
	Ralf Zilligen
	Todd Tilford
Copywriters	Hans-Holger Pollack
	Fiona Grace
Art Directors	Sharon Jessen
	Concetta Milione
	Ton Hollander
	Nicole Hoefer
Photographers	Martin Klimas
	Andrew Zuckerman
Client	Braun Multiquick Culinary

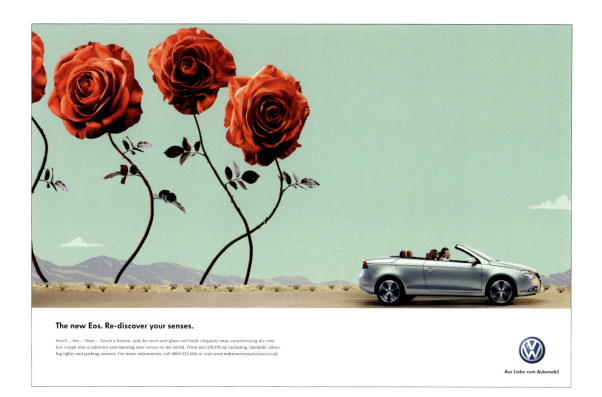

The new Eos. Re-discover your senses.

Smell... See... Hear... Touch a button, and the steel-and-glass roof folds elegantly away, transforming the new
Eos coupé into a cabriolet and opening your senses to the world. From just £19,370 rrp including 'Adelaide' alloys,
fog lights and parking sensors. For more information, call 0800 333 666 or visit www.rediscoveryoursenses.co.uk

Aus Liebe zum Automobil

Breaking up with the Joneses
The painful collapse of a marriage told from both sides
Thursday 9pm

Agency	DDB London	Agency	4Creative, London
Creative Director	Jeremy Craigen	Creative Director	Richard Burdett
Copywriter	Simon Veksner	Photographer	Peter Dazeley
Art Director	Nick Allsop	Client	Chanel 4
Photographer	Nadav Kander		
Client	VW Eos		

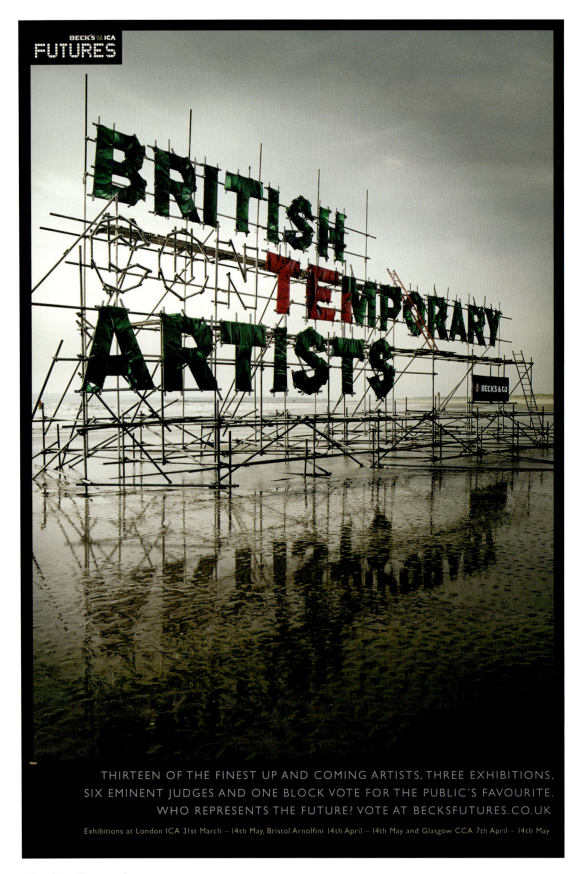

342   **Advertising Photography**

Agency	Leo Burnett, London
Creative Director	Jim Thornton
Copywriter	Tony Malcolm
Art Director	Guy Moore
Photographer	David Hiscock
Client	Beck's Beer

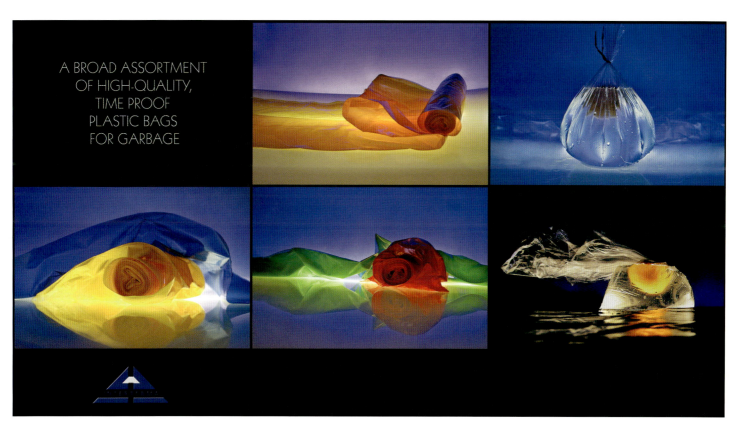

A BROAD ASSORTMENT
OF HIGH-QUALITY,
TIME PROOF
PLASTIC BAGS
FOR GARBAGE

Agency	Bob Helsinki		**Agency**	Vetre Studio, Vilnius
Copywriter	Iina Merikallio		**Creative Director**	Vetre Antanaviciute
Art Director	Zoubida Benkhellat		**Photographer**	Vetre Antanaviciute
Photographer	Blaise Reuterswärd		**Client**	Interma Plastic Bags
Client	Helmi			

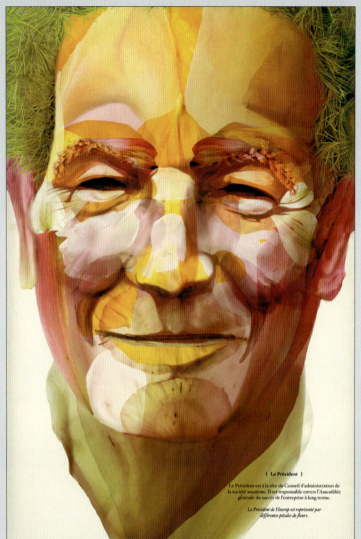

{ Le Président }

Le Président est à la tête du Conseil d'administration de la société anonyme. Il est responsable envers l'Assemblée générale du succès de l'entreprise à long terme.

Le Président de Fleurop est représenté par différentes pétales de fleurs.

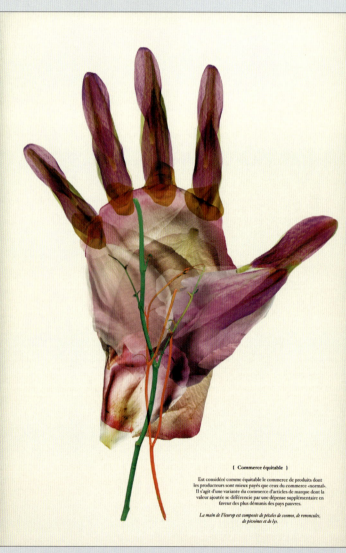

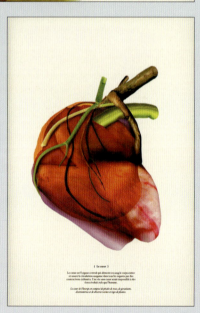

{ Le cœur }

Le cœur est l'organe central qui alimente en sang le corps entier et assure la circulation sanguine dans tous les organes par des contractions rythmées. Une vie sans cœur serait impossible à des êtres évolués tels que l'homme.

Le cœur de Fleurop est composé de pétales de rose, de géranium, d'alstroemeria et de diverses racines et tiges de plante.

{ Commerce équitable }

Est considéré comme équitable le commerce de produits dont les producteurs sont mieux payés que ceux du commerce «normal». Il s'agit d'une variante du commerce d'articles de marque dont la valeur ajoutée se différencie par une dépense supplémentaire en faveur des plus démunis des pays pauvres.

La main de Fleurop est composée de pétales de cosmos, de renoncules, de pivoines et de lys.

---

344   **Illustration & Graphics**

Agency	Walker, Zurich	All the images and graphs in the Fleurop-Interflora annual report are made up exclusively from flowers, buds, stems, roots and petals.
Creative Director	Pius Walker	
Copywriter	Sabine Manecke	
Art Director	Mieke Haase	
Illustrator	Martin Müller	
Client	Fleurop-Interflora	

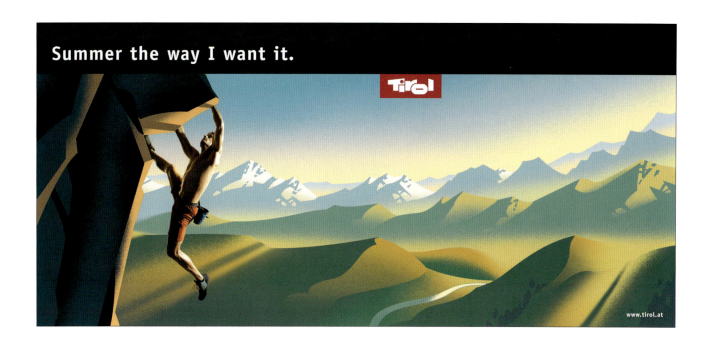

Agency	Demner, Merlicek &Bergmann, Vienna	Agency	Publicis, Zurich
Creative Director	Gerda Reichl-Schebesta	Creative Directors	Ralf Kostgeld
			Markus Gut
Copywriter	Alistair Thompson	Copywriters	Johannes Jost
Art Director	Bernhard Grafl	Art Director	Ralf Kostgeld
Illustrator	Michael Pleesz	Illustrator	Markus Wyss
Graphic Design	Roman Steiner	Client	Optimedia
Client	Tirol Tourism		

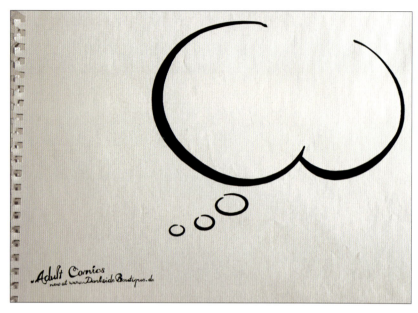

346 **Illustration & Graphics**

Agency	Grand Annonsbyrå, Stockholm		Agency	Scholz & Friends, Hamburg
Creative Director	Mikael Friberg		Creative Directors	Marcus Korell
Copywriter	Alex Molin			Gerrit Kleinfeld
Art Director	Jörgen Lindqvist		Copywriters	Dirk Silz
Illustrator	Jörgen Lindqvist			Bastian Otter
Client	Kaishinkan Aikido School		Illustrator	Marcus Korell
			Client	Darkside Boutique

| MARCH | 01 | 02 | 03 | 04 | 05 | 06 | 07 | 08 | 09 | 10 | 11 | 12 | 13 | 14 | 15 | 16 | 17 | 18 | 19 | 20 | 21 | 22 | 23 | 24 | 25 | 26 | 27 | 28 | 29 | 30 | 31 |
| APRIL | 01 | 02 | 03 | 04 | 05 | 06 | 07 | 08 | 09 | 10 | 11 | 12 | 13 | 14 | 15 | 16 | 17 | 18 | 19 | 20 | 21 | 22 | 23 | 24 | 25 | 26 | 27 | 28 | 29 | 30 | |

MAE AMSER MWG AIL-LAW AR BEN
TIME'S UP FOR SECOND-HAND SMOKE

Agency	KNSK Werbeagentur, Hamburg		**Agency**	Golley Slater, Cardiff
Creative Directors	Tim Krink		**Creative Director**	David Abbott
	Niels Holle		**Copywriters**	Phil Hickes
Copywriter	Berend Brüdgam			Martin Bush
Art Director	Oliver Fermer		**Client**	COI – Welsh Smoking Ban
Client	Jeep			

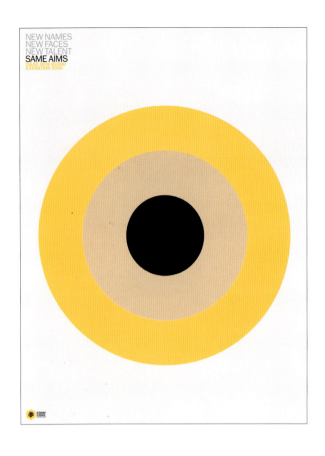

Agency	Love, Manchester		Agency	Scholz & Friends, Hamburg
Creative Director	Phil Skegg		Creative Directors	Marcus Korell
Copywriters	Phil Skegg			André Klein
	Simon Griffin		Art Director	Carolin Rathgeber
Art Director	Phil Skegg		Illustration	Insect, London
Illustrator	Phil Skegg		Graphic Design	Mareike Ledeboer
Client	D&AD New Blood Exhibition		Client	Hänsel & Gretel Foundation

Agency	BeetRoot, Thessaloniki	Agency	Lunar Communications, London
Creative Director	Alexis Nikou	**Creative Directors**	Daryl Corps
Art Directors	Vagelis Liakos		Ben Kay
	Yiannis Haralambopoulos	**Copywriter**	Ben Kay
Client	Republic 100.3	**Art Director**	Daryl Corps
		Client	Marmalade Magazine

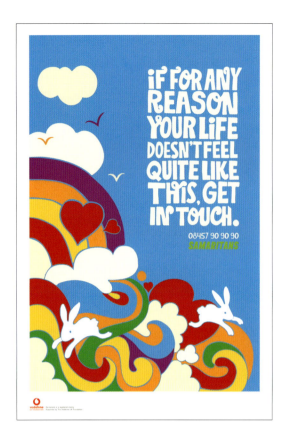

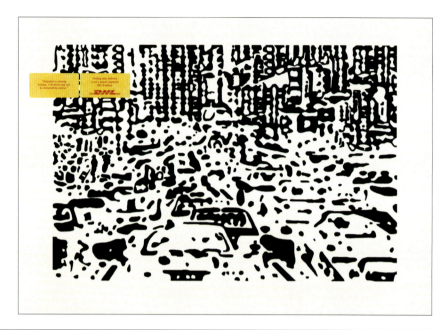

Agency	Lunar Communications, London		**Agency**	Ogilvy & Mather, Frankfurt
Creative Directors	Daryl Corps		**Creative Directors**	Helmut Himmler
	Ben Kay			Lars Huvart
Copywriter	Ben Kay		**Copywriters**	Joerg Schrod
Art Director	Daryl Corps			Jens Frank
Client	Samaritans		**Art Directors**	Jens Frank
				Joerg Schrod
			Graphic Design	Jens Frank
			Client	DHL Track & Trace

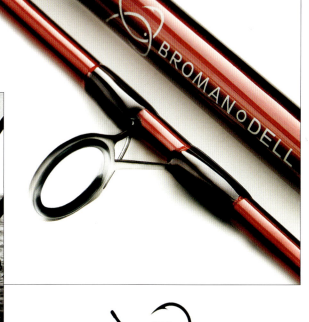

BROMAN○DELL

TACKLE DESIGN

Agency	Redmanwalking, Stockholm	Agency	Ligalux, Hamburg
Creative Director	Fredrik Lewander	**Creative Director**	Claudia Fischer-Appelt
Art Director	Fredrik Lewander	**Copywriter**	Marina Klepka
Illustrator	Fredrik Lewander	**Art Directors**	Thomas Kappes
Client	Broman & Dell Fishing Tackle		Hana Sedelmayer
			Arne Schmidt
		Illustrator	Thomas Kappes
		Client	Mamamoto

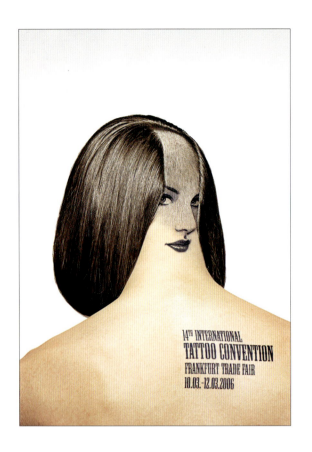

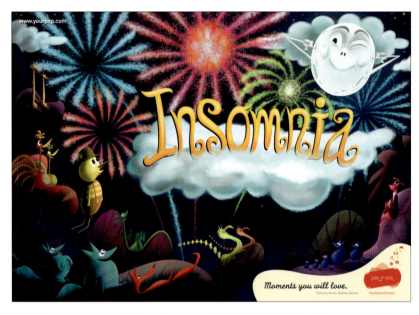

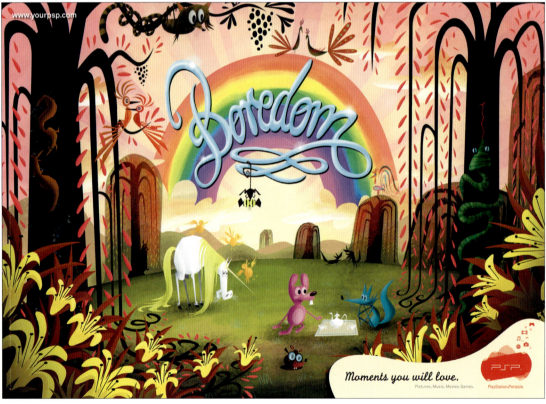

352   **Illustration & Graphics**

Agency	Saatchi & Saatchi, Frankfurt	Agency	TBWA\Germany, Berlin
Creative Director	Burkhart von Scheven	**Copywriter**	Dirk Henkelmann
Copywriter	Michael Causemann	**Art Director**	Philip Borchardt
Art Director	André Sendel	**Illustrator**	Dan Krall
Client	Frankfurt Tattoo Convention	**Design**	Arnaud Loix Van Hooff
		Client	PlayStation Portable

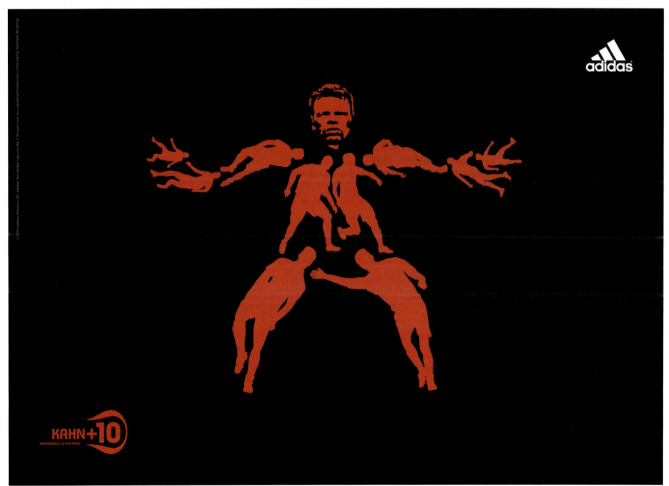

Agency	TBWA\Germany, Berlin
Creative Directors	Stefan Schmidt
	Kurt Georg Dieckert
Copywriter	Helge Blöck
Art Director	Boris Schwiedrzik
Illustrator	Jutta Kuss
Client	Adidas

STUDIO PIN-UPS

2005

354   Publications

Agency	Lida, London	How do you reach lots of agency creatives
Creative Director	David Harris	when you've got a tiny budget? Put your
Copywriter	Peter West	message on something they stare at all
Art Director	David Harris	day long: the wall. This makeover of the
Typographers	David Harris	traditional 'studio pin-up' calendar not only
	Justin Shill	demonstrated Taylor Lane's expertise in
	Stuart Addy	typography, it also acted as a perpetual
	Jan Hansen	reminder throughout the year while
Client	Taylor Lane Typographic	refreshing itself every month.
	& Artwork Studio	

Agency	SCP, Gothenburg
Creative Director	Jan Frankfeldt
Photographer	Håkan Ludwigson
Client	Volvo Cars

The purpose of this book, "Photographs from an Open Car", was to share the feeling of driving a convertible with the top down. You become closer to the people and experience both cities and the countryside more fully. The camera was connected to a GPS, so all pictures in the book come with a longitude and latitude, which gives owners of the book a chance to follow the route. Just log in to Google Earth and type in the coordinates and you will see where in the world the photo was taken.

Agency	Dolhem Design, Stockholm
Creative Director	Christophe Dolhem
Copywriters	Sara Helmersson
	Christophe Dolhem
Art Director	Jan Vana
Client	Dolhem Design
	Logo Book

The agency wanted to publish a selection of the logotypes and symbols it has created over a period of nine years, treating them as small works of art. "It is with pride that we see [our logos] adorning façades in Stockholm; or in the case of Save the Children, as a symbol of something positive for children the world over."

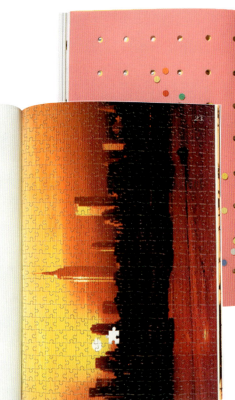

Agency	Garbergs Reklambyrå, Stockholm
Copywriter	Stefan Pagréus
Art Directors	Malin von Werder
	Karin Ahlgren
Photographer	Magnus Magnusson
Client	Södra Cell

Södra has a mission: to spread the gospel of paper in the name of love, joy and goodness. Paper is a symbol of knowledge, communication and culture. But despite its makers' best intentions, paper sometimes causes anger, sadness and suffering. This book brings 25 flagrantly shocking examples to public attention. Every piece of paper may become a milestone in human history: a peace treaty or a life-affirming poem. A blank page has the power to change the world.

Agency	Futura DDB, Ljubljana
Creative Directors	Žare Kerin
	Marko Vičič
Copywriter	Almira Sadar
Art Director	Mateja Podmenik
Photographer	Saša Hes
Client	Almira Sadar

		This calendar depicts Meissen porcelain figurines in a surprisingly modern way, making them look as attractive as pin-up girls.
Agency	Scholz & Friends, Berlin	
Creative Directors	Martin Pross	
	Raphael Puettmann	
	Mario Gamper	
Copywriter	Stephan Deisenhofer	
Art Director	Anje Jager	
Photographer	Attila Hartwig	
Client	Meissen Porcelain	

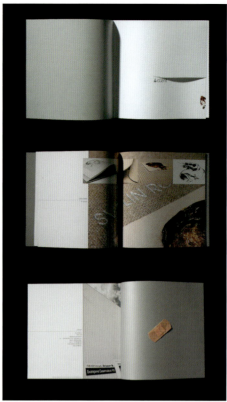

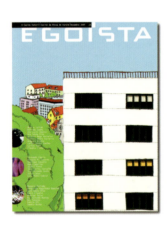

Agency	Noble Graphics Creative Studio, Sofia	Accent is a high quality print-house specialising in sharp, realistic print production. The catalogue with sharp razors on the cover was placed in hand-cut envelope. The idea of the sharp print is further exploited within the catalogue.
Client	Accent Printing House	

Agency	Atelier 004, Lisbon	Egoista Magazine contains regular contributions from leading Portuguese and international photographers, journalists, artists and novelists. Clara Ferreira Alves made her fiction debut here. Other contributors have included the writers Nick Hornby and Frank Ronan and photographers Sebastião Salgado and Annie Leibovitz. A special edition dedicated to a Portugal's future included contributions by the Prime Minister, three of his predecessors and two former presidents.
Creative Director	Patrícia Reis	
Art Directors	Henrique Cayatte Filipa Gregório Hugo Neves Rita Salgueiro Rodrigo Saias	
Producers	Francisco Ponciano Cláudio Garrudo	
Client	Egoista Magazine	

Agency	Silver, Stockholm	Kreativa Byråer 0506 (Creative Agencies
Creative Directors	Eva Aggerborg	0506) is an annual compilation of Sweden's
	Ulf Berlin	leading creative agencies. The cover, intro
	André Hindersson	pages and editorial section are traditionally
Art Director	Eva Aggerborg	designed by one of Sweden's leading
Illustrator	Eva Aggerborg	graphic designers. The goal was to create
Client	Kreativa Byråer 0506	a design that catches the eye in design

bookstores and will become a coffee
table book for the primary target group:
marketing managers at Sweden's 100
biggest companies.

Agency	Serviceplan, Munich	Charity calendars are all very well, but
Creative Directors	Winfried Bergmann	picturesque photos won't stop the hunger.
	Christoph Everke	To reinforce this point, The Munich Table
Copywriter	Tim Strathus	(Münchner Tafel) – which has started a new
Art Director	Matthias Mittermüller	campaign to feed many of the 160,000
Photographer	Heinz Gebhardt	needy people in the city – printed its entire
Graphic Design	Andrea Gärtner	calendar on edible paper.
Client	Münchner Tafel	

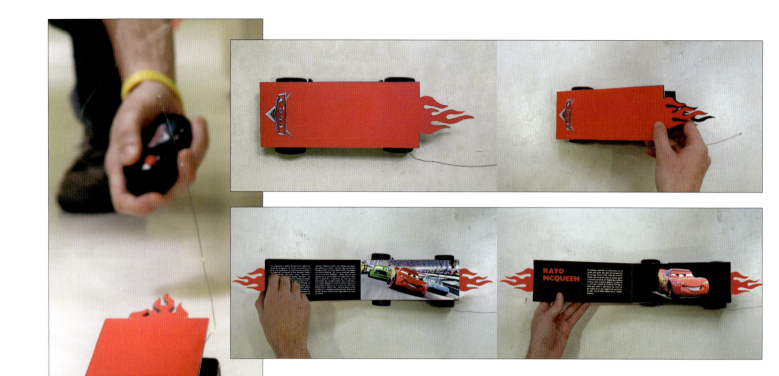

Agency	Zapping, Madrid
Creative Directors	Uschi Henkes
	Manolo Moreno
	Urs Frick
Copywriter	Manolo Moreno
Art Directors	Uschi Henkes
	Jenny Nerman
Client	Buena-Vista,
	"Cars" Press Book

"Cars" is an animated movie with cars as the protagonists. For the worldwide launch of the film the press book was mounted on a remote controlled car that journalists could play with like characters in the movie.

Agency	Zapping, Madrid
Creative Directors	Uschi Henkes
	Manolo Moreno
	Urs Frick
Copywriter	Manolo Moreno
Art Directors	Uschi Henkes
	Jenny Nerman
Client	Buena-Vista,
	"The Guardian"
	Press Book

Disney Buena-Vista's movie "The Guardian" tells the story of a special group of coast guards who put their lives on the line to save others under extreme conditions; storms, floods and tidal waves. Miniature figurines are glued to the cover of the press book which contains all the information on this movie premiere.

Agency	Section.d, Vienna
Creative Director	Chris Goennawein
Art Director	Chris Goennawein
Client	Parabol AM Art Magazine

Agency	Scholz & Friends, Hamburg
Creative Directors	Matthias Schmidt Suze Barrett Tobias Holland
Copywriter	Dennis Lueck
Art Director	Marcin Baba
Client	Schalke 04 Football Club

This calendar was a gift mailing to members of the Schalke 04 supporters club. Each day of the month represents another goal scored against rival club Dortmund.

SCEPTICAL

Never taking anything for granted
is without doubt a valuable attitude
to have in your professional life.
But being too sceptical might
make you less curious to find new
ways of doing things. The perfect
combination of curiosity and
scepticism is often worth striving
for in many situations in life.

Agency	K2design, Athens	Nostalgic artwork and print methods
Creative Director	Yiannis Kouroudis	were combined with stitches rather than
Art Director	Yiannis Kouroudis	the usual metal binding. The design
Client	Kontorousis	incorporates a leaf to reflect the client's
	Printing House	slogan: everything is on the leaf (the
		Greek for "paper" also means "leaf").

Agency	Ehrenstråhle BBDO,	Every month in this 2007 agenda
	Stockholm	features a different "Natural Expression"
Copywriter	Pär Pärsson	by UK photographer Paul Thompson.
Art Director	Lotta Hjalmarson	Each portrait is printed using a different
Photographer	Paul Thompson	technique to enhance the expression in
Client	Munken Paper	question; angry, happy, sceptical, worried,
		hesitant etc. Fragrances are also used to
		stimulate the senses and several qualities
		of Munken paper are used in the book.

Agency	Love, Manchester	This book is about Umbro control technologies. The brief was to take the information and make it simple, transforming science into sense. There are four control technologies: motion control, climate control, impact control and touch control. The book is based on a conversation between the 'control freak' and someone who knows nothing.
Creative Director	Dave Palmer	
Copywriter	Simon Griffin	
Illustrator	Paul Davis	
Design	Adam Rix	
Client	Umbro	

Agency	McCann Erickson, Athens	The Looking Busy Calendar is an oversized coffee table book about truth. It contains 52 pages illustrating creative ways of how to look busy at work.
Creative Director	Anna Stilianaki	
Copywriters	Katerina Bekirou	
	Ioanna Deimezi	
	Maria Alexiou	
	Dimitris Doussis	
Art Directors	Popi Dimakou	
	Sonia Haritidi	
	Nikos Perialis	
	Tina Marouli	
	Flora Petraki	
	Noelle Zografou	
Client	McCann Erickson, Athens	

Agency	Depot WPF Brand & Identity, Moscow	The round stickers on these paint cans describe the type of paint they contain,
Creative Director	Alexey Fadeyev	but there is no brand name – only the
Art Director	Alexey Fadeyev	distinctive star ("zvezda" in Russian).
Client	Zvezda Paint	

neova Pellets
8 MM / 16 KG / 80 KWH

Kvicksilvret kryper nedåt. Ett av höstens sista regn smattrar mot rutan. Efter en arbetsdag är det skönt att sjunka ner i soffan med Irving och Earl Grey.

– Det har varit en härlig dag.

8

neova Pellets
8 MM / 16 KG / 80 KWH

Höststormen sliter i äppelträden. De nykrattade löven yr runt i trädgården. En dubbel espresso och en bit criollo vid köksbordet. Hoppet om pulkarace med Albin väcks.

– En härlig tid.

8

neova Pellets
8 MM / 16 KG / 80 KWH

Första dagen med Moa på ryggen. Skärgårdsisen låg blank och solen gnistrade. Varm choklad i en vik. Skönt att få låta milen rinna ur i ett varmt bad.

– En fantastisk dag.

8

neova Pellets
8 MM / 16 KG / 80 KWH

Mörkret sänker sig runt huset. Och rimfrosten kryper upp i fönstret. Tur att jag la på vinterdäcken i helgen. Nu kan vi njuta av en sen middag på tu man hand.

– Vilken skön kväll.

6

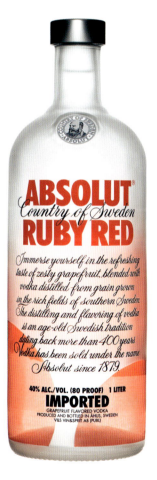

Agency	Clara, Karlstad	Sample text: The autumn storm shakes the apple trees. Recently raked leaves fly around the garden. A double espresso and some criollo at the kitchen table. A sledge race with Albin, now that will be fun. A great time.
Copywriter	Rolf Harju	
Art Director	Erik Nilsson	
Client	Neova House Pellets (Bio Fuel)	

Agency	Blidholm Vagnemark Design, Stockholm	Absolut Ruby Red contains blood grapefruit juice. The challenge was to integrate the bottle into the Absolut Vodka range in a distinctive way while maintaining the traditional brand values.
Creative Director	Catrin Vagnemark	
Art Director	Rikard Ahlberg	
Client	Absolut Ruby Red Vodka	

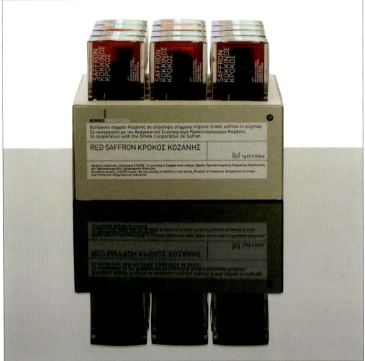

Agency	K2design, Athens	The saffron is packed in plexi-glass cases
Creative Director	Yiannis Kouroudis	with paper sheath safety closures that are
Art Director	Dimitra Diamanti	posed on a carton stand with white hot foil
Photographer	Tasia Voutyropoulou	stamping.
Designer	Helen Prablanc	
Client	Korres Saffron	

Agency	Turner Duckworth, London	Root One tells the story of the original
Creative Directors	David Turner	engrafted Cabernet Sauvignon rootstock,
	Bruce Duckworth	extinct in Europe and now only found in
Copywriter	David Turner	Chile. The rich history of this woodstock is
Art Director	Shawn Rosenberger	visually linked to the final glass of wine, an
Illustrator	Shawn Rosenberger	image of which is hidden in the vine. As
Client	Root: 1	you read the story the root leads you down
	Cabernet Sauvignon	to where it all begins, beneath the soil. A

gardener's tab creates a unique neck label and emphasises the horticultural theme.

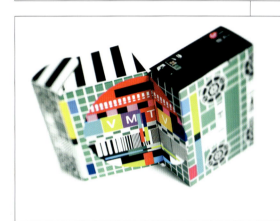

Agency	Start Creative, London	The pack design for Virgin Mobile's first TV phone borrows from iconic graphic
Creative Directors	Darren Whittingham	elements connected to Television, such
	Mike Curtis	as the test card. This pack is a bespoke
	James Sterling	box, but in order for it to work as part of a
Art Director	Chris Bennett	series, a black sleeve has the Lobster logo
Illustrator	Scrawl Collective	and phone name die-cut on opposite sides.
Client	Virgin Mobile	The sleeve can then be carried across any
	Lobster 700TV Phone	future boxes that bear the Lobster name.

The sleeve also adds an element of intrigue as only a section on the test card design is visible. Taking the sleeve off is like turning the Television on.

Agency	Amore Systems, Stockholm	The package design of EasyLooks is meant to encourage young women
Creative Director	Jörgen Olofsson	to try new makeup looks as willingly
Art Director	Karin Larsson	as they try different fashion looks.
Photographer	Henrik Bonnevier	The premiering lineup consists of five
Designer	Anna Johansson	different looks, tailored for the Fall and
Client	EasyLooks	Winter season 2006/07. New looks are

scheduled to launch three times a year.

Agency	Sek & Grey, Helsinki	To celebrate the 100th anniversary of Valio milk six famous Finnish artists were selected to interpret the Valio cow. With sales of over 30 million cartons per month this represented the most popular art exhibition in the country.
Creative Director	Jari Peltonen	
Copywriter	Julia Vuori	
Art Directors	Jari Peltonen	
	Juha Murremäki	
Illustrators	Outi Heiskanen	
	Mauri Kunnas	
	Rosa Liksom	
	Kaj Stenvall	
	Juba Tuomola	
	Julia Vuori	
Graphic Designer	Kari Sandell	
Client	Valio Milk	

Agency	Turner Duckworth, London	Bootleg celebrates the creativity and style of a new generation of Italian winemakers by offering a collection of daring interpretations of classic Italian wines. Many Italian wine labels follow the usual formula of a hard to pronounce name and an illustration of the winery. The agency wanted to give a new twist to the tired cliché of the shape of Italy as a boot. The result is a sexy expression of contemporary Italian style that appears to wrap the bottle in skin-tight zippered leather.
Creative Directors	David Turner	
	Bruce Duckworth	
Art Director	Shawn Rosenberger	
Illustrator	Jonathan Warner	
Client	Bootleg Wines	

Agency	BeetRoot, Thessaloniki	Red Water products contain thermal spring water, herbs, fruits and olive oil. The front of the packaging is all white with the name of the product incorporated into a bubble that is part of the logo and coloured according to the ingredients. Finally, an uncoated paper is used to give a natural feeling when holding the product.
Creative Director	Yiannis Haralambopoulos	
Art Directors	Vagelis Liakos	
	Alexis Nikou	
Photographers	Vagelis Liakos	
	Yiannis Haralambopoulos	
Client	Red Water Dermocosmetics	

Agency	Turner Duckworth, London	Waitrose canned vegetable and pulses are store cupboard staples for most consumers. The range had not been looked at in its entirety for a number of years resulting in a fixture that had become confused and difficult to shop. The solution focused on using the vegetables and pulses to create graphic panels of the products shot against complementary backgrounds that would allow the consumer to not only stock up on their favourites but also find new ingredients. Typographic style was kept as simple as possible to further aid communication.
Creative Directors	David Turner	
	Bruce Duckworth	
Art Director	Sarah Moffat	
Photographer	Andy Grimshaw	
Client	Waitrose Canned Vegetables & Pulses	

Agency	Lewis Moberly, London	Akvinta Vodka was developed by Adriatic Distillers and launched in August 2006. The name Akvinta is derived from Aqua (water), Vino (wine) and Quinta (five). A unique five filtration process purifies the vodka through marble, silver, gold, platinum and charcoal. Vibrant use of colour illuminates the heavy base and crowns the capsule. The 'v' of Akvinta is inspired by the alchemy symbol for spirit. Highlighted in gold, the logo forms the centre piece of a dimensional gilded seal.
Creative Director	Mary Lewis	
Designers	Joanne Smith Paul Cilia La Corte	
Client	Akvinta Vodka	

Agency	Publicis, Frankfurt	This shopping bag was given away to customers when purchasing fitness accessories or nutritional supplements at the fitness centre.
Creative Director	Gert Maehnicke	
Copywriter	Merlin Kwan	
Art Directors	Mia Caroline Stirm Anika Malz Merlin Kwan	
Photographer	Peter Duettmann	
Client	Fitness Company	

Agency	Pemberton & Whitefoord, London	**Agency**	Turner Duckworth, London	Packaging for the Liz Earle Christmas gift range took inspiration from the winter landscape and the feeling of excitement and anticipation of the forthcoming Christmas season; simply open the the lid to reveal silhouetted trees against a snowy horizon. Happy Holidays!
Creative Directors	Simon Pemberton Adrian Whitefoord	**Creative Directors**	David Turner Bruce Duckworth	
Designer	Lee Newham	**Art Director**	Jamie McCathie	
Client	Tesco Flavoured Milk	**Client**	Liz Earle Cosmetics	

372   Websites (Durables)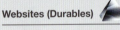

Agency	Euro RSCG 4D, Amstelveen	Sponsoring Disney's Pirates of the Caribbean: Dead Man's Chest, Volvo organizes a global treasure hunt. A Volvo XC90 was buried: find it and it's yours. Having picked up a treasure map at your dealership, The Hunt continues online. Hopping from website to website, a 30-day journey across the Seven Seas unfolds. Unravel an old man's tale on Madeira, match broken china off Africa's coast, decipher Maya murals on Cozumel and be the first to return to Port Royal harbour. Seven finalists were flown to an island in the Bahamas for the final event: the recovery of the buried car.
Creative Director	Sicco Beerda	
Copywriter	Bram de Rooij	
Art Director	Martijn Sengers	
Designers	Antonio Costa	
	Feike Kloostra	
	Edwin Nikkels	
	Jurgen Nedebock	
Production	Framfab, Copenhagen	
Client	Volvo XC90, "The Hunt"	

Agency	Forsman & Bodenfors, Gothenburg	Plan your dream kitchen and organise it the way you want, aided by a couple of virtual hosts.
Creative Director	Mathias Appelblad	
Director	Fredrik Kallinggård	
Copywriters	Fredrik Jansson	
	Anders Hegerfors	
Art Directors	Andreas Malm	
	Anders Eklind	
	Karin Frisell	
	John Bergdahl	
Designers	Mikko Timonen	
	Nina Andersson	
	Jerry Wass	
	Viktor Larsson	
Production	Sammarco	
	Kokokaka	
Producers	Eva Råberg	
	Martin Sandberg	
	Åsa Jansson	
	Magnus Kennhed	
Client	Ikea Sweden, "Dream Kitchens"	

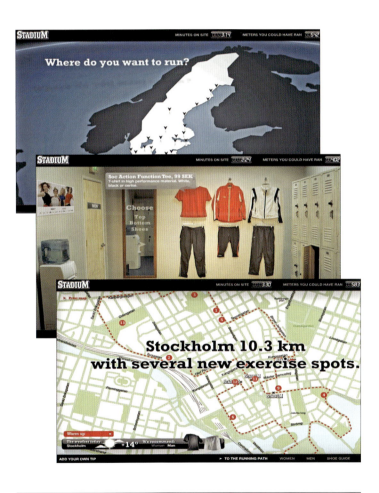

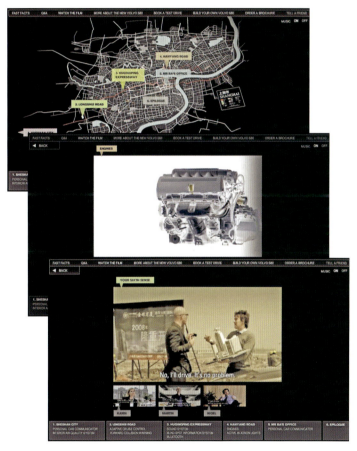

Agency	Forsman & Bodenfors, Gothenburg	Stadium is one of Sweden's leading sports retail chains. The agency prepared a communication platform called The City Is Your Stadium. As part of the campaign a unique running track was designed for 33 different Swedish cities, with details provided on the campaign site (thecityisyourstadium.com) and supported with signposts in real life. Maps for the 33 tracks were featured alongside tips on suitable clothing for the day's local weather conditions. (See also page 95).
Creative Director	Mathias Appelblad	
Copywriters	Rebecka Osvald	
	Jörgen Gjaerum	
Art Directors	Andreas Malm	
	Pål Jespersen	
	Pål Eneroth	
Designers	Jerry Wass	
	Mikko Timonen	
Production	B-Reel	
Producer	Martin Sandberg	
Client	Stadium Sports Stores	

Agency	Forsman & Bodenfors, Gothenburg	So what happened in Shanghai? The site supports a TV ad documenting the adventures of three architects on their way to a business meeting they absolutely can't miss. On their journey they have the opportunity to benefit from all the technological innovations built into the car like bluetooth, the forward collision warning and blind spot information systems. On the web site we get to hear their personal views about what happened, why it did, and what role the new Volvo S80 played.
Creative Director	Mathias Appelblad	
Copywriter	Jacob Nelson	
Art Director	Johan Eghammer	
Designers	Lars Jansson	
	Mikko Timonen	
	Jerry Wass	
Production	Acne	
	Kokokaka	
Producer	Charlotte Most	
Client	Volvo S80, "A Sixth Sense"	

Agency	Plan.Net Concept, Munich	Want to know how the new Mini was really created? The revolutionary new developments for the Mini Revision 56 came from the top secret Mini Lab. Here Mini scientists and engineers just follow their inspiration, however far out it might be: rocket power for the engine, chemical fusion for the lights system and an incredibly sophisticated machine to create the interior…discover them all here. The website was made to introduce the new Mini to BMW employees.
Creative Director	Danusch Mahmoudi	
Copywriter	Mick Schneider	
Art Director	Felix Wolf	
Designer	Paul Schlichter	
Client	Mini, "The Secret Mini Laboratory"	

Agency	Foreign, Stockholm	TV commercials featuring two kids named José and Pedro broke down the barrier between reality and fantasy as they selected players for a "fantasy" backyard match – with the real stars showing up to participate in the game. The site elaborated on the idea by allowing football enthusiasts to enter the world of José and Pedro and wander around their magical neighbourhood. (See also page 211)
Creative Director	Johan Ronnestam	
Copywriter	Jeff Salomonson	
Art Director	Jonas Theder	
Photographer	Mattias Nygren	
Designers	Nicola Smanio	
	Joel Vikström	
Project Manager	Sofia Ojde	
Producer	Annika Tersmeden	
Flash Designers	Oskar Sundberg	
	Per Forsberg	
	Johan Öberg	
Client	Adidas, "+10 Impossible Team"	

374 Websites (Durables)

Agency	Argonauten G2, Düsseldorf	For a relaunch of the Sprite brand, the aim was to create an authentic link between the soft drinks Sprite and Sprite Zero and the urban lifestyle, via basketball. This was partially achieved through a TV spot. The site continued the theme with a virtual city and four street artists who provided personal insights into street trends. In the Sprite Street Battle, members of the young target group submitted their own personal street skills for judgment by the audience.
Executive CD	Sven Kuester	
Creative Director	Monika Ebert	
Art Director	Frank Müller	
Client	Sprite/Sprite Zero	

Agency	Euro RSCG 4D, Amstelveen	The online Volvo C70 guidebook is a journey in itself. Each virtual page offers a new surprise and an entertaining way to discover the car. The pages misbehave; the content breaks the boundaries of the physical book. Watch extracts from the TV ad; meet animated crash test dummies; read the floating poetry…experience a brand campaign on a whole new level.
Creative Director	Sicco Beerda	
Copywriter	Daniel Lutz	
Art Director	Chris Pacetti	
Designers	Feike Kloostra	
	Roland Lamers	
Production	Framfab, Copenhagen	
Client	Volvo C70, "Feel Volvo C70"	

Agency	MRM Worldwide, Frankfurt
Creative Director	Christoph Mayer
Copywriters	Stefan Kursawe
	Philipp Franz
	Alex Miller
Art Directors	Martin Biela
	Roger Knöhr
	Cerstin Scheuten
	Al Dhanab
	Philipp Karger
Production	SaasFee
Client	Opel Corsa

The website for the new Opel Corsa featured the C.M.O.N.S. – a colourful and enigmatic rock group. In fact they are five friends who just happen to be made of fabric and are taking their love of street art to the urban canvas of Barcelona. Fans of the band could find numerous interactive features on the official website. They could download free ringtones, wallpapers and screensavers for their cell phones, order a C'MON! newsletter or choose from a selection of stylish fan gear.

Agency	Lowe Brindfors, Stockholm
Creative Director	Magnus Wretblad
Copywriter	Stephen Whitlock
Art Directors	Tim Scheibel
	Johan Tesch
Producers	Caroline Déas-Ehrnvall
	Anna Kjellmark
	Motion Design
	Daniel Isaksson
Production	Zermatt
Client	Saab 9-5, "Animal Vision"

It's winter. It's freezing. It's the middle of the night. You are alone in a dense forest somewhere in Sweden. Except that you are not alone. You are surrounded by wild animals, including one extremely exotic creature: the new Saab 9-5. By clicking on the eyes of the animals, visitors to the site could switch between different perspectives. Then they could prowl around the car. How they approached it depended on the animal they had become.

Agency	Berger Baader Hermes Digital, Munich
Creative Director	Markus Beige
	Joerg Janda
Copywriter	Tim Sobczak
Art Director	Markus Beige
Designer	Markus Gimenez
Client	Lamy Writing Instruments, "Write it with Lamy"

The website was created for Germany's leading manufacturer of writing instruments and was aimed at young people between the ages of 14 and 19. The strategy was to forge links between young people and introduce them to the Lamy brand. A variety of themed areas addressed issues likely to interest youngsters: falling in love, future careers, games, communicating with others. The overall interactive theme tied in directly with the "Write it with Lamy" claim, created specially for a younger audience.

Agency	Publicis Net, Paris
Creative Directors	Philippe Simonet
	Nathalie Huni
Copywriters	Grégory Papin
	Barbara Soumet-Leman
Art Director	Marc Guillaumin
Client	Wonderbra, "Experience Wonder You"

Wonderbra wanted to break the classic communication codes used by lingerie. Print ads showed the effect provoked by the product and not a model wearing it. The brand asked Publicis Net to take the idea online. Visitors were given a first-person view of the "Wow!" effect. With film production company Partizan, the agency produced short web movies capturing the "Wow!" effect in real life situations. The various product benefits are also presented – with both dressed and undressed explanations.

How to drink without losing your
head or damaging your body.

A NIGHT OUT
Join us on a rewarding round on town.

ENTER SITE

376   **Websites (Non-Durables)**

Agencies	Farfar, Stockholm	The aim was to teach Swedish youngsters
	TBWA\Stockholm	to handle alcohol more responsibly. Embark
Production	Farfar, Stockholm	on a night out and learn about how much
Client	Swedish Alcohol Committee,	fat there is in alcohol, the truth behind some
	"How to Party"	myths and why you get a hangover.

Agency	Great Works, Stockholm
Creative Director	Ted Persson
Copywriter	Kristoffer Triumf
Art Director	Jacob Åström
Illustrator	Benedita Feijó
Flash Designer	Jocke Wissing
Producer	Eva Nilsson
Music	Håkan Lidbo
Client	Absolut Ruby Red Vodka

This brand new flavour from Absolut gets a musical tribute via a website that follows the grapefruit through its evolution into Absolut Ruby Red.

Agency	Great Works, Stockholm
Creative Director	Ted Persson
Copywriter	Kristoffer Triumf
Art Director	Jacob Åström
Designers	Jacob Åström
	Fredrik Karlsson
	Björn Wissing
Producer	Eva Nilsson
Animation	Wreck
Music	Jonas Quant
Client	Absolut Vodka, "The 100 Absolutes"

Absolut launched two commercials in which 14 cultural phenomena were named "absolutes". Great Works took the concept to the internet and made it The 100 Absolutes. Visitors uploaded their own absolute favourites in categories such as film, the internet, books, fashion, food, drinks, travel and so on. Users then voted to arrive at 100 Absolutes.

Agency	Great Works, Stockholm
Creative Directors	Ted Persson
	Frédéric Sebton
Copywriter	Kristoffer Triumf
Art Director	Ted Persson
Designers	Fredrik Karlsson
	Jimmy Poopuu
Producer	Johan Magnusson
Flash	Fredrik Karlsson
	Jocke Wissing
	Oskar Sundberg
Client	Absolut Vodka, "Absolut Drinks"

There are other drink recipes websites, but Absolut Drinks aims to be the best in the market. Visit yourself and learn how to mix killer cocktails.

Agency	Great Works, Stockholm
Creative Directors	Ted Persson
	Sebastien Vacherot
Copywriter	Kristoffer Triumf
Art Director	Jimmy Poopuu
Illustrators	Nicolas Boyer
	Alexis Dernov
Designers	Jimmy Poopuu
	Jocke Wissing
Producer	Eva Nilsson
Client	Absolut Vodka, "Absolut Search"

Join Absolut Search and try to find 82 hidden bottles. Even if you don't find them all, you will be rewarded with some nice wallpaper to decorate your desktop. (See also page 49)

Agency	Great Works, Stockholm
Creative Director	Ted Persson
Copywriter	Kristoffer Triumf
Art Directors	Ted Persson
	Fredrik Karlsson
Designers	Fredrik Karlsson
	Jimmy Poopuu
Producer	Johan Magnusson
Flash	Fredrik Karlsson
	Jocke Wissing
	Oskar Sundberg
Client	Absolut Vodka, "Absolut.com"

This is the official Absolut portal that took 18 months to develop. It provides access to all the Absolut mini sites, describes the company, allows visitors to download music and drink recipes, subscribe to the Absolut newsletter, receive press releases etc.

Agency	Springer & Jacoby, Vienna
Creative Directors	Paul Holcmann
	Murray White
Copywriters	Hans Juckel
	Mario Pirker
Art Director	Katharina Haines
Photographer	Tim Georgeson
Illustrator	Tim Georgeson
Client	Betandwin, "Magic Moments of Sports"

Online betting platform betandwin.com wanted to reconnect people with their passion for sport, while transferring these old-fashioned values to a new media brand and building trust. The idea was to bring together 12 of the greatest athletes from all fields to talk about sport and their own personal "magic moments". The website hosted the resulting TV spots, as well as "making of" films, biographies of the legends and a picture gallery.

Agency	McCann Erickson, Prague
Creative Director	Lars Killi
Copywriter	Vojtech Untermuller
Art Director	Michal Kotulek
Client	Lidice Memorial, "Total Burn-Out"

Lidice is a Czech village that was burned to the ground during World War II. In order to draw attention to the Lidice memorial and raise awareness of this horrifying event, the agency created a controversial fake computer game. Click on the banner and you suddenly become a Nazi officer with a brief to destroy the Lidice village and its Czech inhabitants. When you are armed and the game would normally start, you read an anti-Nazi message referring to the Lidice memorial.

Agency	Arc Warsaw/ Leo Burnett Group, Warsaw	
Creative Directors	Rafal Gorski	
	Martin Winter	
Copywriter	Michael Lars	
Art Directors	Rafal Gorski	
	Adam Smereczynski	
	Jakub Zielecki	
Designer	Konrad Grzegorzewicz	
Client	Wolontariat,	
	"Helping Makes you Stronger"	

The site encourages people to volunteer to help others. When the visitor enters the site, a series of pop-ups appear. The central pop-up is Mariusz Pudzianowski, the world's strongest man, holding the leashes of two little dogs. One of the dogs allows visitors to sign up to volunteer and the other provides a search engine for visitors seeking help. The remaining pop-ups display other campaign elements. (See also page 138)

Agency	OgilvyOne Worldwide, London	
Creative Directors	Cordell Burke	
	Candace Kuss	
	Colin Nimick	
Copywriters	Emma Poole	
	Rae Stones	
Art Directors	Mariota Essery	
	Fiona Sanday	
Designer	Andrew Mackay	
Client	American Express,	
	"VIP Room"	

The brief was to fully leverage the American Express sponsorship of the Rolling Stones "A Bigger Bang" tour in Europe and reinforce the value of being an American Express card member. The solution was The VIP Room – a rock 'n' roll website where visitors could "get closer to the Stones", hang out and watch exclusive videos and interviews with the band. Visitors were also invited to vote for their favourite Rolling Stones tracks of all time. They could enter a contest to become a Stones roadie for a day and win tickets to see them live.

Agency	Bloc, London	
Creative Directors	John Denton	
	Liam Owen	
Art Director	Tom Jennings	
Client	EMI,	
	"The Concretes – in Colour"	

The brief was to create an interactive album sampler for the band The Concretes. Record label EMI also wanted to encourage audience participation, which would make users listen to all the album tracks while generating strong word of mouth. The site offered a set of tools allowing users to create their own personal, unique Concretes-inspired artwork, to be displayed in a virtual gallery, and available to download as PC or mobile phone wallpaper.

Agency	Garbergs Reklambyrå, Stockholm
Copywriter	Martin Johansen
Art Director	Karin Ahlgren
Photographers	Bohman
	Sjöstrand
Director	Henrik Eriksson
Production	Kokokaka
Client	Södra Cell, "Quiz Walk"

Södra is a Swedish company that manufactures and sells pulp to paper mills throughout Europe. It also offers a range of related services through its sub.brand. PulpServices. The purpose of the website was to tell clients and customers more about these services. The solution was an interactive Quiz Walk in the company's own surroundings: the mysterious forests of Småland. Five lucky winners were chosen from the participants to spend a vacation in same area.

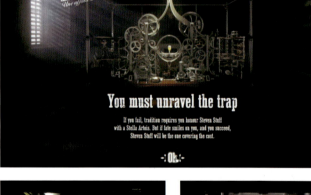

Agency	Lowe Tesch, Stockholm
Creative Director	Matthew Bull
Copywriters	Cissi Högkvist
	Stephen Whitlock
Art Director	Patrik Westerdahl
Producer	Marcus Sundqvist
Production	Stink Productions, London
Directors	Joakim Eliasson
	Daniel Isaksson
Client	Stella Artois, "L'Etranger"

You are the stranger (l'étranger) entering the Brassérie Le Cercle. Soon the bartender challenges you to demonstrate your skills in pouring the perfect Stella Artois. In trying to master the pouring ritual, instruct the bartender and get instant feedback on your performance.

Agency	Lowe Tesch, Stockholm
Creative Director	Matthew Bull
Copywriter	Martin Bartholf
	Ryan Spelliscy
Art Directors	Patrik Westerdahl
	Johan Tesch
	Motion Design
	Daniel Isaksson
Production	Against All Odds
Client	Stella Artois, "Le Défi"

In an old castle, a vicious trap protects a precious chalice of Stella Artois. There are six ways of disarming the trap, equally challenging to the mind. The user can challenge a friend to a duel. If they manage to avoid the trap, Belgian tradition requires that you honour them with a Stella Artois at a venue of their choice.

Agency	Forsman & Bodenfors, Gothenburg
Creative Director	Martin Cedergren
Director	Tomas Jonsgården
Copywriters	Anna Qvennerstedt
	Johan Olivero
Art Director	John Bergdahl
Photographer	Carl Nilsson
Designers	Lotta Dolling
	Nina Andersson
Production	Flodellfilm
	B-Reel
	Kramgo
Producers	Magnus Åkerstedt
	Martin Sandberg
	Charlotte Most
Client	Apoteket, "Sneeze Aid"

Imagine you've got a sick kid at home, and you're not sure if it's the common cold or if you should see a doctor. This tool, developed in collaboration with doctors, helps you decide and offers personalised advice, including a list of relevant products.

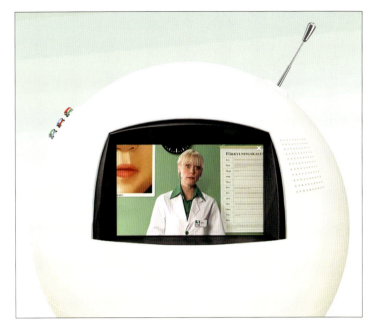

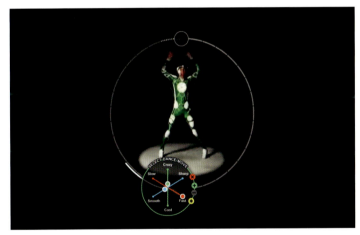

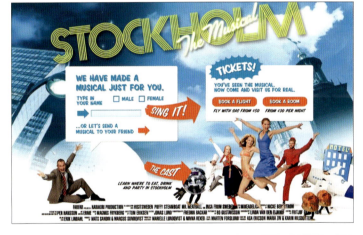

Agency	Farfar, Stockholm
Production	Colony
	Freecloud
Directors	Mikeadelica
	Harakiri
Client	Nokia N91, "Pjotro"

In order to create some buzz around the launch of the Nokia N91 music phone, the agency created a somewhat odd character by the name of Pjotro. He loves music so much that he became music. A viral clip of his breakthrough performance on TV led to a site where you could explore his background and test his greatest innovation: The Musical Suit.

Agency	Farfar, Stockholm
Production	Colony
	Freecloud
Directors	Mikeadelica
	Harakiri
Client	Visit Sweden, "Stockholm, The Musical"

In order to encourage Londoners to visit Sweden, the site gave them the chance to make customised versions of "Stockholm, The Musical" for their friends.

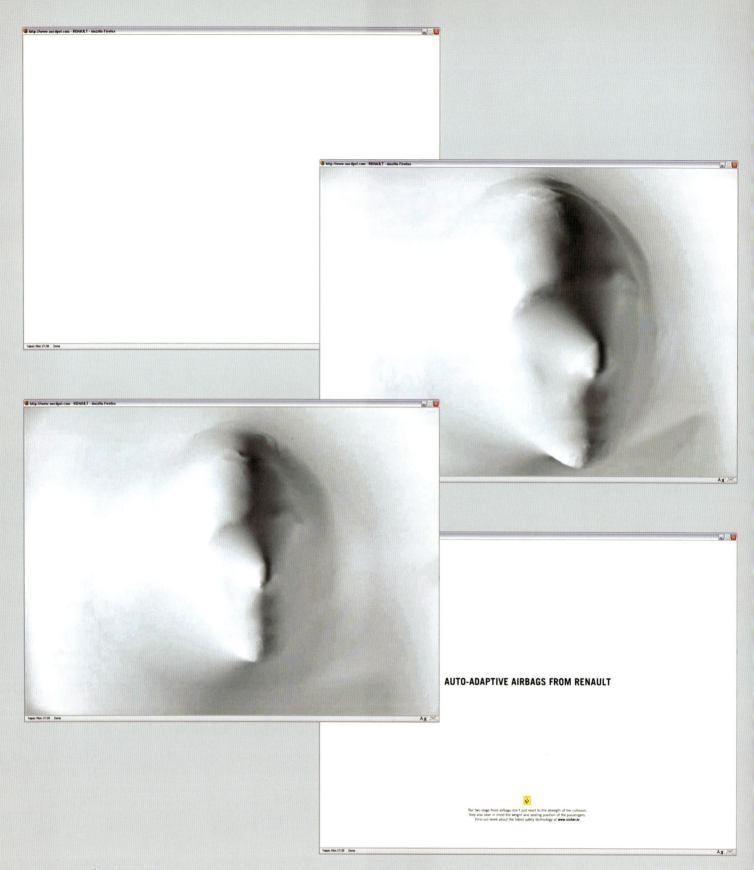

AUTO-ADAPTIVE AIRBAGS FROM RENAULT

Our two stage front airbags don't just react to the strength of the collision, they also bear in mind the weight and seating position of the passengers. Find out more about the latest safety technology at www.sicher.tv

Agency	Nordpol+ Hamburg	As a way of demonstrating the safety of a Renault, a TV spot takes the audience inside an airbag during a car crash. This leads to a website incorporating a "safety calculator". By simply entering the brand, the year of construction and the model of their current car, users can find out how it performed in European safety tests. Renault offered a special deal to owners of cars with less than five stars.
Creative Director	Ingo Fritz	
Copywriter	Ingmar Bartels	
Art Directors	Dominik Anweiler	
	Gunther Schreiber	
Designer	Mark Hoefler	
Director	Silvio Helbig	
Client	Renault, "Car Crash"	

Agency	Tribal DDB Germany, Hamburg
Creative Director	Friedrich von Zitzewitz
Art Directors	Daniel Könnecke
	Gregory Jacob
	Justin Landon
Client	Hamburg-Mannheimer Insurance, "Missclicked"

The ad demonstrates how easy it is to unintentionally cause massive damage. With one click, an entire website collapses like a house of cards. This amusing online ad is for personal liability insurance.

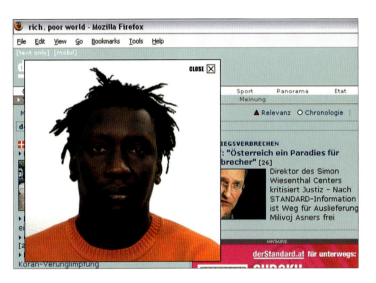

Agency	Wien Nord Pilz, Vienna
Creative Directors	Eduard Boehler
	Edmund Hochleitner
Copywriter	Felix Fenz
Art Director	Andreas Lierzer
Client	Austrian EU-Platform of NGOs, "Please Don't!"

A pop-up box reveals the face of a young black man. When users try to close the box, the man says, "Please don't!" He explains that many people want to ignore him, but as long as there is poverty and violence in the world, people like him will come to Europe to try to make new lives. Instead of pretending that they don't exist, why not try to help?

Agency	Elephant Seven, Hamburg
Creative Directors	Dirk Ollmann
	Daniel Richau
Copywriter	Benjamin Bruno
Art Director	Kai Becker
Designer	Till Hinrichs
Flash	Rouven Laurien
Client	Mercedes-Benz M-Class, "Splatter"

The campaign for the launch of the new M-Class bore the strapline: "Built for the road. And for getting that far." Taking a different approach to car advertising, the screensaver / pop-up generated interest in a bold way, without showing the vehicle instantly. Small dots appearing on a blank screen turned out to be flies splattering on a windscreen. When the screen is almost entirely covered with dead insects the windscreen wipers come on the reveal the new Mercedes M-Class.

Agency	Saatchi & Saatchi, Frankfurt
Creative Director	Sebastian Schier
Copywriters	Peter Huschka
	Sebastian Schier
Art Directors	Christian Bartsch
	Georg Cockburn
Designers	Christian Bartsch
	Georg Cockburn
Client	T-Mobile Web'n'Walk, "T-Shirt"

A banner leads to a website – which then walks away, revealing that it is a design on a t-shirt! This simple idea gets across the virtues of T-Mobile's web 'n' walk mobile internet service.

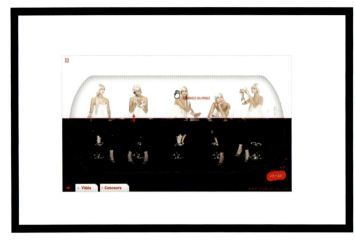

Agency	Duke, Paris
Creative Director	Aurelie de Villeneuve
Copywriter	Laurent Vidal
Art Directors	Thomas Porthé
	François Duval
Client	Playstation Portable, "PSP White"

Do you prefer your PlayStation Portable in white or black? This intriguing banner offered both options, thanks to a split-screen film showing young women sitting at a bar in either an all-white or all-black environment. Users could seamlessly switch between the two by dragging their mouse over them.

Agency	Publicis Dialog, Amstelveen
Creative Director	Bram Holzapfel
Copywriter	Paul Hillesum
Art Director	Paul Bakker
Designer	Arnold de Kok
Client	The Red Cross, "Pakistan Snowdome"

In a traditional snowdome, a cute Alpine hut suddenly collapses. The Dutch Red Cross helped victims of an earthquake in Pakistan survive the freezing winter of 2005/6. Funding was needed and this confrontational and cost-efficient internet banner collected more than 300,000 euros in online donations.

Agency	Profero, London
Creative Director	Matt Powell
Art Director	Scott Clark
Designer	Johan Arlig
Client	Mini, "The White Rabbit"

The campaign enticed users to break from their daily surfing habits and join Mini for a random tour of the World Wide Web. Entitled "The White Rabbit", the campaign took users on an unexpected journey to eccentric British websites, instead of taking them to the Mini site like most online campaigns. A pop-up appears on the home page of each participating niche site, the Mini then zooms out, spins around and zooms off to another site when the user clicks on "this is not the way to the Mini site", "this way", "down her", "through here" etc.

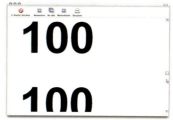

Agency	Contrapunto, Madrid
Interactive Director	Juan Corrales
Creative Directors	Antonio Montero
	Alberto Barragán
	Jaime Chávarri
	Iván De Dios
Copywriter	Jaime Chávarri
Art Director	Iván De Dios
Designer	Alberto Barragán
Client	WWF, "Gorilla"

WWF/Adena is an organisation that fights for wildlife worldwide. Its basic strength lies in the coordinated action and energy of individuals who share the same vision. The organisation's most recognised icon is the gorilla. Click on this online ad and your cursor joins thousands of others to form the shape of a gorilla.

Agency	Nordpol+ Hamburg
Creative Director	Ingo Fritz
Copywriter	Ingmar Bartels
Art Director	Dominik Anweiler
Designer	Mark Hoefler
Client	Renault Mégane Sport, "Sport Mailing"

The Mégane Sport is the sportiest vehicle in the Renault range. It is also equipped with cruise control as standard, enabling the driver to maintain a constant speed. These two important characteristics are portrayed in a surprising way using nothing but emails. The first mail encourages readers to start at 0 and drag the cursor at top speed down to 100. The second email remains at a constant 100 on every line. The newsletter was devised to attract potential buyers to the Mégane Sport website and offer them a test drive.

JOIN THE CHAIN

00:00:06 / 01:47:53
Ronaldinho, Brazil

CHOOSE. MIX. PLAY.

TODAY'S SUBMISSIONS   GETTING STARTED

HALL OF FAME
TODAY'S MOST POPULAR CLIP
SELECTED 809 TIMES

MIX TOMORROW'S CHAIN: CLICK AND DRAG THE BEST 10 HERE

SUBMIT

VIEW: ALL VIDEOS   SEARCH: ENTER NAME

00:00:46 / 01:43:08
Mikey Pauls, Canada
Now playing: Que

WHO'S NEXT?

THE WINNING MIX WILL BE ADDED TO THE CHAIN TOMORROW AT 12PM CET.

START HERE

Players in the chain	912
Countries	83
Total running time	01:43:08

UPLOAD YOUR VIDEO HERE

VIEW: ALL VIDEOS   SEARCH: ENTER NAME

00:00:26 / 01:47:53
Paul, France

VIEW: ALL VIDEOS   SEARCH: ENTER NAME

00:02:08 / 01:47:53
edú, Spain

VIEW: ALL VIDEOS   SEARCH: ENTER NAME

00:00:28 / 01:43:08
Ludwig Seibel, Germany

386   Online Films

Agency	Framfab Denmark, Copenhagen	Via nikefootball.com, users could become part of the world's longest football video by submitting their personal contribution to The Chain. Football crazy kids are invited to film themselves passing a ball and submit it to the site. The rules are simple: the ball has to enter the frame from the left and disappear out of frame on the right. New submissions are uploaded each day and users can mix their own favourites for the next day's chain.
Creative Director	Lars Cortsen	
Copywriter	Thomas Robson	
Art Directors	Rasmus Frandsen	
	Kristian Grove Møller	
Producers	Simon Ryhede	
	Michael Amsinck	
Client	Nike, "The Chain"	

Drive for free, all over the country!
Yes, it's true but really not so strange...

Our cars are rented "one-way", and must be returned to the rental station were they came from. Therefore you got the opportunity of a free ride between two cities.

Read more here!

Hertz

youwantafreeride.org

SUNSILK

Fab hair, it's all you need to turn him on!

Play again

For tips on how to get great hair visit www.sunsilk.co.uk

P.S. Sunsilk accepts no responsibility for men throwing themselves at your feet.

Agency	Pool Interactive, Stockholm
Creative Director	Jenny Åberg Hüttner
Copywriter	Jenny Åberg Hüttner
Art Director	Anders Ramström
Production	Keeppunching, Stockholm
Director	Erik Lindwall
Producers	Arvid Axland
	Jim Carlberg
	Mattias Kullstrand
Client	Hertz Car Rental, "Do You Want a Free Ride?"

Lucas, Taylan and Eric are three bumbling youngsters who've apparently set up a video blog describing their exploits as they try to bum "free rides", either by attaching themselves to moving vehicles or hijacking ostriches on a farm. Hertz occasionally needs to transfer cars between two cities. And it needs volunteers to do that – effectively enabling them to rent a car for free. By clicking on the ads next to the viral films users could book their rent-free cars.

Agency	OgilvyOne Worldwide, London
Creative Director	Bo Hellberg
Copywriter	Yasmin Quemard
Art Director	Sanni Sorma
Director	Olivier Rabenschlag
Client	Sunsilk, "Shower Slave"

With Sunsilk Colour Enhancement, redheads, blondes and brunettes will intensify their hair colour and live life to the max. The agency created the interactive Shower Slave just for these vibrant Sunsilk girls. The viral combines humour, sex appeal and shock value. The user selects an outfit, a dance routine and a persona for her Shower Slave. He can't help but obey the ladies, underlining the message that all they need is fab hair to turn guys on.

Agency	Spillmann/Felser/ Leo Burnett, Zurich	Based on the idea that "equipment this good can cause loss of common sense," outdoor brand Mammut invented 85-year-old British lady Mary Woodbridge, who bought a Mammut jacket and suddenly decided she was going to climb Mount Everest. She documented her crazy plans on her website and over 250 media outlets worldwide ran with the ball. Mammut then began using Mary Woodbridge in print ads, brochures, on the internet and at points of sale as an example of how equipment this good can cause loss of common sense.
Creative Directors	Martin Spillmann Peter Brönnimann	
Copywriter	Peter Brönnimann	
Art Director	Raul Serrat	
Production	Plan B Films	
Client	Mammut Sports Group, "Mary Woodbridge"	

The VW Fox is small and fun.

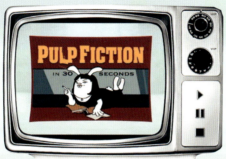

Agencies	DDB Germany, Berlin	**Art Directors**	Jörg Meyer
	Tribal DDB Germany, Hamburg		Jennifer Shiman
Creative Directors	Jennifer Shiman		Christian Brenner
	Amir Kassaei		Karin Schmidt
	Eric Schöffler		Daniel Könnecke
	Tim Jacobs		Sabrina Schumacher
	Hartmut Kozok	**Production**	Angry Alien Productions
	Martin Drust		VCC Perfect Pictures
Copywriters	Tim Jacobs	**Director**	Jennifer Shiman
	Sandra Illes	**Producers**	Marion Lange
	Katja Behnke		James Strader
		Client	Volkswagen Fox,
			"Short but Fun"

The challenge was to enrapture a very young target group with the new VW Fox. In order to do so takes bravery and originality. Take six funny cartoons that reduce film classics to 30 seconds. Give them the claim "Short but fun – The Fox". Put them online. Run them for one weekend only on music stations MTV and Viva, with an URL, and watch the viral machine go to work. (See also page 224).

Agency	Agency.com, Amsterdam
Creative Director	Kay Hofmeester
Copywriter	Alain Dujardin
Art Director	Jaz Lim
Designer	Kiril Nachev
Client	Heineken Experience Amsterdam, The Secret H-Sign"

The concept revolved around The Heineken Experience, a museum-style attraction at the original Heineken brewery in Amsterdam. The brand and its agency came up with a secret "H-sign". When visitors make this freemason-style gesture at the reception of The Heineken Experience, they gain the right to taste a special beer. The rumour was spread with an "internal" email that "accidentally" ended up in the mailbox of 45,000 newsletter subscribers. It was followed up by a hasty denial. But by then the story had been picked up by bloggers worldwide. Pretty soon, people started turning up at the Heineken Experience and making the H-sign...

Agency	Forsman & Bodenfors, Gothenburg
Creative Director	Martin Cedergren
Director	Tomas Alfredsson
Copywriters	Johan Olivero Anna Qvennerstedt
Art Director	Joakim Blondell
Photographers	Henrik Gyllenskiöld Göran Hallberg
Designer	Lotta Dolling
Production	EFTI & B-Reel
Client	Systembolaget, "Dear Mr B"

Systembolaget believes alcohol problems in the country have been reduced thanks to its monopoly system. In order to encourage other European countries to do the same, it created a special web film aimed specifically at European Commission President José Manuel Barroso. To draw his attention to it, he was sent a letter and ads were placed in newspapers like the Financial Times. The online film asked why, when alcohol is clearly dangerous, it is treated like any other commodity – rhubarb, for example.

Agency	Forsman & Bodenfors, Gothenburg
Creative Director	Jonas Sjövall
Copywriter	Jonas Enghage
Art Director	Kim Cramer
Designer	Karin Nolmark
Production	B-Reel
Producer	Martin Sandberg
Client	Statoil, "Unattended Petrol Stations"

In Sweden there are a large number of unattended petrol stations on the outskirts of cities. They are usually desolate, but as they don't have to employ staff they can offer much lower prices than full service stations like Statoil. The new Statoil loyalty card changes the situation by offering great prices and full service. In order to demonstrate this, Statoil created viral ads showing frightening things happening to people at unmanned stations. Chainsaw-wielding bunnies, wild dogs, serial killers and mad bikers were all on offer.

Agency	i-merge, Leuven	On December 24 i-merge clients and prospects received an email telling them a new agency employee had made them a Christmas card. The mail directed them to a microsite where they were introduced to Freddy the Hamster. The "Hamstercam" showed a "live" video of Freddy sleeping. To view their personal Christmas card, visitors had to send a text message saying "Wake up Freddy".
Creative Director	Vincent Jansen	
Copywriter	Peter Vijgen	
Art Director	Petra Sell	
Client	i-merge, "Hamstercam"	

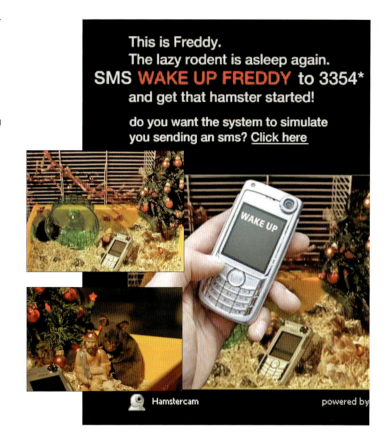

Agency	Lemz, Amsterdam	The use of Axe may encourage sinful behaviour. To promote the Axe shower gel range – which helps dirty boys get clean – young men were invited to confess their sins via a website or a telephone number. They were encouraged by a 15-second TV spot featuring a mysterious woman who urged them to reveal their dirty secrets. The confessions flooded in and awareness of Axe shower gels soared.
Creative Directors	Remco Marinus Peter de Lange	
Copywriter	Ilona van de Laarschot	
Art Director	Carianne van Raak	
Photographer	Arjen Went	
Designer	Fleur van Maarschalkerwaart	
Director	Daan Noppen	
Production	Gr8 Films Us Media	
Client	Axe Shower Range, "Confessions"	

Agency	Åkestam Holst, Stockholm	The agency used a series of media supports to promote the extraordinarily thin TV sets stocked by cutting edge electronic retailer Pause. Bookmarks, ultra-thin posters, a clever press ad and even gingerbread biscuits given away on the street all reinforced the slenderness of the TVs available at Pause. (See also page 153).
Copywriter	Mark Ardelius	
Art Directors	Andreas Ullenius Johan Landin	
Photographer	Philip Karlberg	
Illustrator	Torbjörn Krantz	
Client	Pause Ljud & Bild, "Unusually Thin TV Sets"